IMMIGRANTS RAISING
CITIZENS

IMMIGRANTS RAISING CITIZENS

Undocumented Parents and Their Young Children

Hirokazu Yoshikawa

Russell Sage Foundation • New York

The Russell Sage Foundation

The Russell Sage Foundation, one of the oldest of America's general purpose foundations, was established in 1907 by Mrs. Margaret Olivia Sage for "the improvement of social and living conditions in the United States." The Foundation seeks to fulfill this mandate by fostering the development and dissemination of knowledge about the country's political, social, and economic problems. While the Foundation endeavors to assure the accuracy and objectivity of each book it publishes, the conclusions and interpretations in Russell Sage Foundation publications are those of the authors and not of the Foundation, its Trustees, or its staff. Publication by Russell Sage, therefore, does not imply Foundation endorsement.

Library of Congress Cataloging-in-Publication Data

Immigrants raising citizens : undocumented parents and their young children / Hirokazu Yoshikawa.
    p. cm.
Includes bibliographical references and index.
  ISBN 978-0-87154-986-0 (hardcover)   ISBN 978-0-87154-971-6 (paperback)
  1. Immigrant children—United States—Social conditions.   2. Immigrant children—New York (State)—New York—Social conditions.   3. Children of immigrants—United States—Social conditions.   4. Children of immigrants—New York (State)—New York—Social conditions.   5. Illegal aliens—United States—Social conditions.   6. Illegal aliens—New York (State)—New York—Social conditions.   7. United States—Emigration and immigration—Social aspects.   I. Title.
  JV6600.Y67 2011
  305.9′069120973—dc22   2010050216

The paper used in this publication meets the minimum requirements of American National Standard for Information Sciences—Permanence of Paper for Printed Library Materials. ANSI Z39.48-1992.

Text design by Genna Patacsil.

RUSSELL SAGE FOUNDATION
112 East 64th Street, New York, New York 10065
10   9   8   7   6   5   4   3   2   1

Contents

About the Author

Hirokazu Yoshikawa is professor of education at Harvard University's Graduate School of Education.

Acknowledgments

This book is the product of years of collaboration and support. When Catherine Tamis-LeMonda, Niobe Way, Diane Hughes, and I were funded by the National Science Foundation to start two longitudinal studies of child and youth development in New York City, we envisioned research on how culture and context intersect to influence unfolding lives. As principal investigators of the Center for Research on Culture, Development, and Education at New York University, we were developmental and community psychologists interested in the contexts of home, child care, school, peers, and parental work as they intertwine in the development of children. I did not foresee that the cornerstone of the study—the intensive qualitative study of families' lives that represented the first years of our center's work—would ultimately result in a book on documentation status and its effects on children's learning. I am grateful to the National Science Foundation for providing core funding for this set of studies and am most thankful to Catherine Tamis-LeMonda, my principal collaborator on the birth cohort study that provides all of the data for this book. Ronit Kahana-Kalman, a crucial collaborator on our birth cohort study, directed the survey and child data collection and provided excellent scientific input into all aspects of the study. Work on this book was also supported by generous grants from the William T. Grant Foundation, through a Scholars fellowship and a supplemental grant. That foundation, through the vision and leadership of Robert Granger, Edward Seidman, and Vivian Tseng, has informed the work presented here in innumerable ways.

My main intellectual and motivational support for the writing of this book was Niobe Way, a fellow principal investigator of the Center for Research on Culture, Development, and Education. Our many conversations in downtown Manhattan about every aspect of the books we were working on stretched my thinking, challenged me to communicate the stories of the families in this study, and kept me motivated to complete the book. In addition, David L. Eng provided constant support and encouragement as well as vital critical analysis for many parts of the book.

This project was my first experience in collecting longitudinal ethnographic data. I am indebted to two friends and mentors in ethnography and mixed qualitative-quantitative work: Thomas S. Weisner and Ajay Chaudry. Weisner has contributed unfailingly supportive guidance and wisdom to my qualitative and mixed-methods work since 2001 and, like many superlative mentors, became a collaborator. (We co-edited a 2006 Russell Sage Foundation book based on the New Hope Ethnographic Study and experimental demonstration, a model in many ways for the mixed qualitative-quantitative approach that Tamis-LeMonda and I took for the birth cohort study.) Chaudry and I co-led the first qualitative study of the Center for Research on Culture, Development, and Education until he left to direct early childhood policy for New York City. As a researcher interested in many of the same policy, employment, and immigration issues that I was, but with a much deeper understanding of ethnography, Chaudry was both a colleague and a mentor for all of the qualitative work presented here. As the supervisor to my own fieldwork for the study, he provided additional guidance for my field notes and interviewing.

For the center's qualitative studies, field-workers spent hours interviewing and hanging out with families across the city of New York. Their incredible dedication to the task of recording the daily struggles and triumphs presented in this volume was motivated not only by the desire to learn about and master the research process but also by love and respect for the families they visited. I owe an incalculable debt to Renelinda Arana, Bronwyn Becker, Monica Brannon, Margaret Caspe, Ajay Chaudry, Francisco Gaytan, Erin Godfrey, Carolin Hagelskamp, Yanli Liang, Gigliana Melzi, Boon Ngeo, Ximena Portilla, Maria Ramos Olazagasti, Maria Reyes Lopez, Ann C. Rivera, Eva Ruiz, Jing Sun, Kimberly Torres, Nia Ebon West-Bey, and Qing Xue. The supervisors of the qualitative studies, who provided painstaking and creative mentorship and leadership, were Ajay Chaudry, Francisco Gaytan, Karen McFadden, Gigliana Melzi, Ann C. Rivera, Kimberly Torres, Niobe Way, and Qing Xue. Maria Clara Barata and Madeleine Currie, doctoral students at Harvard, ably directed the transcription and coding of all of the qualitative data.

This book was born during a year of qualitative analysis conducted away from the pressures of academia. The Russell Sage Foundation provided a fellowship during the 2008 to 2009 academic year, and I am grateful to Eric Wanner and all of the staff at the foundation for their support. I am also grateful for the collegiality and friendship of the other RSF scholars that year. I am particularly indebted to those who shared a focus on immigration—Krista Perreira, Virginia Parks, and Donna Gabaccia. During our lunchtime conversations, they were the first to hear about the focus of my work, and they added a breadth and depth of insight from their own work in immigration that enriched many parts of this book. For her wise and efficient oversight of the review and publication process, I thank Suzanne Nichols, director of publications for the foundation. Galo Falchettore provided wonderful assistance with the maps in chapters 2 and 4. The two anonymous reviewers of the book provided detailed, meticulous reviews that greatly improved it.

For support with the quantitative analyses and editing of this book, I thank two talented and dedicated students at the Harvard Graduate School of Education, Jenya Kholoptseva and Lindsey Lockman. For all of her generosity and mentorship, not only during my fellowship year at Russell Sage but more generally during my career since moving to Harvard, I thank Kathleen McCartney.

Several scholars and colleagues provided helpful and thought-provoking feedback on early versions of the data presented here. They include Richard Alba, Randy Capps, Nancy Foner, Andrew Fuligni, Ariel Kalil, Robert Smith, and Ruby Takanishi. I also benefited from many thoughtful comments from participants at colloquia and conferences where I presented data from the book, including meetings at the National Institute for Child Health and Human Development, Fuzhou Normal University, the Radcliffe Institute of Harvard University, the School of Public Affairs at Baruch College of the City University of New York (CUNY), the immigration seminar at CUNY, the immigration series at the University of California–Los Angeles, Duke University, the Harris Graduate School of Public Policy Studies at the University of Chicago, Teachers College of Columbia University, the Eliot-Pearson Department of Child Development at Tufts University, the "On New Shores" conference in Guelph, Ontario, and several colloquia at the Harvard Graduate School of Education.

An amazing group of colleagues, friends, and mentors gave their time and input by reading drafts of chapters or the entire manuscript. They include Ajay Chaudry, Greg Duncan, David L. Eng, Vanessa Fong, Francisco Gaytan, Shinhee Han, Mae Ngai, Maria Ramos Olazagasti, Patricia Ruiz Navarro, Mica Pollock, Kimberly Torres, Niobe Way, Thomas Weisner, Richard Weissbourd, Qing Xue, doctoral advisees at New York University's Departments of Psychology and Applied Psychology, and members of my research lab at the Harvard Graduate School of Education during the 2009 to 2010 academic year. My students are the daily inspiration for my work.

Finally, I would like to thank my family for their unwavering support. My brother Takaaki Yoshikawa, my brother-in-law Larry Freeman, and my mother-in-law Sue Freeman were always supportive of the work I was doing on this book. My life partner, Stuart Freeman, offered extensive and wonderful feedback on the book. More importantly, he provided the love without which I could not have completed it.

This book is dedicated to all the immigrant families who contributed their time and their voices to this study of citizen children in the United States, and to one more—the family that my parents, Akiko and Takatoshi Yoshikawa, immigrants from Osaka, Japan, started in the great city of New York in 1958.

Chapter 1

Emiliana, Elena, and Ling Raise
Citizens in New York City

The A train links lives across the city of New York. It has done this for nearly a century. In the 1930s, Billy Strayhorn named his new composition, "Take the A Train," after directions that Duke Ellington had given him to his home in Harlem. At that time the subway line carried New Yorkers from Harlem to eastern Brooklyn. By the turn of the twenty-first century, the line had been extended up past Harlem to Washington Heights, down the full length of Manhattan Island, and over to the farthest southeastern corner of Queens.

On July 18, 2005, if you were on the A train in the right subway car at the right time, you would have seen two Latina women and one Asian woman. The subway ride was a crucial part of each of their daily routines. These three women's homes spanned the entire length of the A—the two terminal neighborhoods of Far Rockaway, Queens, and Washington Heights in Manhattan, and one neighborhood in between, the oldest and most famous of the four Chinatowns of New York City. The women shared certain characteristics: all three were roughly the same age, in their late twenties to early thirties; all three had infants; and all three were part of a longitudinal study of child development. They would have all appreciated the air conditioning on the train (and noticed the lack of it on the subway platforms when the train made stops).

You would not have guessed, seeing these three women on the subway, that despite their demographic similarities, they differed on a crucial invisible characteristic: legal documentation status.[1] Differences in this status shaped their everyday experiences in innumerable ways: through differences in their social networks, in the programs and care settings to which their children were exposed, in the quality of their jobs, and, most importantly, in their prospects for full integration into American society. Despite these differences, Emiliana, Elena, and Ling shared one crucial characteristic: their infants were U.S. citizens. In telling the hidden stories of Emiliana, Elena, and Ling, *Immigrants Raising Citizens* shows that the undocumented status of some immigrant parents entering the United

States can have harmful consequences for their children. I focus on the 4 million of our nation's children who are citizen children of undocumented parents—nearly one-third of all children of immigrants, and about one student per classroom in every elementary school in the United States.[2] In an intensive, three-year study of nearly four hundred children recruited hours after birth in public hospitals and followed in the homes and neighborhoods of New York City, this increasingly common but largely unknown part of the American childhood experience emerged as a powerful and unexpected story.

Immigrants Raising Citizens describes the experience of raising very young children as an undocumented parent in the United States. It is also about the ways in which the undocumented status of immigrant parents influences the development of their U.S. citizen children. I argue that the simple fact of coming without legal papers shapes the everyday interactions of young parents with institutions and organizations, as well as their housing, jobs, and households, even when their children are U.S. citizens, with all the rights that that status implies.

I show in this book that the lack of a pathway to citizenship for their parents is harmful to children's development—particularly their cognitive and language skills—as early as ages two and three. Undocumented parents employ a tremendous range of survival strategies to provide opportunities for their children's learning, health, and development. Despite these sources of strength, parental undocumented status represents a risk, not a source of resilience, in the development of these children.

How does documentation status affect such young children's learning? In this study, two sets of influences transmitted the effect of documentation status in lowering children's cognitive skills. At twenty-four months, parents' economic hardship and psychological distress—feelings of depression, anxiety, and worry—were responsible for this effect. At thirty-six months, with more of the mothers having gone back to work, the influence of documentation status on child cognitive skills was conveyed through the disastrous work conditions of the undocumented parents in the sample, combined with lower access to center-based child care.

The undocumented are viewed in current policy debates as lawbreakers, laborers, or victims—seldom as parents raising citizen children. Policymakers generally ignore the development of children of the undocumented. The data from this book suggest that ignoring these children has costs for society. Millions of the youngest citizens in the United States, simply by virtue of being born to a parent with a particular legal status, have less access to the learning opportunities that are the building blocks of adult productivity. The consequences of parental undocumented status, reflected in outcomes as intimate as a toddler's vocabulary at age three, are societal in their importance, because the early cognitive skills of our youngest citizens predict the future productivity and success of the nation.

EMILIANA RAISES VICTOR

On this July afternoon, if you had taken the A train from the familiar territory of midtown Manhattan, it would have taken an hour and a half to get to Far Rockaway, the home of Emiliana and Victor. Ana, a field-worker in our study of early child development in immigrant families, took the A train from Penn Station, after coming in from her home in New Jersey. The neighborhood of Far Rockaway sits on the edge of the Atlantic, in the southeastern corner of the city, past Kennedy Airport. The neighborhood made national news in November 2001 when American Airlines flight 587 to the Dominican Republic crashed there soon after taking off from the airport, killing all 251 people on board. Far Rockaway is a largely black and Latino neighborhood. No single ethnic group predominated there in 2005, and Mexican immigrants were a relatively small proportion of the community. There was quite a bit of commercial activity in the neighborhood of the subway station, including a florist, grocers, a barbershop, a couple of pizzerias, and small convenience stores. Two chain pharmacies—Eckerd and CVS—were located near the subway stop. Some walls were covered with graffiti. The street life was relatively sparse. Emiliana's apartment, several blocks away from the station, was in a three-story house converted into three apartments. The houses on these quiet streets had well-kept lawns. Most of the homes, including Emiliana's, had gates and bars on the windows.

Nine years before, in her late twenties, Emiliana had arrived from a village in Mexico's state of Puebla, the region of origin for most Mexicans in the recent and first large wave of Mexican immigration to New York City.[3] Also like most in this wave of immigration, she had come to the United States undocumented.[4] She had two U.S.-born children with her husband, Victor Sr.: a four-year-old daughter named Luz, and Victor, the focal child in our study, an eight-month-old baby with a calm and energetic disposition.

Emiliana greeted Ana at the door. She had long straight hair, brown eyes, and medium-brown skin. She was dressed casually in sweatpants on the first visit. Although Emiliana described herself as a shy person, she had a friendly personality. Like many of the parents during the first visit of our ethnographic study, she said that she was not sure she would have anything interesting or important to say. By the end of this visit, however, she would tell Ana that she was surprised to have had so much to say about her experiences.

3

The apartment was a one-bedroom. During the two years that Ana visited Emiliana's apartment, the number of people living there ranged from eight at the first visit to a maximum of twelve at one point. The bedroom, about twenty square feet, was the only place where the interview could take place in the apartment because Emiliana's sister-in-law, together with her husband and two children, lived in the living room. The bedroom was just large enough to fit a queen-sized bed, a crib for Victor, a smaller twin bed for Luz, a bookcase for a headboard, a TV atop the dresser, another dresser for clothes, and Victor's changing table; there was only a tiny bit of room to walk. The only places for Ana and Emiliana to sit were two corners of a bed, about three feet apart. This made for intimate conversations.

Ana was amused by Emiliana's initial introduction of baby Victor: waving her arm like a magician pulling a rabbit out of a hat, she exclaimed, "Y aquí esta Victor." Victor was chubby, with black hair, fair skin, and brown eyes. During the first visit, there were not many times when he did not have a smile on his face. He was quite playful, trying to kiss, hug, or bite his mom's and Ana's faces. He would be calm for a bit, looking at his surroundings, and then, quite suddenly, he would laugh or jump up and down. By his second year, Emiliana had given him a buzz cut and was dressing him in fashionable outfits—one combined a green sweater, brown slacks, and blue shoes.

Although Emiliana had some relatives in the city, they were not concentrated in any one neighborhood. She had arrived early in a great wave of migration, and so there was not yet a single large concentration of Mexicans in New York City (although Mexicans were a growing presence in East Harlem, the legendary barrio of a huge prior wave of migration to New York from Puerto Rico, as well as several other neighborhoods in the city). Although many people from Emiliana's village in Puebla had come to New York, she told Ana, they were "scattered all over the city."

Emiliana was one of the first in her family to come to the United States. Among her large family of eight siblings, only she and her next youngest brother had undergone the "adventure" of the border crossing. Her father had been the very first in the family to come; he stayed in the city for three years before returning to Mexico. She herself was sent to New York by her father immediately after she completed ninth grade in order to start working and send remittances back to the rest of the family in Puebla. In this classic path to social mobility in the sending regions of Mexico, the eldest siblings usually sacrifice the rest of their education. In Mexico, ninth grade is the end of "secundaria" (secondary education), and an age when teenagers are often considered old enough to emigrate by themselves. The path to middle- and upper-middle-class jobs would have been further study past ninth grade ("preparatoria"), but this path was closed to her when she came to the United States. She spoke of this interruption in her education wistfully and related to Ana her hopes of eventually picking up her education. First she would have to strengthen her English. She had taken a few weeks of English classes near Penn Station soon after arrival, but the unrelenting schedules of low-wage work and then parenthood took over her life.

Emiliana and Victor Sr.'s working lives and schedules were grueling. Victor Sr. worked in a restaurant as a line cook, putting in twelve-hour days, six days a week. Undocumented himself, he had been dutifully paying taxes for eleven years and waiting for a work visa; none was forthcoming. The few times that Ana saw him during her visits, he looked exhausted. Emiliana woke up every day around six, prepared her children for preschool and child care, went to work cleaning houses, came home, prepared dinner, put her children to bed, did housework, and then waited up for Victor Sr. to return home, often after one in the morning. When he arrived, she gave him his dinner, went to bed, and woke up only a few hours later. Ana observed in more than one visit that Emiliana seemed listless and sad, though when asked about it, she always said that things were "fine."

Emiliana's older child, her daughter Luz, was in preschool, but this had happened almost accidentally. Like many undocumented parents in our study, Emiliana had not been aware that free preschool is provided to low-income families in the United States through programs like the federal Head Start program. Ana in fact was the one who told her about Head Start, although by that time of the year it was too late to enroll Luz. Emiliana subsequently had concerns about Luz's language development. (She spoke relatively few words and mumbled, so it was extremely difficult for even her mother to understand her.) When Emiliana spoke with her pediatrician about these concerns, he helped to have Luz evaluated. In this way, Luz was found to qualify for services through the federal early intervention program, and she began attending a preschool with a special focus on children with delays. She also started receiving intensive speech therapy.

Emiliana had few social supports to help take care of Victor or Luz. Neither of her parents was in New York City, and no one in that generation was available in her family. She also did not report much support from neighbors, either in her building or in the area. She was committed, however, to supporting the early learning of her children. She provided Luz with a preschool desk, which she picked up for twenty dollars at a garage sale, as well as books, markers, and crayons. From time to time she also bought English-language DVDs to play for her children (*Dumbo* was one). These forms of investment in materials for children's learning can improve early cognitive development. In her work as a housekeeper,

Emiliana learned about "structure" as U.S. parents conceive it, with children's time divided into distinct periods: playtime, homework time, dinnertime. She wanted to provide these forms of stimulation to her children and also said that she wanted them to grow up not spoiled ("mimados") but independent.

ELENA RAISES ALBERTO

On this same humid July afternoon, Elena Espinal, a woman in her late twenties who had arrived in the United States from the Dominican Republic eleven years before, was coming home. She was on the A train in the far northern part of Manhattan, where she would pick up her son Alberto, eight months old, from her aunt's house. Then she would try to make it home by six, when she had scheduled a first meeting with Patricia, a field-worker from our research project who was assigned to interview Elena for the next two years.

Elena had just come from her job taking care of an elderly Dominican woman in the same neighborhood, Washington Heights, the historic center of Dominican life in New York City since the 1960s. The child care provided by her aunt, despite being close in terms of blood relations, entailed a subway ride and so was a bit too far away to fit into her busy schedule with Josefina, her ten-year-old daughter. So Elena had recently been thinking about switching to government-subsidized infant day care. One program was within a short walk from her apartment in the Heights. She worried, however, that she might not be able to trust someone who was not a relative of Alberto's. After all, he was so young.

At that moment, Patricia, the field-worker, was taking the subway up to Washington Heights from downtown Manhattan. She was reading her notes on what to do on the first visit to a family. This was one of her first ethnographic visits, so she felt both nervous and excited to be starting after the months of discussion and training on the project. The A train was packed with people of all racial and ethnic backgrounds, most of whom got off at Penn Station. A man came through the train, shouting, "Batteries, two dollars!" in Spanish and English. From Penn Station all the way up to Washington Heights, blacks and Latinos outnumbered whites on the train. Patricia had never been so far north in Manhattan; her friends had told her in recent days that she should be very careful because "that's not a nice neighborhood." Patricia was worried about her return home in the evening after her visit, when she would walk by herself back to the subway.

Walking straight ahead from the subway station, Patricia felt nostalgic as she listened to the music coming from the stores she passed. They were playing merengue, salsa, and bachata. The music, the voices of people speaking Spanish on the streets, four older men playing dominoes on the sidewalk—it all reminded Patricia of Rio Piedras, a part of San Juan in her native Puerto Rico. The streets were congested in the middle of the evening rush hour, but there was not a single taxi in sight.

Washington Heights is one of the liveliest residential neighborhoods in New York City. Its commercial core is an unending parade of small businesses lining upper Broadway, a thoroughfare that was once the Wickquasgeck Trail, used by American Indian tribes for centuries to make their way through the swamps and ridges of the island of "Manahatta." Within two blocks of the subway station closest to Elena's home, on Broadway, were several restaurants, both fast-food and ethnic, a bakery that advertised DOMINICAN CAKE, and an ice cream store. National small-box stores like Radio Shack and Payless Shoes coexisted with inexpensive clothing stores that put racks out on the sidewalk. There was an H&R Block and three banks—Washington Mutual, Banco Popular (a Puerto Rican bank), and Chase. The banks had big banners shouting WE CASH CHECKS. In another storefront was a little "multi-purpose" travel agency that dealt with immigration issues, insurance, and "envios" (money sent overseas). Unlike Far Rockaway, a substantial proportion of the small businesses in Washington Heights focused on hiring, serving, or selling to immigrants, Dominicans in particular. And as these businesses suggested, the concentration of Dominicans in this part of Washington Heights was very high—over 50 percent, according to the 2000 U.S. census. In contrast, no Mexican family in our study lived in a census tract with more than 27 percent Mexican families.

The density of commercial activity in this part of Washington Heights was matched by the density of socializing between adults and children: there was far more activity and monitoring of children on the streets of Washington Heights than Ana ever saw in Far Rockaway. Elena's street was very lively—about eight children on small bikes were playing under the supervision of several adults, who were sitting on beach chairs that they had put out on the sidewalk. An older man was fixing one of the kids' bikes, and the children were getting impatient because they wanted to ride. Patricia also saw from a distance a group of men playing dominoes and laughing. She did not at that point know that one of the men was Alberto's father, Ramon, but she would recognize him there on later visits.

Elena was a little chubby, had her hair up in a ponytail, and wore black leggings and a white T-shirt that said MIAMI. Her hair was dyed a reddish color, though its natural color was dark brown. She had gold jewelry on, but wore no makeup. She had come to the United States, at the age of eighteen, from the large, fertile Cibao region north of Santo Domingo, the origin of many of the Dominican families in New York City. As was common for many Dominicans who came to New York late in the 1990s, several decades after the great wave of immigration that had begun after Trujillo's death in 1961, Elena was not the first of her family to come to the United States; many of her family members were already here, including two of her three siblings and both of her parents. She had come initially on a tourist visa, but eventually her father was able to sponsor her for her green card.

During the first visit, her son Alberto kept making a lot of funny faces that everyone laughed at. He had learned how to wave "bye-bye" and did it all the time when family members told him to. He waved in slow motion, and his gesture looked more like flamenco than a good-bye. He also smiled at everyone, and after a few minutes of intently observing Patricia, he smiled at her too.

What was most memorable to Patricia about this first visit with Elena—aside from her own relief at the relative safety of the neighborhood—was the ease with which she, a research interviewer and stranger to the household, was integrated into the large network centered on Elena and her children. Even before her first visit, as Patricia was scheduling it on the phone, she could hear Elena's husband Ramon interjecting that if she came on such-and-such a day they could make "asopao" (a Dominican stew) for her. About twenty minutes into the first visit, Lola, Elena's aunt, arrived without notice and kissed Patricia in greeting as if unsurprised to see her there. Then, about an hour later, Maria Graciela, Elena's mother, arrived. She also kissed Patricia hello as if she were part of the family. Elena did not introduce Patricia to either woman; perhaps she said, "This is Patricia," but she did not say who she was or why she was there. Neither Lola nor Maria Graciela asked. It turned out that this was nothing unusual for the family. Over the course of the next nine visits, Patricia was to observe again and again visits from relatives and other people, both within the building and around the neighborhood. Alberto's godmother, Elena's cousin, visited at least once a week. At various times Elena's great-uncle and Maria Graciela's husband visited. Maria Graciela came herself every day right after she completed her work as a home care attendant. These visitors interacted regularly with Alberto. Maria Graciela, in particular, was a major figure in his life. As Alberto grew into toddlerhood, Patricia observed that Maria Graciela read to him regularly.

Not only were the extended networks rich in social interactions in the Espinal household, but they were important in their work lives as well. Elena had obtained her job through her mother: they worked at the same home health care agency. Unlike Emiliana's and Victor's jobs, this was a unionized job, so that when Elena had to undergo an emergency C-section at Alberto's birth, she was able to take off three paid months to recover. Elena's extended network formed a web of supports that was centered on her work and the children's care and school schedules but was also available for the unexpected needs that came up. Elena's sister, who lived down the block, visited the family nearly every day and took care of Alberto when Elena needed to run errands.

How might these support figures in Alberto's life have mattered for his development? Multiple figures in the Espinal household provided Alberto with not only love and affection but also stimulation in the form of early language activities. Right from birth, Alberto was exposed to both Spanish and English. Elena and Ramon tended to watch Spanish-language TV, but when Josefina, Alberto's nine-year-old sister, entered the room, she would switch the TV to English-language programs. She also spoke both Spanish and English to Alberto, unlike Elena and Ramon, who spoke only Spanish. As is common in the later development of the second generation, by age ten Josefina had started to respond to her mother in English.

Patricia observed book-reading activities in the Espinal household. One book in English had thick cardboard pages with big pictures and large-font text. During a visit when Alberto was twenty months old, he flipped the pages of this book and "talked" as if he were reading. He said "guaw guaw" ("woof woof") when he saw a picture of a dog in the book. Whenever he did this, Elena would smile back and say in Spanish, "What's that? The guaw guaw? Show me where it is." Maria Graciela did this too. Studies show that these forms of conversation—elaborating on children's speech and linking objects in everyday life with the words that refer to them—help support vocabulary development.

Alberto's learning was aided not only by multiple generations of adults in the household but by his older sister. Josefina was skilled in interacting with her younger brother. In one visit, Patricia observed Josefina teaching Alberto how to play with a puzzle. She began by showing him the puzzle deconstructed, but Alberto had no idea of what it should look like. When she realized this, she started to put the right pieces in the right positions, close to where they belonged, so that Alberto could just put them where they went. Whenever he was unsuccessful at putting the right piece in the right space, she would take his hand and move and direct his action in such a way that he would be able to put it where it belonged. This kind of teaching by "scaffolding"—gently directing a child in actions that are just out of his or her developmental reach—supports language development in young children.

LING RAISES GUANG

Yong, our field-worker assigned to Ling, a mother in her thirties from China, will never forget his second meeting with her family. He had tried to arrange the meeting for midafternoon on a weekday. Two days before the meeting, Ling called. She was abrupt in her Mandarin: "Can you come meet us in midtown at this address at 7:45 Wednesday morning?" The address was not near her home, which was in Chinatown. Yong, who had been trained to be flexible and responsive to the often shifting and nonstandard schedules of parents in our study, immediately said yes. Much to his surprise, the meeting place that Ling had chosen was an administrative office of the New York City Department of Education. The meeting would not be what Yong had expected: a relaxed chance to hang out and observe the daily routine of Ling, her husband Wei, and their son Guang. Instead, he was being recruited as a translator to help transfer Guang to another school. Lacking a large network of extended family like Elena's, Ling, a mother from Fujian province on the eastern coast of China, was adept at recruiting the relatively few members of her social network for instrumental aid.

Guang, an eleven-year-old with a prematurely dry sense of humor, was the older of Ling and Wei's two children. As a language broker in training, Guang would wink occasionally at Yong while he was translating for Ling. Ling and Wei felt that Guang was much less close to them emotionally than their younger child, their daughter Mei. They thought this might have been because they sent him back as an infant to China for several years, between the ages of four months and four years. In one of the big surprises of our study, we were unable to follow the Chinese infants we recruited at birth because the vast majority of them were taken on this very same journey in the first years of their lives. Guang's story was therefore our only ethnographic window into the experience of these infants and how they fared after their return to the United States, usually at the age of four or five.

Guang often asked his parents, "Why did you send me back?" He did not know that Ling and Wei had sent about $1,500 a year back in remittances to Ling's parents to help raise him. At entry into preschool, shortly after his return from Fujian province, a teacher in his Manhattan Chinatown preschool asked Guang, "Did your parents treat you nice?" He replied, "No—only my grandparents." The transition from grandparents he trusted and loved to parents he had never known was not easy, and even seven years later this separation was steadfastly lodged in his psyche.

Ling had come to the United States at the beginning of the 1990s, early in the wave of immigration from Fujian province that came to dominate low-income Chinese immigration to this country in that decade.[5] This was exactly the same period when Mexican migration to New York swelled from a trickle to a steady stream. Like the Cantonese who had come during the previous decades and had formed the majority of Chinatowns in U.S. cities, the Fujianese came from largely rural backgrounds in one of the eastern provinces. (Fujian province is just north of Guangdong, or

Canton, province.) Ling left because "there was nothing to do—no jobs there" (that is, in the town near Fuzhou city where she lived). She was the first in her immediate family to go to the United States, her connection there being Wei, to whom she was already married. She had met her husband at a tire factory, and Wei had left for New York three years before her. Like most of the Fujianese wave of migrants to New York, they were undocumented and arrived in the city with the assistance of the "snakeheads" to whom they paid enormous sums to make the crossing. Sums of tens of thousands of dollars are impossible for most emigrants to pay at once, and so they incur large debts. The combined pressure of these debts and the high cost of infant child care in the United States compelled many in this wave of pioneers, who did not have their own parents around, to send their babies born within the first several years of arrival back to Fujian province to be raised by their grandparents. Ling, like most of her female counterparts from Fujian prior to 9/11, worked in the garment industry to pay off the debt. Her husband worked in Chinese restaurants. After several years of twelve-hour work shifts, six days a week, Fujianese immigrants are usually able to pay off their debts.[6]

Guang's family lived at the edge of Manhattan's Chinatown, the far downtown historic center of many waves of Chinese immigration since the nineteenth century, though only one of several Chinese ethnic enclaves in today's city. East Broadway is the center of the most recent Fujianese settlement, and the area is as important to that community as upper Broadway is to the Dominicans. This street is on the eastern border of Chinatown, angled toward the East River, and bears no relation to the better-known Broadway. The ramp to the Manhattan Bridge looms over this part of Chinatown. The neighborhood is a mix of public housing projects and private apartments in tenement walk-ups. On Ling's block, a couple of blocks away from East Broadway, Yong saw two nail salons, a McDonald's, and a ninety-nine-cent store. There were many people out on these streets at the border of Chinatown and the Lower East Side—Chinese, black, Latino, white, and Jewish Orthodox. Yong did not see a predominance of Chinese immigrants in the area. But within ten blocks were many organizations with decades-long histories of serving the Chinese immigrant community, including social service, faith-based, and political organizations.

Like nearly all of our Chinese and Mexican families, Ling lived in a cramped private apartment outside the housing subsidy system. As an undocumented immigrant, the key in-kind support of public housing or Section 8—a lifeline in the most expensive city in the United States—was not accessible to her. Her apartment was in a crumbling, five-story walk-up with a broken front-door lock.

Like Emiliana, Ling had few support figures in her life to help with

11

important tasks such as navigating New York City schools and other institutions. Her life was quite isolated: she did beading work at home, while her husband Wei worked long days stretching into the evenings at a Chinese restaurant in Brooklyn. She did not appear to have many friends or visitors to the apartment. Ling did say that financial support in the form of loans—sometimes even very large amounts in the thousands—was common practice among family networks of the Fujianese. She reported, for example, that she had loaned large amounts of money to her brother to assist in the down payment for an apartment, and she described that loan as an "unquestionable duty." She also reported the existence of formal lending pools—做会, or zuohui—in the Fujianese community that extended beyond family to friends and other nonrelatives. However, she did not trust the zuo hui—"It's like they will give you money if you need, and then we give the money bit by bit. But if you run away, there goes the organization. I dare not try it." The extended social networks available to the Dominican families in our study were characteristic of neither our Chinese (largely Fujianese) families nor our Mexican families. So when Yong entered Ling's family's life as a field-worker who would interview them ten times, he was immediately recruited as a language broker.

Ling had a mixed—sometimes laissez-faire, and sometimes very proactive—attitude toward Guang's learning. She did not have very high expectations for his school success: "I told my husband, I think we don't have the talent: we didn't have people who studied in the last generation." She pointed out the family across the hall in their Chinatown building: the father had graduated from Qinghua University, one of the top four universities of China. She felt certain that her neighbor's children would succeed in school without even trying: "Now his children all play the video games, and his mother wouldn't care about him, but he could pass the exam and got in the secondary school, you see, how terrific he is?" Despite these statements, her actions generally showed her commitment to facilitating Guang's learning and education. With Yong's help, she enrolled her son in what she felt was a better school. Earlier in his life, she had felt that it was very important to enroll Guang in preschool, and she had made sure that he returned to the United States in time to enter preschool and receive this early exposure to English. She berated him if he did not help his seven-year-old sister Mei with her homework. However, she enrolled him for only a brief time in "shadow schooling," or Chinese language school—a common way for immigrant parents to bolster their children's schooling and maintain their Chinese fluency.[7] Ling reported that she "got lazy" about making the extra commute that was involved in getting Guang to the weekend school. Contrary to the findings of many scholars of East Asian parenting, Ling seemed to believe that innate ability matters more than effort in children's school success.

ORGANIZATION OF THE BOOK

The stories of Emiliana, Elena, and Ling suggest striking differences in their everyday experiences as mothers of young children. Despite sharing the same city and subway line, many features of their daily routines—support from social networks, work conditions, access to in-kind supports like housing or child care subsidies, knowledge about preschools and schools, and neighborhood resources—were different. These features are all important influences on children's learning in the first years of life. The *developmental contexts* of Victor, Alberto, and Guang—not only the settings in which they spent their own days and nights but also their parents' settings, which indirectly affected them—were very different. These differences occurred even though we chose families for our sample to be as similar as possible on traditional indicators of socioeconomic status, such as income, parental education, and employment. Newborns were recruited from public hospitals serving largely low-income families; they were all born in the United States, nearly all of them to first-generation immigrant mothers; and they all lived in New York City. They represented the three immigrant groups we sampled for our study: Dominicans, Mexicans, and Chinese.

When our research team recruited these mothers at the time of their children's birth, we did not realize that they would differ on a key legal marker that appears to have a profound influence on the everyday routines and resources in these households: undocumented status. This story emerged from the qualitative interviews and became an important part of the study as our fieldwork team realized the impact that documentation status can have on children's development.

Emiliana's and Ling's undocumented status and Elena's documented status fit a pattern that was common at this point in the history of New York City and U.S. immigration policy. Their statuses were representative of their respective immigrant groups. The majority of low-income Mexicans and close to a majority of the low-income Chinese who arrived in New York during the period our families came were undocumented.[8] The undocumented immigrants, arriving after both the federal amnesty of 1986 and passage of the highly restrictive immigration and welfare reform laws of 1996, had no clear path to citizenship.[9] Victor Sr., a taxpaying immigrant working twelve-hour days, six days a week, had been waiting for a work visa for eleven years—in vain. Ling and her husband Wei came to New York bearing crushing debts of tens of thousands of dollars to the smugglers who brought them into the country. Their long work hours in their first years in the United States (like Victor Sr.'s, they typically worked twelve hours a day, six days a week) were devoted to fighting their way up to a zero balance in their finances. On the other hand, Dominicans who came to New York during this period included a much smaller proportion of undocumented because, having arrived late in a decades-long wave of immigration, this group was much more likely to have relatives with permanent resident or citizenship status already in the States.[10] Many of the Dominican parents in our study were therefore able to enter under family reunification provisions or with work or tourist visas obtained with the help of these older pioneer generations.

Despite the differences in the legal statuses of their parents, the children of Emiliana, Elena, and Ling, as well as all of the focal children in our study, shared a single status: U.S. citizenship. Our study recruited newborns in New York City, so by definition these children were born with all the rights of U.S. citizens. In this respect, too, our families were representative of their counterparts across the nation. In nearly all U.S. families with at least one undocumented parent and a child under six (91 percent), that child is a U.S. citizen.[11] Many families in this study shared this most common type of "mixed status"—undocumented parent with citizen child—with the households of roughly 4 million children in the United States.[12]

Emiliana, Elena, and Ling came to New York with the hopes of economic success. They also came during their prime childbearing years. The average age of our Mexican mothers when they came to the United States was twenty; for the Dominicans the arrival age was seventeen, and for the Chinese it was twenty-three. There was a larger range of ages for the Dominicans (stretching from early childhood into adulthood), with smaller ranges for the Mexicans and Chinese, who generally came as adults. Although we did not obtain information on their decision to have children in the United States, one cause for the widely observed "immigrant optimism" among the recently arrived—optimism concerning future prospects, economic success, and even lower perceptions of discrimination—may be the future potential not only to become U.S. citizens but to raise children who are citizens from birth and thus fully integrated into U.S. society.[13] Within the first decade of their arrivals in New York, Emiliana, Elena, and Ling had children. (On this front we do not have any comparison group of childless immigrants, as our study by definition was of babies born in New York City hospitals.)

Should we be concerned about the development of the children of Emiliana, Elena, and Ling—Victor, Alberto, and Guang? Hundreds of studies suggest the importance of early cognitive, social, emotional, and attentional skills for later school and life success.[14] Owing in part to the foundations of brain architecture being laid in the first years of life, infancy and early childhood is a developmental period that is highly sensitive to environmental influence. Without adequate cognitive stimulation and resources from adults, proper nutrition and health care, and the constant "serve and return" of early responsive and nurturing caregiving, child development can be delayed or go off track. In this book, I ask whether parental undocumented status, by altering the everyday experiences and resources available to households, harms children's development above and beyond the effects of relatively low parental income and education.

The public view of children of undocumented immigrants is not rosy. Some policymakers decry their use of public resources, such as welfare or health care. From this vantage point, these children are burdens to the nation, taking resources away from other families. On the other hand, these children are likely to spend the bulk of their lives in the United States, and therefore as a society we must care about their future success, well-being, and productivity.

Young children are particularly important to consider because early cognitive skills are important for lifetime success. At as early as three years of age, these skills are linked to later school readiness, subsequent achievement, and even adult earnings. Although cognitive skills are one of the most stable individual characteristics,[15] in the first years of life they are malleable and sensitive to environmental influence.[16] The Nobel Prize–winning economist James Heckman posits that because early skills beget later skills, investment in cognitive development in the first years of life provides greater long-term returns, in the form of later economic productivity, than investment in middle childhood or adolescence.

In this volume, I aim to describe the story of how undocumented parents raise their citizen children in the United States. This story, ignored in the public and scholarly domains, reframes the undocumented as parents of current and future citizens of the nation. By focusing on the everyday experiences of parenting and child development in these families, I also am able to describe the consequences of undocumented status for the developmental contexts and early learning of children in the first years of life. Using a mix of ethnographic, survey, and child assessment data collected between birth and age three, I present both detailed descriptions of the everyday experiences of being an undocumented parent and quantitative analysis of how such experiences matter for the actual developmental status of children.

The Development of Young Children of
Undocumented Parents: What We Know

How are young children of undocumented parents faring? Although data on this population are hard to come by—most survey studies do not ask about documentation status per se—we can glean some patterns from a few studies that have asked about the citizenship status of parents. And as a rough proxy, we can examine the relative developmental status of children from groups that differ in proportions of undocumented in the

United States. In interpreting these findings, we need to examine how differences among groups hold up after adjusting for traditional indicators of socioeconomic status (SES), since undocumented immigrants are likely to have lower SES than those who arrive with permanent resident or citizenship status.[17]

National data show that children from immigrant groups with higher proportions of undocumented are faring less well, especially on early cognitive school readiness, than their counterparts from groups with lower proportions of undocumented. One of the national studies is the Early Childhood Longitudinal Study–Kindergarten Cohort (ECLS-K). Data from this study, which recruited more than twenty thousand young children in a nationally representative sample in 2002, show some reason for concern about the early development of children in Mexican families, who have the highest proportion of undocumented parents among immigrant groups in the United States. Young children of Mexican immigrant parents are generally performing less well on standardized reading and math skills at kindergarten entry relative not only to white children of native-born parents but also to African American children and children of Dominican immigrant parents.[18] The contrast to Dominican children is striking in that Dominican immigrant parents have lower levels of undocumented status than their Mexican counterparts (as we will see in chapter 2) but share with them relatively low SES and Latino backgrounds. These differences are of moderate to large magnitude (about 0.40 standard deviation relative to African American and Dominican children and about 0.90 standard deviation relative to white children). The differences are reduced, but do not disappear, after adjusting for traditional indicators and correlates of socioeconomic status, such as parental education, employment, income, and family structure.[19] Using data from a parallel study that started at nine months of age, the Early Childhood Longitudinal Study–Birth Cohort (ECLS-B), Bruce Fuller and his colleagues found, similarly, that Mexican children are at particular risk: they scored lower on overall cognitive development (the Bayley mental index) at twenty-four months than children from other Latino, African American, white, and Asian groups.[20] In their study, the difference of about half a standard deviation between Mexicans' and whites' cognitive scores is barely reduced after controlling for indicators of family structure, father presence, parent cognitive stimulation, parent depression, feeding practices, parental education, and parent full- and part-time employment.

However, these and other national data sets, such as the twenty-city Fragile Families and Child Well-Being Study, show that on measures of behavioral development and infant health, Mexican children are performing at the same levels as white children. These include measures of attentiveness and persistence, early behavior problems such as withdrawn or aggressive behaviors, and birth and early health outcomes, such as birth-weight.[21] Some of these findings may be driven by what is known as "positive selection": those who emigrate are healthier, on average, than their counterparts who do not emigrate, and healthier even than their U.S.-born counterparts in the same ethnic group. For example, more recently immigrated or first-generation adult Latino populations are healthier, on average, than their second-generation counterparts, even controlling for socioeconomic status and neighborhood residence.[22] Although these studies do not distinguish documented from undocumented immigrants, they suggest that this "immigrant health paradox" applies to the undocumented. This may be true because, even within the poorer regions of countries of origin with high rates of sending the undocumented, emigrants are often of somewhat higher educational and economic status than their peers who do not leave the country.[23]

In addition to doing well on early behavioral and health measures, children of immigrant parents from East Asian countries (those from China and Korea being the most numerous) perform at higher levels than white children on reading and math skills in kindergarten.[24] In the long run, however, there is some reason to worry about the emotional well-being of this group. Several recent studies show that Chinese adolescents, while performing very well academically, report higher levels of depression and social isolation than their black, Latino, and white counterparts. Although most studies showing this pattern focus on Chinese in urban, multiethnic public schools,[25] some are national studies.[26]

None of these studies directly measures undocumented status and links it to children's development. The only large-scale study to date to do so, by Alexander Ortega and his colleagues, explored parent documentation status and parents' reports of their children's development in a large sample of California residents.[27] Parents of children under age six were interviewed not only about their documentation and citizenship status but also about the general developmental status of their children, using a ten-item scale. (Unfortunately, this study does not distinguish between different domains of child development.) In this study, the authors were able to compare undocumented and documented Mexican immigrant parents and both Mexican and white U.S.-born parents. After adjusting for confounding characteristics such as parental education, income, and language spoken at home, the researchers found that children of Mexican undocumented parents are at higher developmental risk than children of U.S.-born white parents.[28]

Why might children of undocumented parents perform less well than children of documented parents in their early learning and cognitive skills? Here the scholarly literature provides almost no clues. The only research that sheds some light on this question considers the roles of food insecurity, work conditions, and access to preschool education. For example, Jennifer van Hook and Ariel Kalil, in studies conducted on two different national data sets, found that children of noncitizen parents are more likely than children of citizen parents to experience food insecurity.[29] This difference holds up even after controlling for education, employment, and income. In studies conducted in Chicago, Los Angeles, and New York comparing documented to undocumented workers, all in low-wage jobs, researchers found higher rates of wage violations and unsafe working conditions among the undocumented.[30] In a study of adult Mexicans in California who either were citizens, had a green card, or were undocumented, the undocumented reported lower levels of use of health care and lower rates of having a usual source of health care than did the documented, but they also reported lower levels of difficulty finding care.[31] And several studies have found that young children from Mexican backgrounds are less likely than children in other Latino groups and white non-Hispanic, black non-Hispanic, and Asian children to attend preschool.[32] The data do not permit the conclusion that higher proportions of undocumented parents among Mexicans are responsible for this difference. But the fact that enrollment is lower than it is for other Latino groups, together with controls for other indicators of disadvantage, suggests that this characteristic may be playing a role.

A Conceptual Model of How Parental Undocumented Status Affects Developmental Contexts and Early Learning

In this book, I provide a comprehensive picture of how parent undocumented status can harm the development of children in the first years of their lives. I argue that undocumented status is an often unobserved factor that helps explain disparities in cognitive skills—emerging as early as twenty-four months in national studies—between groups with high rates of undocumented status and those with lower rates. Ethnographic data are ideally suited to the task of unearthing the everyday experiences of undocumented status that might affect children. In gathering that data, we focused on the struggles and triumphs of parenthood and child development between the first and third years of life; the methodology of visiting every ten weeks or so proved ideal to the task of tracking the full range of home and community settings within which each family lived. From the ethnography, several sets of experiences most clearly distinguished the undocumented from the documented within our immigrant groups. They are outlined in the conceptual model underpinning this book (figure 1.1).

Figure 1.1   Conceptual Model of Parent Undocumented Status and the Developmental Contexts of Children

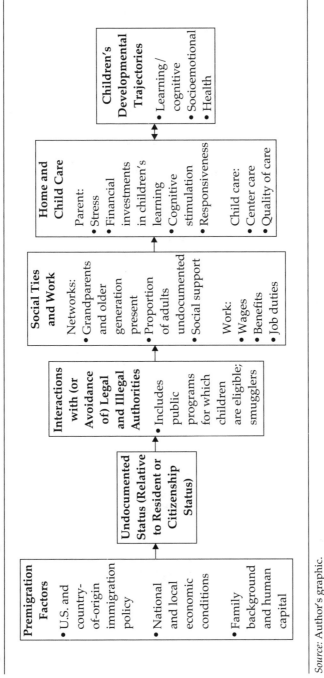

Source: Author's graphic.

From one scholarly perspective, the model depicts what sociologists refer to as experiences of incorporation—the gradual integration of new-comers into the networks, organizations, and institutions of the host country.[33] In conveying these mothers' experiences of New York and the United States, ranging from neighborhood organizations and social net-works to public policies, these data address some of the central aspects of incorporation. The large, seminal studies on youth of the second genera-tion conducted in the past twenty years have considered incorporation from such standpoints as peer relationships, discrimination, ethnic iden-tity, work opportunities, and quality of schooling.[34]

I focus more narrowly on aspects of incorporation that might be linked in particular to undocumented status, on the one hand, and to early child-hood development, on the other. The flip side of incorporation—exclu-sion—is in many ways more characteristic of the undocumented experi-ence. I also conceptualize developmental contexts as not just those settings and interactions that children directly experience, like parenting and child care, but also those everyday experiences of parents that influence chil-dren indirectly, like job quality or program eligibility. The developmental contexts that influence children more indirectly are listed on the left side of figure 1.1, and those that influence children more directly are on the right side.

From another scholarly perspective, the concerns of this book are also closely related to research on the assimilation of the post-1965 second gen-eration.[35] Sociologists of assimilation consider the contexts that influence the very diverse patterns of youth educational attainment and success among the second generation. Neighborhood factors in the United States ("contexts of reception") such as concentrated poverty, the presence of or-ganizations and peer networks that can facilitate or impede youth learn-ing, and family relationships and supports are all hypothesized to explain why some immigrant youth succeed spectacularly well and some have difficulties, even coming from the same immigrant groups with similar levels of parent education and skills. In this scholarly literature, documen-tation status has been presented as an instance of political exclusion that can affect assimilation.[36]

One other literature relevant to this book comprises qualitative studies of the everyday experiences of undocumented immigrants. Several stud-ies of undocumented Mexican immigrants in California, conducted in the 1980s and the 1990s, examine the contexts of migration, work, and family life.[37] Experiences of incorporation—whether in networks of family mem-bers and other households living in close proximity or through the accul-turative experiences of U.S.-born children in adolescence—were specific to an area of the country with a long-standing pattern of undocumented migration from Mexico. In both cases the settlements were characterized by very high concentrations of fellow Mexicans. In contrast, as I show in this volume, the undocumented Mexicans in our study were part of a much more recent wave of migration to New York City; for the most post, this group did not live in a concentrated enclave. Robert Smith has documented the new Mexican migration to New York, though from the different standpoint of transnational ties of communities and families and the experiences of youth who travel back and forth between the two countries.[38] As for Asian undocumented immigrants, work on the Fujianese in New York has been conducted by Peter Kwong and Zai Liang.[39] Again, none of these researchers have focused on undocumented parents or the effects of parental undocumented status on children.

Unlike these prior studies of incorporation, assimilation, and undocumented adults, I focus on the experiences of families with infants and toddlers. Many of the influences on youth development that have been explored in the sociological and psychological studies of the second generation are not relevant to this much earlier developmental period. After all, infants and toddlers are not choosing their own peer networks for the most part; they are not in school; they have not developed their ethnic identities; and they do not perceive that their parents are immigrants, let alone that they are documented or undocumented. The influences of parents' documentation status on the youngest must occur through a different set of developmental contexts than those that are studied in much of the literature on incorporation or assimilation.

Proceeding from left to right in figure 1.1, I first acknowledge (under "Premigration Factors") the fact that a complex mix of push-and-pull factors in both the country of origin and the host country drives flows of undocumented migration to the United States. In chapter 2, I outline the particular forces that led Emiliana, Elena, Ling, and their Mexican, Dominican, and Chinese counterparts in our larger study to come to the United States when they did, and with the particular family backgrounds and legal statuses that they had. I tell this back story by describing the recent waves of low-income migration from Mexico, the Dominican Republic, and China to New York. The push-and-pull factors include economic factors in countries and regions of origin; the recent history of immigration policies in the United States and emigration policies in the three sending nations; and the network and human capital resources of migrant families. These forces shaped the dramatic, and sometimes harrowing, narratives of how Emiliana, Elena, and Ling came from Puebla, Cibao, and Fujian to the great metropolis of New York City.

The rest of the model outlines four kinds of developmental contexts that, I argue, can transmit the influence of parents' undocumented status on early child development. Each of these sets of influences is discussed in chapters 3 through 6. The first set of experiences includes the interactions with legal and illegal authorities that become an everyday part of undocumented immigrants' experiences the minute they set foot in the United States or overstay a visa. Legal authorities represent the local, state, and federal agencies that can determine whether a parent is deported, as well as those that can offer a variety of forms of aid to citizen children. The central paradox here is that the very same government that legally excludes undocumented parents from various social institutions also offers help to their citizen children in the form of benefits and programs. Undocumented parents in this study reported avoiding contact with most government authorities, whether they were associated with deportation, like U.S. Immigration and Customs Enforcement (ICE), or with help, like the agencies administering child care subsidies or food stamps programs, for which their citizen children were usually eligible. This avoidance unfortunately results in low rates of enrollment of citizen children in programs that we know could help foster their early learning, such as center-based child care. I discuss these experiences relating to legal authorities in chapter 3. I also discuss the debts that undocumented parents often owe to illegal authorities (smugglers) early in their lives in the United States and the impact of such debts on their financial well-being, their overall level of hardship, and even the transnational migration of their infants. These interactions with legal and illegal authorities are primary channels for transmitting the influence of being undocumented to children because these experiences are so specific to that status.

The second set of experiences is embedded in more informal social ties. Although the daily routines of undocumented immigrants might appear at first glance to be the same as those of documented immigrants, the parents in our study told us about crucial differences in their households, their social networks, and the community organizations in their neighborhoods. First, in virtually all of the households of undocumented parents in our study, it appeared that all other adults in the household were also undocumented. Thus, lack of access to resources that require identification, such as savings and checking accounts and driver's licenses, characterized entire households, not just the parents in the study. Second, as recent arrivals, these parents had less social support available in their larger networks. Despite having more adults in the household, the undocumented in our sample reported having fewer people available to help with child care and making ends meet than were available to the documented. Grandparents were also much less likely to reside in the United States, in the city, or down the street. Finally, many of our undocumented parents lived in neighborhoods with few organizations serving their group and even fewer responding to the needs and potential organizing power of the undocumented. However, the picture was not all bleak: most of the Chinese families and a few of the Mexican families lived in established or emerging ethnic enclaves. The Mexican families in our study who lived in the growing enclave of East Harlem provided a picture of greater access to the coethnic community resources, networks, and organizing that may represent the future of this group, which is currently scattered across the city in neighborhoods with low proportions of fellow Mexicans. And the Chinese, despite being part of a regionally specific wave of migration from Fujian province, had relatively easy access to a variety of organizations and providers with at least fluency in Mandarin, if not Fujianese. (Most of the Fujianese immigrant mothers in our study spoke Mandarin.)

The third set of experiences that distinguished the documented from undocumented members of our ethnographic sample centered on work conditions. Experiences of work differed dramatically depending on parents' documentation status. Exploitation in employment in the first months after arrival, an extremely high number of hours worked, wage stagnation, lack of access to job benefits, and low levels of autonomy in job duties were much more common among our undocumented than documented parents. High rates of wage violations (hourly wages below the legal minimum) among our undocumented parents indicate that many of them worked at the very bottom of the urban labor market. In chapter 5, I draw on the field of work-family research to examine how the work lives of parents appear to differ depending on their documentation status.

These three sets of experiences associated with parents' undocumented status—interactions with legal and illegal authorities; everyday social ties with households, networks, and organizations; and work conditions—affect children's early development through the intimacy of the settings in which infants and toddlers spend the most time—specifically, home and child care settings. These settings represent the fourth set of developmental contexts that link parent undocumented status to children's development. I list these factors in the column at the far right of figure 1.1; they represent hypotheses drawn from decades of research in developmental psychology.

First, the broader developmental contexts linked to undocumented status may act as stressors to parents and increase their levels of distress, anxiety, and depression. Everyday experiences such as poor work conditions, lowered availability of social support, or fear of deportation may result over time in higher levels of psychological distress in parents who are undocumented, relative to those who are documented. Parental depression has been linked to lower levels of learning, because parental distress can reduce the quantity or quality of language in the home.[40] As a result of distress, parents may become withdrawn or harsh in their parenting of young children.[41] Parental stress may also affect children's biological responses and risk for disease through chronic overactivation of biological stress mechanisms or the immune system.[42] As I show in chapter 4, parents' economic hardship and distress transmitted the influence of undocumented status on children's cognitive skills at twenty-four months of age.

Second, undocumented parents may be less able to purchase learning materials for their children and engage in cognitively stimulating activities with them. Many studies have shown that this investment pathway links economic disadvantage to children's early cognitive skills. Undocumented status, above and beyond traditional indicators of socioeconomic status such as parental education or income, may reduce parents' ability to purchase learning materials for their children. Undocumented parents, for example, are less likely to enroll their citizen children in in-kind programs that could increase their disposable household income, such as food stamps or child care subsidies. Parents with less disposable income are less able to purchase learning materials. Cognitively stimulating interactions, such as reading or storytelling, may also be affected by a lower ability to purchase books, a higher number of work hours, or parental stress. These factors robustly predict early cognitive skills in young children.[43]

Finally, a third mechanism through which parents' everyday experiences of being undocumented could affect child learning is lower use of center care. This form of care is associated with higher early cognitive skills in children, especially for lower-income families.[44] This may be because, relative to other forms of out-of-home care in the first year, centers usually have caregivers with higher levels of training and skills and a greater variety of stimulating materials. Nonrelative home-based care, in particular, tends to be of lower quality than center-based care, as measured by the presence of responsive and language-rich interactions with young children.[45]

In chapter 6, I draw on our full-sample data to examine the family experiences through which undocumented status can affect children's development. I also include some of the broader contexts discussed in chapters 3, 4, and 5 when information about them is available in our survey data. In these quantitative analyses, I find that the best proxy for documentation status in the survey, household access to resources requiring identification like checking accounts, savings accounts, and driver's licenses, does indeed distinguish our groups: Mexican parents reported much lower access to such resources than Dominicans or African Americans. (Because the vast majority of Chinese infants were sent back to China in the first six months of life, we were not able to follow up the Chinese sample; I tell the story of why this occurred in chapter 2.) Lower household access to these resources, in turn, was associated with lower job autonomy and wages, lower rates of center care use, and ultimately lower cognitive skills in children at thirty-six months. These links in the quantitative data are not explained away by other potentially confounding characteristics, such as parental education, family structure, years in the United States, preferences in child care, primary language in the home, or even earlier levels of child cognitive skills as measured at fourteen months.

Interestingly, I find little support for cognitive stimulation as a pathway through which undocumented status affects three-year-old children's cognitive skills. Indeed, parents of the different ethnic groups in this study, as the stories of Emiliana, Elena, and Ling show, were equally likely to engage in stimulating activities with their children. They showed equal dedication to supporting the learning of their citizen children. There is no support in the data for cultural differences in mothers' support of their children's learning, as reflected in rates of reading to children, storytelling, or playing with toys and other stimulating materials.

In the final chapter, I spell out the implications of this work for three areas of practice and policy. First, I explore the potential benefits for undocumented parents and their children of providing a pathway to citizenship in immigration policy. Second, I suggest improvements in labor law enforcement and other routes to improving the terrible job conditions of undocumented parents. Finally, I suggest ways in which community-based programs and organizations can provide responsive services and venues for advocacy and organizing that undocumented parents will trust.

THE STUDY METHODS

All the data reported in this book are drawn from the work of the Center for Research on Culture, Development, and Education, a project funded by the National Science Foundation since 2002 and directed by Catherine Tamis-LeMonda, Diane Hughes, Niobe Way, Ronit Kahana-Kalman, Ajay Chaudry, and myself. This book is based on data from one of the two major longitudinal studies that are part of the center's work, a study of infants from 375 Dominican, Mexican, Chinese, and African American families in New York City (109 Dominican, 97 Mexican, 56 Chinese, and 113 African American). The infant study has been co-directed by Tamis-LeMonda, Kahana-Kalman, and myself; the other study (of adolescents) is directed by Hughes and Way. In 2004 and 2005, mothers of healthy newborn infants were recruited on maternity wards of public hospitals in New York City during the first day or two of their baby's life by a team of multilingual research assistants. All of the Mexican and Chinese mothers, and 85 percent of the Dominican mothers, were first-generation immigrants. All of the African American mothers were U.S.-born. The children have been followed over the course of their early development, and this book focuses on the first three years of their lives.

Several sources of data form the basis of the findings reported in this book—mainly longitudinal qualitative interviews and participant observation, but also direct child assessments and parent surveys. (For more details regarding the methodology of this study, see the appendix.) A large team of researchers administered surveys as in-person structured interviews with mothers, first on the maternity ward and then at one, six, fourteen, twenty-four, and thirty-six months. Home visits, including direct child assessments of cognitive skills, were also conducted at the fourteen-, twenty-four-, and thirty-six-month time points. All of these assessments were conducted in the language of preference of the parent and the dominant language of the child.

A sample of twenty-three families from our three immigrant groups—eleven Mexican, nine Dominican, and three Chinese—form the basis for all of the qualitative data presented in the book, including the data concerning Elena, Emiliana, and Ling. This embedded qualitative study was co-directed by Ajay Chaudry and myself. Most of these families were randomly chosen from the larger cohort of 376. The rest were drawn from an initial ethnographic study, conducted in 2002 and 2003, that preceded the recruitment of the birth cohort. Each of these families was visited between six and twelve times. Our field-workers engaged in participant-observation at home and in a variety of neighborhood settings at every visit. In addition, semistructured, recorded interviews occurred at every other visit. Visits were made when the infants were between the ages of seven and thirty months, on average once every ten weeks. Our qualitative data consist of interviews transcribed and translated from Spanish and Mandarin as well as field notes written in English by our multiethnic, multilingual team of field-workers.

The primary comparison in this book is of undocumented and documented first-generation immigrant parents. I make distinctions among the documented—that is, between legal permanent residents and citizens—in a few places where it is relevant, primarily in the sections of the book on policy access. There were no parents with refugee status in the qualitative sample. The ethnic groups in this study appeared to differ markedly in their likelihood of being undocumented, with high proportions among Mexican and Chinese parents and relatively low proportions among Dominican parents. Ten out of eleven Mexican mothers in the qualitative study were undocumented, including the vast majority of the fathers; in contrast, only one out of nine Dominican mothers was undocumented, and only one family with a Dominican mother had an undocumented father. (He was of Mexican origin.) Because there were only three Chinese in our ethnographic sample, I have no meaningful estimate of this status among them; however, 72 percent of the Chinese mothers recruited at birth sent their babies back to China within a few months. As we will see later, it is likely that the majority of this 72 percent were un-documented, as Ling was when she and Wei sent Guang back to Fuzhou. Because of this sending-back phenomenon, we stopped recruiting the Chinese sample midway through the recruitment period. We did not fol-low up this group with surveys and child assessments; I therefore lack information on how this group's children fared. The very few Chinese cases in the qualitative sample had not sent their young child back to China; however, one family (Ling's, as it turns out) had already gone through the sending and return of an older child. Therefore, Ling and Guang have particular prominence in the presentation of qualitative data on the Chinese families. Information about Guang, who was much older than the infants and toddlers in the sample, is presented to illustrate the transnational experience of children being sent back to China as newborns and returning to live with parents they do not remember having known.

The African Americans in the sample, all U.S.-born mothers, were therefore all citizens. They were not an immigrant group, although a very small proportion of these mothers were second-generation immigrants from families of West Indian backgrounds. Owing to my focus on a com-parison of documented and undocumented first-generation immigrants, I do not present qualitative analyses of the African American families. In a few places where I present quantitative comparisons of the ethnic groups, however, the African American families are included because they repre-sented the largest low-income, native-born racial-ethnic group among parents in New York City.

Documentation status is a difficult topic to research quantitatively.[46] We did not ask about undocumented status directly in any of our survey vis-its with families in the larger sample. I therefore can present neither data from the survey sample on rates of undocumented status nor quantitative estimates of its effects on parents or children. In the many discussions with field-workers about their everyday lives, however, Mexican, Domin-ican, and Chinese parents in the ethnographic sample were open about this aspect of their experience. Everyday experiences that might be associ-ated with undocumented status are the focus of this book. To protect the identities of our families, many details have been masked or combined, and direct quotes are kept to a minimum, but this has been done in such a way that the relevant patterns in the data are retained.

Chapter 2

The Hidden Face of New York: Undocumented Immigrant Parents' Routes to the City

Flood-tide below me! I see you face to face!
Clouds of the west—sun there half an hour high—I see
    you also face to face.

Crowds of men and women attired in the usual cos-
    tumes, how curious you are to me!
On the ferry-boats the hundreds and hundreds that
    cross, returning home, are more curious to me than
    you suppose.
And you that shall cross from shore to shore years
    hence are more to me, and more in my meditations,
    than you might suppose.

—Walt Whitman, "Crossing Brooklyn Ferry" (1856)

In 1647, there were already eighteen languages being spoken on the narrow streets of the fledgling settlement of New Amsterdam at the southern end of Manhattan Island.[1] In the 1850s, when Walt Whitman, the great sage and bard of New York City, wrote "Crossing Brooklyn Ferry," he saw throngs of immigrants, from the newest group—Irish escaping the Great Hunger of the 1840s—to Germans, English, and forced migrant African slaves as well as free African Americans, making their way to work from Fulton Street in Brooklyn to Fulton Street in Manhattan from his vantage point on the ferry. By the late nineteenth century, two-thirds of the city was foreign-born. As the central city for commerce in North America, blessed with the best harbor on the Eastern Seaboard, New York has drawn the peoples of the world for 450 years.

The particular countries represented in the crowds of humanity on the streets, ferries, streetcars, and subways of New York varied dramatically from decade to decade. Let us fast-forward to 1970. If you were making your way to work on the A train—the Brooklyn ferry of the twentieth century—you would have been relatively unlikely to hear a foreign language other than Spanish. If you did hear a foreign tongue, chances were it was a European language. At that time, New York City was just beginning to undergo a demographic shift that would radically change the face of the city. Eighteen percent of the city's population in that year was born outside the United States, and the ten leading countries of origin of the city's foreign-born were largely European: Italy, Poland, the Soviet Union, Germany, Ireland, Cuba, the Dominican Republic, the United Kingdom, Australia, and Jamaica (in that order). Fifteen percent of the city was Latino (largely Puerto Rican). About one-quarter of the city's population was black or African American. This was the tail end of three great waves of migration in twentieth-century New York City: the waves of European migration that had transformed New York starting in the mid-nineteenth century; the wave of Puerto Rican migration from the commonwealth to New York that started in the 1930s and had begun to decline by 1970; and the Great Migration north of black Americans from the South, starting in the 1890s and ebbing as well by the 1970s.

On the same subway line thirty years later, in 2000, you would have been roughly twice as likely to hear a foreign language as in 1970. If you were sensitive to differences in the Spanish language, you might have heard several different dialects in a single subway car. The indigenous languages of Central and South America were now more likely to be part of the mix, and you also would have heard a range of Caribbean languages and dialects. As in 1970, just about one-quarter of the city's population was black or African American. However, at 37 percent, twice as large a proportion of New Yorkers in 2000 were foreign-born.[2] More than 60 percent were either immigrants or children of immigrants. Latinos had by 2000 overtaken blacks as the largest panethnic "minority" group in the city. The list of leading countries of origin had almost completely changed: the Dominican Republic, China, Jamaica, Mexico, Guyana, Ecuador, Haiti, Trinidad and Tobago, India, and Colombia.

Shifts in documentation status among immigrant groups in the city played a hidden but powerful role in this transformation of New York City over the thirty years before our study took place. This story, largely untold in studies of the changing face of the metropolis, affects many parts of a New Yorker's daily experience. The demographics of the undocumented explain the surprisingly few ethnic backgrounds of the busboys, deliverymen, and line cooks who serve the much wider array of ethnic foods served in restaurants, delis, and groceries; the affordability of a housekeeper for middle-class New Yorkers; and the unusually low (and stable) price of a piece of fruit from a street cart, a lunch special at the local

Chinese takeout, or flowers from a street vendor. These regularities of New York's social fabric are a result of the demographic, policy, and economic forces that have shaped undocumented migration to the city in recent decades. And in turn, these regularities affect the everyday experiences of undocumented immigrant parents and their children.

The top five immigrant groups in the city in 1970 came to the city largely through legal channels—either under the hemisphere-specific quotas for immigration established in the Hart-Celler Act of 1965 and expanded in 1990 or as refugees. In contrast, in 2000 a large proportion of immigrants from Mexico, a substantial minority of immigrants from China, and a small minority of those from the Dominican Republic had entered the country without documentation or had become undocumented at the point when they overstayed a work or tourist visa.

With their origins in three of the top four immigrant groups in the city in the 2000s, Emiliana, Elena, and Ling represent the face of the new New York. The differences in their documentation status as parents of young U.S. citizens were representative of their groups as well. We cannot consider how undocumented status affected their daily lives without acknowledging that a variety of societal and policy factors in their countries of origin and the United States accounted for their migration in the first place. This chapter tells the story of these push-and-pull factors in Mexico, the Dominican Republic, China, and the United States. I show how the dramatic stories of how Emiliana, Elena, and Ling each came to New York City reflected a much larger narrative of Mexican, Dominican, and Chinese migration to the United States at the turn of the twenty-first century.

THE UNDOCUMENTED IN
U.S. FEDERAL POLICY

As of 2010, there were 10.8 million undocumented immigrants in the United States, representing a slight decline from 2008, due to the global recession, but still almost one-third of the foreign-born.[3] This number amounts to 4 percent of the nation's population and just over 5 percent of its workforce. The public's concerns about a recent rise in the number of undocumented are supported by the numbers: in 2000 an estimated 8.4 million were in the country, and the increase to 10.8 million represents a 29 percent increase over ten years.

The households of undocumented migrants in the United States are dominated by the voices of children. Over half of undocumented adults have children, and so the bulk of their households are made up of families, not single adults. Children of undocumented immigrants represent a significant segment of Americans. They are estimated to make up 6.8 percent of U.S. children in elementary or secondary school and nearly one-third (31 percent) of children of immigrants in schools.[4] In other words, on average, there is more than one child of undocumented parents in every public school classroom. In gateway cities like New York, the proportions are likely to be much higher.

Some recent policy debates have concerned whether the undocumented cross into the United States while pregnant in order to have a child born as a U.S. citizen. The national evidence, calculated by the demographer Jeffrey Passel, shows that, to the contrary, more than half of U.S. births to the undocumented occur five years or later after immigration.[5] Thus, rather than being "anchor babies" who give their undocumented parents a foothold in the United States, these children have immigrant parents who have generally been living and working in their new homeland for years prior to giving birth to their first U.S. citizen child.

Despite recent increases in nontraditional gateway communities, New York City continues to be a major draw for immigrants to the United States, including the undocumented.[6] Between 1892 and 1954, the city was the primary gateway for all immigration to the United States, with millions making their way through the halls of Ellis Island. In the decades since, California, the Southwest, Florida, and Illinois have also become gateways for both legal and undocumented immigration. The undocumented immigrant population was much more dispersed in 2008 than it was in 1990. Despite this scattering of new undocumented immigrants to many states that have not been traditional gateways of immigration, New York State, from which all of the parents in our study were drawn, remains a major draw. The state was eighth in the nation in the proportion of undocumented workers in the labor force in 2008, with an estimated 6.7 percent of its labor force undocumented.[7]

A common misconception is that all undocumented immigrants in the United States are Mexicans—and conversely, that nearly all Mexicans are undocumented. This belief is not accurate: border-crossers include not just those crossing the U.S.-Mexico border but also those who arrive from the sea or across the Canadian border. Approximately 45 percent of the undocumented are visa-overstayers who technically become undocumented at the point when their visa expires.[8] The two most common types of visas that are overstayed are tourist and work visas; the majority of undocumented from the Dominican Republic, for example, have overstayed a tourist or work visa.

Why are there so many undocumented immigrants in the United States now? Much of the answer lies in changes in federal policy, which have affected particular immigrant groups in different ways. Three major waves of legislation, enacted in 1965, 1986, and 1996, altered the mix of countries from which immigrants to the United States came, as well as immigrants' access to residency and citizenship.

The watershed federal immigration law of the last fifty years was the 1965 Hart-Celler Act. In place of the unequal nation-specific quotas for immigration of the 1924 Johnson-Reed Act, based on racial and regional preferences, the Hart-Celler Act instituted equal quotas and extended them to the Western Hemisphere. The 1924 law, for example, included much higher annual quotas for northern European immigrants than for their Asian, Jewish, and southern and eastern European counterparts. The numbers of Chinese, Japanese, and East Indian immigrants allowed into the country, for example, were minuscule. The 1924 law retained many of the features of the racial exclusion laws of the late nineteenth and early twentieth centuries, such as the Chinese Exclusion Act of 1882—which created, for the first time in the history of the United States, the category of "illegal immigrant."

The Hart-Celler Act also retained the priority given to family reunification in allowing immigrants into the United States legally, and it included occupational preferences. Both priorities had the purpose of favoring European immigrants; people from these countries were more likely to have relatives already living in the United States and to have advanced skills of interest to American employers.[9] However, the 1976 amendment to the Hart-Celler Act closed a loophole that had allowed children of the undocumented to sponsor their parents for legal residency. Since then, only at the age of twenty-one can a citizen child of an undocumented parent sponsor that parent for legal residency. To start that process, the parent must return to the country of origin and apply for citizenship from there.

The most far-reaching effect of the Hart-Celler Act was to increase immigration from Latin America and Asia. Hart-Celler in large part produced the "new second generation" of children born of Latino and Asian American immigrants to the United States, a demographic that has profoundly changed the face of America. In New York City, the transformation of immigrants from the still largely European list of countries of origin in 1970 to the largely Latin American and Asian list in 1990 was a direct result of this law.

Our story, however, is not yet complete. Policy changes since Hart-Celler have drastically altered the access of undocumented immigrants to legal residency. The Immigration Reform and Control Act (IRCA) of 1986 instituted for the first time sanctions for employers who knowingly hire undocumented immigrants. In addition, it provided amnesty to undocumented immigrants who could provide proof of continuous residency and employment since 1982. This law was an odd mix of punitive and generous, reflecting conflicts among the interests of several concerned parties: conservative policymakers trying to stem the tide of illegal immigration; advocates and Latino and Asian rights groups fighting discrimination; agribusinesses trying to attract more foreign, low-wage labor; and the broader business sector, which was concerned about potential sanctions against employers who unknowingly hired illegal immigrants.[10] Between the initial bills and the passage of the legislation, employers' concerns were lessened by a provision that they would not be required to check the authenticity of immigrant workers' documents. The sanctions against employers have therefore largely not been enforced since 1986, although the Obama administration is currently moving toward stronger enforcement. The amnesty provisions of IRCA ultimately resulted in legalization for the majority of the undocumented then residing in the United States (roughly 1.7 million, or 70 percent).[11] It also reduced the flow of migrants across the U.S.-Mexican border in the two years following enactment of the legislation.[12] As we will see later in the chapter, this law was largely responsible for the low rates of undocumented status among recently arrived Dominicans in New York.

The second major shift since Hart-Celler occurred after a majority Republican Congress swept into power in the 1994 midterm elections. Republican net gains of fifty-four seats in the House and nine in the Senate dramatically altered the policy landscape for legal and illegal immigrants in the United States. Two major laws subsequently restricted access to federal programs as well as to residency and citizenship and broadened the circumstances leading to deportation. The federal welfare reform legislation of 1996 (the Personal Responsibility and Work Opportunity Reconciliation Act, or PRWORA) sharply restricted eligibility for federal means-tested programs for legal immigrants arriving after 1996. Guidelines differed by program.[13] For example, post-enactment (after 1996), legal immigrants became ineligible for welfare and Medicaid in the first five years after their entry into the United States. To receive food stamps, legal immigrants had to prove that they had worked in the United States for at least ten years. A few select groups were not subject to this restriction (refugees or asylees in the first seven years post-entry, children who arrived before 1996, and some elderly and disabled). States could provide their own funding to replace these programs for post-enactment immigrants; they have varied in the degree to which they have done this.[14] Undocumented immigrants' federally funded benefits were restricted to Medicaid emergency care. U.S. citizen children continued to be eligible for these programs, even if one or both of their parents were not.

In New York State, the focus of this study's data, the restrictions on Medicaid for legal immigrants were lifted through the New York State Court of Appeals in June 2001 in the *Aliessa v. Novello* decision.[15] The state restored full Medicaid eligibility to legal immigrants who met the program's income guidelines, with benefits paid for entirely by the state. The welfare reform law did not change eligibility regulations for undocumented immigrant parents in New York. They remained ineligible for the majority of means-tested programs in the state, except for emergency care and prenatal and postnatal (up to six months) care.

Although PRWORA's immigrant provisions were aimed at restricting access for recently arrived legal immigrants, the policy produced a "chilling effect" on take-up of programs for a wide range of eligible populations among immigrants.[16] This broader impact of the law is relevant to our story. In the next chapter, I present the enrollment rates of citizen children of undocumented parents in programs and benefits for which they were eligible.

The Illegal Immigrant Reform and Immigrant Responsibility Act (IIRIRA), passed in the same year of 1996, instituted additional restrictions in many areas governing migration. The law responded to concerns that increases in illegal immigration to the United States were harming, not helping, the economy. The uneasy balance between the demands of agriculture and the service economy and lawmakers tilted toward exclusion and deportation. Under IIRIRA, anyone who had been in the United States unauthorized for a year or more and who had left the country became inadmissible with any legal status for a period of ten years. Prior to the law, individuals who overstayed their visas could become legal permanent residents by paying a fee.

The 1996 IIRIRA legislation greatly expanded the circumstances under which immigrants suspected of being undocumented could be deported. For the first time, local law enforcement and other officials could declare individuals to be inadmissible to the United States, thus initiating deportation without judicial oversight or review. IIRIRA also greatly expanded the definition of prior "aggravated felonies," which made a legal resident subject to deportation, to include crimes more minor than under previous laws (for example, perjury, failing to appear in court for a crime where the potential sentence was two years or more, drunken driving, and shoplifting). Serving a sentence for a crime prior to 1996 also qualified an immigrant for deportation. Finally, "public charge" provisions to ensure that immigrants applying for citizenship did not rely on government assistance were made more demanding. Relative sponsors of legal immigrants (except for immigrant spouses or children of U.S. citizens) were required to provide a legally enforceable affidavit of support indicating that they took responsibility for ensuring the immigrant's income for ten years following the entry of that person into the United States.

Overall, the sequence of laws since IRCA in 1986 has made pathways to citizenship more difficult. But the ways in which the Hart-Celler law and its amendment, IRCA, and the laws of 1996 affected flows of migration from particular nations depended in part on economic and immigration policies in those countries of origin. The causes and course of undocumented flows of Mexicans, Dominicans, and Chinese in twenty-first-century New York City cannot be told as a single story. Thus, the narratives of how the mothers from these groups in our study came to the United States are dramatically different. Both the overall demographic characteristics of arriving immigrants from these three countries and each immigrant's "adventures," as one Mexican mother euphemistically called the circumstances of her crossing, were shaped by the policy and local economic contexts in Mexico, the Dominican Republic, and China.

MEXICAN PARENTS AND EMILIANA'S JOURNEY

Emiliana's migration to New York City is part of the latest chapter in a long history of migration from Mexico to the United States. The large and recent wave of migration from the Mixteca region of Mexico to the city has fairly high rates of undocumented status and lacks the long-standing ethnic enclaves and associated organizations to which Dominicans and Chinese in the city have access. The high rates of undocumented status in this group are a reflection of the latest phase in a long history of conquest, economic interdependence, and shifting inclusion and exclusion of Mexicans in the States. Emiliana's journey to the United States was typical of the journeys undertaken by the most rapidly growing immigrant group in New York City—a group scattered across the city whose numbers are still relatively low but one that is slowly transforming the economic and cultural life of the city.

Mexicans made up 56 percent of all undocumented immigrants in the United States in 2008. Viewed another way, it is estimated that just over half of the foreign-born Mexicans in the United States—55 percent—are undocumented.[17] Of the remainder of undocumented immigrants, roughly two-thirds are from other Latin American countries (particularly the poorer nations of Central America), and one-third are from Asia (principally China, India, Korea, and the Philippines). Mexican undocumented immigrants usually arrive by crossing the border on foot.

Policy debates about illegal migration are dominated by concerns about Mexican immigration. "Illegal alien" has become synonymous with "Mexican." Some of the policy options floated during the 2006 cycle of policy debate—which ultimately did not result in congressional action—included establishing temporary guest worker status; allowing unauthorized immigrants who had been in the United States more than a certain number of years to pay a fine and progress toward citizenship; and setting employment history requirements (for example, requiring a period of continuous employment). These concerns have roots in the long and complex history of U.S.-Mexico border and immigration policies. I concentrate here on the recent history, since 1965.[18]

The Hart-Celler Act had the paradoxical effect of increasing undocumented migration from Mexico. Because of the new per-country restrictions, the annual quota for Mexico (40,000) represented a large reduction in potential numbers allowed from Mexico compared to the prior Johnson-Reed Act and the "bracero" (guest worker) program in place from 1943 to 1964. Undocumented migration rose as a result.[19] An amendment to Hart-Celler in 1976 placed a further restriction on the Western Hemisphere. Following this new cap of 20,000 per year, huge numbers of Mexicans—over three-quarters of a million in 1976—were deported.[20]

Undocumented migration from Mexico also rose in the 1990s because of what was happening in both the Mexican and U.S. economies. After the peso crisis of December 1994, the Mexican economy was in tatters. The simultaneous sustained expansion of the U.S. economy in the 1990s and early 2000s—the largest and longest period of growth since World War II—provided plenty of job opportunities up north. These two factors drove the extraordinary increases in undocumented migration from Mexico in the late 1990s and 2000s, which occurred despite tougher border enforcement and increasing deportation rates under President George W. Bush. The growth in undocumented migration did not begin to slow until 2008 and 2009, and then only because of the recession of late 2008 and 2009, which hit low-wage immigrant workers particularly hard. Unemployment soared among immigrants in the United States, surpassing unemployment rates among the native-born by early 2009.[21]

How do undocumented immigrants from Mexico compare in their education and work skills to either those who do not emigrate at all or those who arrive with a visa or residency? Studies show that the answer differs depending on the comparison group. Undocumented Mexican immigrants are often of somewhat higher educational status than others in the same geographic region who do not depart, and the former also tend to have more network members in the United States already. This "positive selectivity" has been observed for many immigrant groups.[22] If we compare undocumented to documented migrants, however, the undocumented are more likely to be poorer, to have less education, and to come from a rural area.[23]

Mexican migration to different cities in the United States is specific to particular sending regions in Mexico. Most in the recent group of undocumented migrants came to New York City from the Mixteca region, an area that has in common a set of indigenous languages and cultures. It spans much of the state of Puebla and parts of Guerrero and Oaxaca.[24] The beginning of this migration from Mixteca has been traced to the mid-1940s. By 1980 there were still only 40,000 Mexicans in New York City. Their incomes were quite high relative to other Latino groups—this initial small group of migrants were on a par with Cubans, for example, in their socioeconomic indicators. The big surge in migration from this region did not occur until after the passage of IRCA, when 9,000 Mexicans in New York applied for papers.[25] By 1990 there were 100,000 Mexicans in New York, and by 2000, roughly 275,000. Their average incomes were much lower than those of the group of Mexicans in the city in 1980, which is in accordance with there being a higher proportion of undocumented among them.[26]

Most of the Mexican mothers in our study arrived from the Mixteca region during the mid to late 1990s, when the economy of Mexico was particularly weak and the U.S. economy was soaring (see figure 2.1). The states making up the Mixteca region are some of the poorest in Mexico; in 2000, Puebla, for example, ranked seventh in socioeconomic disadvantage among the thirty-one Mexican states.[27] Of the ten Mexican mothers in the qualitative study who were undocumented (out of a total of eleven), none had an immediate family member with papers. The group in our sample thus had almost no links to the amnesty of 1986 to 1988; this makes statistical sense in that the growth from 40,000 Mexicans in 1980 to 275,000 in 2000 could not have been driven entirely by close relatives of the 9,000 Mexicans who applied for amnesty through IRCA. Instead, a chain-migration process occurred in which family or wider network members who had crossed the border and done well—by sending back remittances that supported their families and communities—spread the word about economic opportunity in New York.[28]

Emiliana grew up in a large family that struggled to make ends meet in a town in the state of Puebla. Their house was a relatively flimsy wooden one that was rebuilt with bricks only in recent years. Emiliana took care of her seven younger siblings while her mother and father worked. Her father, in addition, was "celoso" (jealous) of his eldest daughter and kept her inside. She was not allowed to ever visit friends and was only allowed outside their house to go to school. In 1994 her father went to the United States, crossing the border without papers to seek work. He came back to Mexico with the news that opportunities were good. Despite his emphasis until then on keeping Emiliana indoors, as soon as he felt that she was old enough, he sent her with her younger brother Hector to the United States, telling them that they needed to help out the family. She told Ana, the field-worker, that both she and Hector had wanted to continue their education (she finished secundaria, or ninth grade, but did not go on to preparatoria).

Arriving as single adults, Emiliana and Hector brought a large family's hopes and economic needs with them in their crossing. Emiliana called her journey "the Adventure," and like many of the other Mexican aventuras we heard about, she crossed in the pitch-black of the southwestern desert night into her new life. The journey across the border involved

Figure 2.1 Origins of Mexican Mothers in the Mixteca Region of Mexico

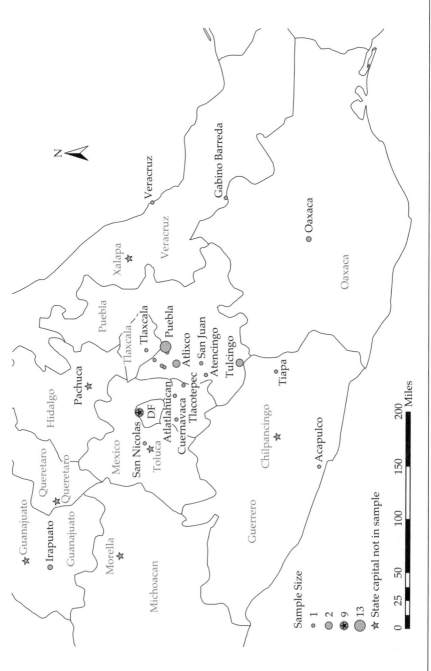

Source: Author's graphic utilizing data from the Early Childhood Cohort Study (Center for Research on Culture, Development, and Education 2009).

walking in the cold over grassy hills, without any clothes except what she was wearing, in a small group of about eight. Nobody carried food or water. Anything heavy would have slowed them down too much if they had needed to run during the several-hour-long night crossing. The coyote who had picked them up guided them and told them on occasion to roll down a hill, "as if we were rocks," in order to evade la migra, who were patrolling in helicopters. As she was walking, Emiliana thought a lot about her mother. It very difficult for her to leave her mother, knowing that she would not see her for a very long time. She felt torn between this loss and the obligation to support her mother financially.

Unlike some of the other Mexicans in our study, Emiliana arrived after only one try. For a few, it took as many as three tries over several weeks, with single crossings taking as long as a week. One of the mothers talked about a friend who had traveled with an infant through a tunnel, crouched over (as in the film *El Norte*, noted the field-worker, who was very surprised that an infant had made the crossing). This friend spoke of her fear of what she might find at the other end—the exit closed up, for instance, or la migra waiting.

When Emiliana came to the United States, a crossing cost about $1,500 a person for an adult and somewhat less for a child. (For those who came in the early 1990s, the cost was roughly $800; by the mid-2000s it had risen to $2,000.) As was common during that time, successful border-crossers were picked up one by one in cars, to be taken to a hotel. At the hotel they could contact their relatives in Mexico, and it was there that they had to pay the coyote. They then received plane tickets to their final destination—in this case New York.

When Emiliana arrived, her first impression of New York was that it was dirty. Although she wanted to go out and explore Manhattan, her brother Hector was protective and did not allow her to leave the apartment during his very long work hours. Other mothers in our Mexican sample reported similar first impressions of New York as they compared it to Mexico. Indeed, the two legendary metropolises of North America, New York and Mexico City, are often compared. For the mothers in our study, New York suffered in the comparison; most who had been to "D.F." (the Distrito Federal, or Mexico City) were not impressed by New York, finding the rats and cockroaches a nasty contrast to the cleanliness they associated with Mexico City. "Filthy" and "not that big a city" were some of the reactions. (Indeed, New York is not that big compared to the largest city in the Western Hemisphere.) Several mentioned how lonely and painful the first weeks in New York were. Husbands or fathers often prevented them from leaving the house in the first weeks.

The women who had come directly from rural areas, most commonly villages in Puebla, were more impressed by the night lights of New York

City, but the transition was more jolting for them. One Mexican mother, Victoria, reported a particularly drastic contrast between life in her village and the transition to the United States. During her border crossing, she saw two animals—ironically, they looked like coyotes—which she called nahuales. These, she said, are animals that used to be children whose parents wanted them to be evil. Such parents take their newborn baby to the mountain and allow an animal (coyote) to lick the baby clean. Then the animal leaves. When the parents want to complete the transformation, they take the child to an ant nest and roll the child in the ants. At this point, the baby takes the form of the animal that licked him or her clean. The nahuales live around people and change to animals when they want to steal them. Victoria was astonished to see nahuales on her walk across the border. When she arrived finally at the airport in Los Angeles for her flight to New York, she was stunned anew by her very first view of airplanes. She thought they were large animals. When she finally got on board, on the first airplane flight of her life, she felt dizzy, as if she would throw up. Another mother, Adelina, said that one of her male relatives, upon seeing his first New York snowfall after arriving from rural Morelos, was amazed and asked when the penguins and polar bears would start to fall. She explained that "that is the way it is when you come from a small town in Mexico where you have not had a lot of exposure to the outside world."

Why did we find such high rates of undocumented status in the Mexican mothers in this qualitative sample, relative to the participants in Robert Smith's study, the largest prior study of Mexicans in New York?[29] There may have been some variation in who agreed to be in the study; however, our recruitment rates for both our main study and its qualitative part did not appreciably differ across ethnic groups. And as we will see in chapter 4, the neighborhoods that the Mexicans in our study lived in were representative of New York City neighborhoods with Mexican residents in the 2000 census. Our population of parents, however, mothers of newborn infants, were much younger than the parents in Smith's sample, and they were also part of a newer generation of migration with lower rates of documentation than the group whose arrival here was linked to IRCA. In addition, most of Smith's sample first came to the United States before IRCA; he describes a large decline in the undocumented status of members of this group between their first trips back to Mexico and 1992, by which time many had achieved documented status thanks to IRCA. Finally, our group was sampled from a public hospital rather than transnational organizations and networks, as was the case in Smith's study of Mexicans from one of the original sending towns in Puebla; Mexicans in our qualitative study did not report the extensive transnational ties and travel depicted in his study.

DOMINICAN PARENTS AND ELENA'S JOURNEY

Unlike the migration story of Emiliana, who had relatively few connections to predecessors who had already come to the United States, Elena's migration story was the latest in a chain of transnational travel in her family. Recently arrived Dominicans in the city like Elena often follow a well-worn path taken by hundreds of thousands of their predecessors from the cities and countryside of the Dominican Republic to the decades-old ethnic enclave of Washington Heights. This path is eased from a legal standpoint by tourist and work visas, as well as by sponsorship of green cards through family reunification provisions, although a small proportion of recent arrivals become undocumented after overstaying a visa. Dominicans now live all over the city, its suburbs, and the Northeast, but the Heights and its neighboring communities continue to represent the hub of Dominican life in the United States, decades after migration began.

The relationship of the Dominican Republic to the United States has been one of violent entanglements—the United States has invaded the D.R. twice, in 1916 and 1965—and economic dependence, especially under the economic policies of the dictator Rafael Trujillo, who ruled the D.R. from 1930 to 1961. During the Trujillo period, the nation's subsistence agriculture was transformed on a massive scale to cash crops (mainly sugar), with accompanying industrialization and the growth of export industry. Consolidation and monopolization of the sugar industry drove the increased mobility of agricultural workers. During this period, however, few Dominicans were allowed out of the country—the ones who did leave were well off and came from the Cibao region, from which some of the mothers in our study also came (see the area between Santo Domingo and San Francisco de Macoris in figure 2.2).[30]

New York City looms large in the Dominican diaspora. Emigration rose from an average of 1,000 a year in the 1950s to an average of 10,000 a year in the 1960s, with the bulk of emigrants going to New York City and other cities in the Northeast.[31] The second U.S. invasion of the Dominican Republic in 1965 was intended to prevent a Communist government and bolster an alliance of military officers, industrialists, and international traders.[32] After that invasion, the two countries encouraged migration in order to siphon off political discontent; most of these legal migrants went to New York City.[33] The economic policies of Joaquín Balaguer—Trujillo's former presidential secretary who ruled the nation from 1966 to 1978—continued to emphasize consolidating land ownership, keeping agricultural prices low, and fostering industrial growth that required investments in capital rather than labor. These policies drove rural-to-urban migration,[34] and the overseas migration encouraged by the Dominican government helped to keep unemployment rates relatively low during those years.

Figure 2.2   Origins of Dominican Mothers in the Dominican Republic

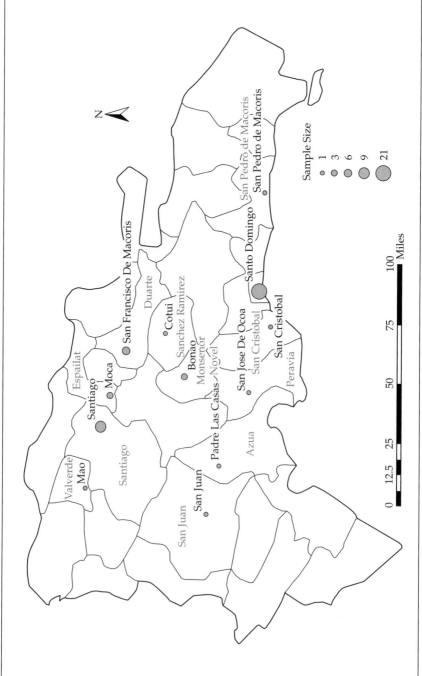

Source: Author's graphic utilizing data from the Early Childhood Cohort Study (Center for Research on Culture, Development, and Education 2009).

In New York, Washington Heights grew as an ethnic enclave for Dominicans during the 1970s and 1980s—so much so that it acquired a mythic status in the Dominican Republic as El Alto (the Heights). Dominicans in New York reached the mainstream milestone of their own Broadway musical—named after an ethnic enclave, just as *West Side Story* had been named for Puerto Ricans fifty years before—with the opening of *In the Heights* in March 2008.

The Heights had been a mix of small farms and larger estates as recently as the early 1900s; it became a neighborhood of Irish immigrants and European Jews in the 1920s and 1930s and then, prior to the Dominicans' arrival, a Cuban and Puerto Rican enclave. Dominican migrants have typically arrived with visas; some become undocumented when their visa expires.[35] At this point in history, after decades of migration, most of the arrivals already have relatives in El Alto or in the neighborhoods of the South and West Bronx, where Dominicans have increasingly moved as rents rose in Washington Heights.

Most of the migrants from the Dominican Republic to the United States have not been the poorest Dominicans from rural areas but rather their somewhat better-off counterparts from urban areas.[36] The bulk of our overall sample of Dominicans came from the country's two largest cities, Santo Domingo and Santiago (see figure 2.2). Many had lived middle-class lives in the Dominican Republic; quite a few mothers in our sample, for example, were registered nurses prior to arriving in the United States.

Between 1986 and 1988, owing to the IRCA provisions, a large number of undocumented Dominicans in New York (an estimate of 12,000) became legal permanent residents.[37] As a result, first-generation Dominicans who arrived in the 1990s—like most of the Dominican mothers in our sample—were more likely to come sponsored by relatives already in New York than had been the case for their predecessors in previous decades. Judging from our qualitative sample, in fact, the majority of our Dominican mothers were legal permanent residents or citizens by the time of our study.

The undocumented among Dominicans in New York are usually visa-overstayers, not border-crossers like the majority of the undocumented Mexicans.[38] Short-term visas are relatively easy to come by in the Dominican Republic, although paperwork requirements have shifted over time and their complexity has fostered a mini-industry of visa preparation.[39] Prior to the 2000s, long-term (up to ten-year) tourist visas were common, with requirements to return to the Dominican Republic every six months. (Long-term visas were also given to some Mexicans, but in very small numbers and generally to the well-to-do.) With increased restrictions after 9/11, long-term visas were no longer issued in the 2000s. This is another reason why the proportion of undocumented among Dominicans in New York has most likely decreased since the mid-1990s.

43

Unlike the Mexican mothers in our sample, most of whom had arrived in the ten years prior to the birth of their child, the Dominican mothers varied a great deal in the timing of their arrival. (Variation in their age at arrival was one-third larger than for the Mexicans.) Some had been pre-schoolers when they arrived in the United States, brought over by a parent or relative. After spending decades in the United States—and most importantly, by arriving before IRCA—most of this group who had arrived in early childhood were residents or citizens by the time our qualitative study started. Others had come as late as in their twenties.

Elena came at the age of eighteen (the mean age of arrival of our Dominican sample). Like most of this group, she was not the first in her family to emigrate. By the time we began our study in 2004, pioneer immigrants like Emiliana—the first in their families to come to the United States—were relatively rare among Dominicans. A long chain of relatives in Elena's family had navigated friendlier immigration policy contexts in the United States in prior years, often first arriving with a tourist or student visa. She had aunts who had come before she was born to find "a better life, a better future." Then, when she was still in school, her father went to the United States for the first time, on a long-term tourist visa. He returned to the Dominican Republic about every six months, as one has to do on a tourist visa. He eventually applied for legal permanent resident (LPR) status and obtained it. With his help, her brother then went to the United States on a student visa. He did not enroll in school, however, but started working.

Elena herself was not sponsored by her father (although her younger sister was). Instead, her husband, who was steadily employed in the Dominican Republic working for the government, got a tourist visa and went to New York in the early 1990s. Then Elena went to New York, with the process facilitated by her husband. So despite migrating at virtually the same age as Emiliana (eighteen), Elena arrived with the security of multiple connections in the new land. The trip itself was relatively easy for her: she reported none of the sort of hardships that were common in the crossing stories of undocumented Chinese and Mexicans. Her husband Ramon, on one of his trips back to the Dominican Republic, helped her gather her documents to get her own tourist visa, and she then accompanied him back to New York City, where she was reunited with her mother and father—her mother telling her she was "gorda" (fat) and she in return telling her mother she looked "flaco" (skinny). Although she did not like New York in her first month, she soon adjusted. After spending a month or two at her aunt's apartment, she moved in with her husband in an apartment in Washington Heights. Eventually, her father was able to sponsor her green card.

The Dominicans in our qualitative sample were much more likely to be documented than the Mexicans. This difference is not explained by the fact that Dominicans have been coming to New York City in large numbers for much longer. In fact, the flow of Dominicans to New York City never went through a period with the very high proportion of undocumented of the recent Mexican flow. There were several other reasons why Dominicans were more likely to be documented: first, much of the initial wave of migration was supported by the U.S. and Dominican governments; second, after the initial waves, the principal mode of entry was a visa under family reunification provisions; and third, the Dominican Republic does not share a land border with the United States.

CHINESE PARENTS AND LING'S JOURNEY

Ling's story, like the stories of other Fujianese in New York City, is part of a pattern of regional succession: mainland Chinese from a specific sending area are remaking the Chinatowns of the city after a long history of Cantonese migration. Exclusion from the United States was followed by the easing of migration restrictions in the United States in the 1960s and in China in the 1970s. Most recently, a surge in low-income migration in the 1990s was spurred by international smuggling organizations operating across Fujian province, Taiwan, and the United States. These forces are the backdrop to Ling and her husband Wei's particularly harrowing story of migration to New York. The couple are representative of the substantial proportion of mainland Chinese immigrants to New York who arrived undocumented (likely close to 50 percent among our sample, recruited in a public hospital serving many low-income Chinese).

The history of undocumented migration from China to the United States has been shaped by the history of Chinese exclusion. Beginning with the passage by Congress in 1882 of laws barring the Chinese from admission and naturalization, and continuing through the Johnson-Reed Act—which put restrictions in place that effectively excluded not only Chinese but East and South Asians (particularly Japanese and Indians) from migrating to the United States—the Chinese case was central to the sea change in U.S. migration policy from nearly unfettered migration in the eighteenth and nineteenth centuries to increasing restriction in the late nineteenth and twentieth centuries.[40] Although the exclusion of this group was relaxed during China's war with Japan in 1937 (then tightened again during the Communist Revolution in 1949), even the repeal of exclusion laws in 1943 restricted legal migration to a mere 105 a year. (Nevertheless, for the first time since 1882, the 1943 repeal allowed for family reunification and sponsorship.) Because of restrictions like these, unauthorized migration represented a substantial percentage of immigration flows from China throughout the twentieth century. In 1950, for example, at least one-quarter of

Chinese in the United States were undocumented.[41] Scrutiny of Chinese immigrants' papers increased dramatically as a result of the Cold War, beginning in the late 1950s and continuing through the 1960s.

The Hart-Celler Act created an enormous new flow of migration from Taiwan and Hong Kong, and then China, that led to huge increases of ethnic Chinese in New York City. The number of ethnic Chinese in 1960 in New York City was 33,000; that number rose to over 300,000 by 1990, and to over 500,000 by 2000.[42] Since China's loosening of emigration restrictions following the death of Mao in 1976, the country has sent hundreds of thousands of young emigrants to the United States to study. In addition, because spouses and children of U.S. citizens are exempt from the 20,000-per-country limit within a hemisphere set by the act, more than 20,000 Chinese come to the United States legally each year. And finally, preferences based on professional skills tend to favor immigrants from Asia over those from Latin America. Legal immigrants from China have therefore come to the United States unusually positively selected on characteristics like educational background.

The recent wave of undocumented migration from China, however, has quite a different narrative. Unlike prior Chinese migration, which was largely from Guangdong (Canton) province, Hong Kong, and Taiwan, this new wave, which began in the 1980s, came primarily from Fujian province. (See figure 2.3 for a map of the origins of our overall sample of Chinese parents.) There were three reasons for this shift: China's loosening of emigration restrictions; the passage of IRCA in 1986; and the ability of an international smuggling industry based in Taiwan and Fujian province to swiftly change its focus from heroin smuggling to human smuggling. From 1949 to 1978, during the Cultural Revolution, Mao's severe border restriction policies allowed very little emigration from mainland China, whether undocumented or documented. Thus, China was not among the top ten countries of origin of immigrants in New York City in 1970, despite the flourishing ethnic enclave of Chinatown. The Chinese government relaxed these policies in the 1980s, however, to allow increased emigration.

Economic growth in Fujian province, as in much of eastern China, was rapid after Mao's death, and it accelerated further in the 1990s. Beijing focused on Fuzhou City, the provincial capital, as a venue for economic development, albeit not at the level of investment that the Shanghai urban area enjoyed. Despite the region's economic growth, the Fujianese tradition of sending migrants overseas, as well as continued large wage differentials with the United States, Europe, Australia, New Zealand, and Japan, drove a process of chain migration.[43] In the United States, this process was greatly accelerated by IRCA's amnesty provisions. The announced deadline of November 1988 for providing documentation for amnesty (in-

Figure 2.3   Origins of Chinese Mothers in Fujian Province, China

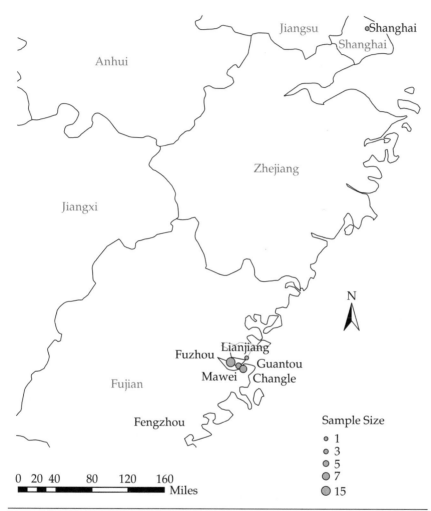

Source: Author's graphic utilizing data from the Early Childhood Cohort Study (Center for Research on Culture, Development, and Education 2009).

cluding proof of residence and employment history in the United States) unleashed a flood of unauthorized migration from Fujian province. Smuggling fees, which had been less than $2,000 as recently as a few years before, skyrocketed to $18,000 by 1990.

As with the migration from the Dominican Republic, most of the migrants came from areas near the capital city (specifically, the counties surrounding Fuzhou). Processes of chain migration drove the "specialization" of particular counties in sending emigrants to particular regions of the world. For example, most of the Fujianese migration to the United States is from Changle County, a county about an hour outside of Fuzhou that includes the city's airport. Other counties send high proportions of emigrants to Japan, Europe, and Australia. Those who went overseas and then returned and spent lavishly, constructing modern new homes and contributing to the infrastructure of Fuzhou City and surrounding counties, created an additional incentive to emigrate. For example, a lavish public gate can be found in one of the high sending neighborhoods in Changle County. We observed this gate on a trip to Changle County in 2007. Emblazoned with Chinese poems on the two marble pillars (for example, THE SUN SHINES UPON MORNING DEWS REFLECTING A THOUSAND RAYS IN THE GOLDEN WORLD), the arch of the gate reads: DONATED AND BUILT BY CHINESE AMERICAN MR. YANG YEZHUN IN OCTOBER 2003.

Smuggling organizations now have well-developed networks across China, Southeast Asia, and the receiving regions of the world. The beginning of the surge of migration was characterized by relatively dangerous modes of passage. Some migrants came in rickety boats. When one vessel, the *Golden Venture*, hit a sandbar off Rockaway in Queens in 1993, with 286 immigrants on board, ten people dived into the rough waters and struggled to swim to shore. This boat had been four months at sea. All on board were told to swim ashore after the pilots of the 150-foot boat intentionally grounded it 200 yards from Queens. Eventually the key smuggler in this case, Cheng Chui Ping, known as "Sister Ping" in the Fujianese community, was sentenced to thirty-five years in prison.[44] This event was one of the first that drew the attention of New York and the United States as a whole to the new wave, post-IRCA, of undocumented migration from Fujian province.

The story of Ling and her husband Wei reflected the hardships of the early phase of Fujianese migration. After Wei left their home, she was "worried to death" for several months. She heard nothing about him. She went regularly to the Stone Bamboo Mountain, about twenty miles south of Fuzhou, to pray at the temple there. This beautiful temple overlooks a lake where for centuries the Fujianese have prayed for safe passage to foreign lands. "If we pray there, only need to wait a few months, or one to two years, we can come to the U.S." It turned out that her husband had climbed the foothills of the Himalayas to get to Thailand. The crossing through the mountains was hazardous; the group of Fujianese were tied together with ropes as they made the trek. About ten people had to share one pot of soup and one chicken. One died during the journey. Once they arrived in Thailand, the group had to stay in fields because the danger of being caught was greater in hotels. In the tropical heat, mosquitoes were everywhere, and it was nearly impossible to sleep. Then Wei was caught by the military in Thailand and spent several months in prison. His money to pay the snakeheads for the rest of the journey was stolen from him; his brother, already in the United States, had to wire him several thousand dollars to cover the rest of his passage.

In contrast, three years later, Ling's own journey was relatively easy. Several relatives and friends already in the United States loaned her several thousand dollars each, enough to help her pay the snakeheads. She told Yong, the field-worker, that it was normal for friends already in the United States, who understood the costs and consequences of migration, to lend such amounts of money. In her first years in New York, she worked twelve-hour days in garment factories near the Manhattan Bridge in Chinatown, repaying her debts. In her words, the Fujianese "are small circles, and very generous" with their close friends and relatives. She herself had loaned her relatives and friends thousands of dollars over the years, all of which had been paid back.

The cost of passage paid to the snakeheads for papers was roughly $25,000 at the time when Ling and her husband came to New York. (It was $30,000 for the privilege of enduring the voyage on the *Golden Venture*.)[45] By the time of our study, this fee had risen to between $60,000 and $80,000, owing to the huge expansion in the Chinese economy, particularly in the eastern provinces, and subsequent rises in income there. The *Golden Venture* incident had largely ended smuggling on boats in favor of individual bookings by air.

The Chinese undocumented from Fujian province are relatively better off in terms of education and income than their counterparts who do not emigrate. As Zai Liang and Wenzhen Ye point out, the high cost of leaving simply requires more financial and network resources.[46] Not surprisingly, in our study the Chinese were the oldest upon arrival in the United States, compared to the Mexicans and Dominicans. In the sending counties of Fujian province, those who leave also increase their social status. Men who do not leave, in particular, are viewed as having "no great future" (mei chu xi). On the other hand, undocumented emigrants from China are of lower socioeconomic status on average than those who leave with papers.

CONCLUSION

Our three groups of immigrants had drastically different rates of documentation status, owing to the very different histories of recent Mexican, Dominican, and Chinese migration to New York. For Mexican immigrants, New York is not a historically important destination city in El Norte, like Chicago and Los Angeles, but rather a relatively new gateway to the United States. New York is a city where Mexican low-income parents of young children are quite likely to be undocumented. The Mexicans in our sample were often pioneers in their families—the first to come to the new land. They arrived after the amnesty provisions of the 1986 IRCA law went into effect. They also arrived without tourist or work visas and thus, before 1996, did not have the option of paying a fine and applying for residency. Their sole path to residency and citizenship will require decades of being Americans in waiting. Under current law, their eldest U.S.-born child will be able to sponsor them for residency when he or she turns twenty-one. At that point, of course, the child's development, together with any influences of parental undocumented status upon it, will largely be over.

For the Dominicans, in contrast, New York has been a destination city—especially the near-legendary neighborhood of Washington Heights —since the midtwentieth century. With decades of undocumented migration behind them, culminating in the 1986 passage of IRCA, the large majority of Dominican parents with young children in New York, as reflected in our qualitative sample, appear either to be residents or citizens themselves or to have a resident or citizen among their close relatives. The proportion of undocumented among arrivals since 1986 is likely to have decreased substantially. As we will see in chapter 4, the proportion of undocumented in the networks of Dominican undocumented adults in our qualitative sample was much lower than among their Mexican counterparts. This difference, I argue, has implications for access to resources and opportunities for learning among the children of these two groups of immigrants.

Finally, the current wave of low-income Chinese migration to New York represents a unique case in the history of this destination city. A transition in Chinese policy from being completely restricted to having more open borders spurred a highly localized (in China) but international smuggling operation aided by transnational investment. The publicized deadline of November 1988 for amnesty under IRCA spurred the smuggling organizations. These far-reaching organizations have also benefited from a strong occupational niche in Chinese restaurant work (which requires little English) in storefront and buffet establishments all over the eastern half of the United States. The amazing concentration of this wave's origins in Changle County, a tiny area near Fuzhou City, testifies to a highly successful marketing strategy and the visible wealth that remittances buy in that area. The personal and economic risks that families undergo, incurring massive debts to smugglers, create in their wake a generation of U.S.-born children with an unusual transnational developmental trajectory. These children spend the first years of their lives in China being raised by their grandparents as their parents work seventy-two-hour weeks in the new land. The percentage of infants sent back was far higher among our Chinese families than among the Mexican or Dominican families. The implications of this unusual transnational pattern for child development are explored in detail in the next chapter.

Chapter 3

Life Under the Radar: Legal and Illegal Authorities and Public Programs

Adelina, a Mexican mother with an infant son, was talking with her field-worker about public programs in the United States that help children. "I tell you, I have very little information, since I don't deal with a lot of people from here." She knew about Medicaid and WIC, because hospital social workers had signed her up for these programs during prenatal care. She knew that she herself had access to care only during and right after pregnancies, while her son Federico had full medical coverage. Adelina had heard about welfare from one friend, an older Dominican woman with grown children. This woman had also told her about "Seccion Ocho" (Section 8), but Adelina did not quite remember what that program was. When asked about a whole list of other programs, Adelina was not familiar with child care subsidies, Head Start or other free preschool programs, benefits for people with disabilities, or unemployment insurance.

Adelina also had heard from a friend that American-born children of undocumented immigrants could be taken from their parents. She feared that if she was caught while traveling, her children would be taken from her. The friend had told her that immigration officials, when deporting an undocumented parent, ask the child whether he or she wishes to remain with the parent and do not send the child with the parent automatically. This friend had also told Adelina that immigration officials might not give her children a choice at all and could just deport the parent and take the children into protective custody. Adelina had a great fear of this horrible moment occurring and ripping apart her family.

The undocumented parents in our study arrived in the United States with hopes and dreams for a better life no different from the good life envisioned by all Americans—owning a home, having a good job, raising children in safe neighborhoods with good schools. But for these undocumented parents, the American dream was tempered by how unlikely it was at this point in U.S. history that they would obtain legal resident status and, ultimately, citizenship status. As we saw in chapter 2, pathways to citizenship in the United States for undocumented immigrants were increasingly restricted between 1986 and the 2000s, to an extent that was unprecedented in the twentieth century.[1] This was the period during which the majority of the undocumented in this sample came to the United States; for them, having a U.S.-born child was their only long-term hope for integration into U.S. society. But they were often reluctant to take advantage of the rights that their children held as U.S. citizens. Keeping out of sight of a range of authorities was part of the daily experience of these immigrants, who quite frequently suffered from depressive symptoms and psychological distress.

The undocumented parents in our sample lived this paradox: the very same government that could deport them also offered resources to their citizen children, in the form of public supports for families in poverty. The children in our sample were generally eligible as citizens in low-income families for a range of U.S. public supports. Many of these resources—the center-based care that child care subsidies can help families purchase, the food and nutritional information provided by WIC and food stamps—are proven to help children's early development. But of course, children cannot walk into offices and enroll themselves in these programs. When parents are reluctant to do so, for a variety of reasons—including reasons related to their legal status—children cannot benefit.

This chapter is about the conflicting experiences of legal and illegal authorities and public programs brought about by this paradox in the lives of undocumented parents and their children. These experiences—ranging from being afraid of deportation and associated distress, to paying off debts that are sometimes in the tens of thousands of dollars, to gathering information and making decisions about programs that citizen children are eligible for—are all related to the paradox of living both inside and outside U.S. institutions that characterizes the daily lives of "mixed-status" families. Far too often, that paradox leads to citizen children of the undocumented being excluded from supports from which their peers with documented or citizen parents benefit.

IMMEDIATE LEGAL AND ILLEGAL CONTEXTS IN THE NEW LAND

Many of the undocumented in our study were well aware that they had arrived during a policy period that allowed them virtually no paths to citizenship. Aurora, for example, said that she had a strong desire to own her own home in the United States. She and her husband Gustavo had been in the United States for a decade. She worked full-time at a restaurant, and Gustavo worked more than full-time at a pizzeria, clocking in twelve-hour days, six days a week. Aurora admitted that she was not very hopeful about buying a home because of her legal status. She was afraid that a potential seller could easily take her money without giving her the home, and that she would then have no recourse because she had no documentation. Pessimism, born from the belief that legal exclusion would last for decades, was equally common among the few immigrants in our sample who had older children who were also undocumented. One mother, for example, confessed to her field-worker that she was unsure whether her school-age daughter, born in Mexico, would be able to go to college, because she was undocumented.

Deportation Fears and Depressive Symptoms

Across the years of our study, the threat of deportation was increasingly on the minds of undocumented parents. "La migra"—the federal Immigration and Customs Enforcement (ICE) agency (formerly the Immigration and Naturalization Service, or INS)—arrested almost twenty thousand undocumented immigrants in the interior of the United States in fiscal year 2006. Although a large number, twenty thousand pales next to the hundreds of thousands of immigrants whom the Department of Homeland Security (DHS) has arrested crossing the border from Mexico in recent years. A recent study of nine hundred adults who experienced workplace arrests in three sites found that five hundred children were affected, with over half of the children under the age of five and 66 percent of them U.S. citizens.[2] The effects on families, which were dramatic, included loss of child care; large losses of income; difficulty in meeting children's basic needs, such as buying food, diapers, formula, and clothing; and the reluctance of remaining parents and caregivers to go to agencies to obtain emergency assistance. Many families sequestered themselves round the clock in their homes, keeping their children out of school, a reaction we usually associate with armed conflict in the developing world. Longer-term effects on families and children included social isolation; depressive symptoms and suicidal ideation among remaining caregivers; and anxiety, depression, and post-traumatic stress disorder in children.

In 1996 the Illegal Immigration Reform and Immigrant Responsibility Act (IIRIRA) made minor crimes, such as shoplifting, grounds for deportation. Prior to this point, only crimes that resulted in five or more years in prison resulted in immediate deportation. The act also allowed states and localities to deputize their police to conduct the federal enforcement required by the act. As a result, more and more cities and states are linking minor-offense databases to federal immigration databases.[3] Like thirty-one other cities in the nation, however, New York City has declared itself a sanctuary city. This means that New York City law enforcement officials do not ask people whether they have documentation of residency or citizenship. The undocumented are still concerned that any brush with the law might result in deportation. As one of our field-workers observed about one immigrant, "I see that being illegal here is what makes up most of her experience of discrimination and prejudice. It is not being able to be free, feeling as she once said that she is an unwanted guest."

The possibility of being deported was a faint but audible hum in the background of everyday life for the undocumented in our study. During the course of our study, President George W. Bush proposed policies to create a pathway to citizenship for undocumented immigrants. When one mother heard the details—the undocumented could register with the government, demonstrate their employment during their time in the United States, pay a fine, and work toward citizenship—she thought that this program was a ploy by the government to get people like herself to register and then deport them. Even if the program was implemented, she would not participate. Another mother put it simply: she wished that she and her husband did not have to go to work fearing deportation.

Fear of deportation contributed to the depressive symptoms that the undocumented mothers in our study reported. The mothers' survey reports of these symptoms were directly related to lower child cognitive skills at twenty-four months.[4] Depressed, anxious, and withdrawn parents are less likely to talk and interact with their children, to respond quickly to communications, or to show warm affect with them. These lower levels of responsiveness then lead to lower levels of early language and cognitive skills.[5] As we will see in the next chapter, depressive symptoms were directly related to the proxy for undocumented status in our survey—not having access to resources requiring identification.

Fear of deportation, mixed with gendered norms about women's safety versus men's, may have accounted for reports of undocumented women in our sample living "underground" in the days immediately after they arrived in the United States. Like Emiliana, several of the mothers who arrived unauthorized had brothers or partners who did not allow them to leave the house in the days immediately following their arrival. Such seclusion can intensify the anxiety and depression that typically accompany transition to a new country.[6] Men who arrived from Mexico tended to look for work immediately; they roomed together in crowded conditions—often five or six men living in two bedrooms. With long and nonstandard work hours, beds were often never empty during any twenty-four-hour period. One of the mothers in our sample arrived and was not allowed to live in such an apartment, even though her husband was in one. She stayed with her aunt until she and her husband were able to find an apartment where they could live together as a couple.

Illegal Authorities and Debts

For some parents in our sample, it was not so much the long arm of the law that cast a shadow over their lives as the long arm of smuggler organizations. The degree to which our families owed money to smugglers varied widely among the different groups. The undocumented Dominicans generally did not rely on smugglers to bring them from the Dominican Republic, but instead obtained tourist or work visas (through the help of family or friends in both the Dominican Republic and New York) and then overstayed then. For the most part, by the time they had children in the city, Mexican undocumented parents had paid off any debts they owed smugglers.

Debts owed to smugglers affected our Chinese undocumented migrants the most—with dramatic consequences for their infants. The Chinese in our sample had paid by far the largest sums of money to come to the United States, and their survival strategies were the most drastic. For Ling, who came to the United States in the early 1990s, the total cost of $28,000 included debts to friends already in the United States. (She and her husband Wei paid smugglers up front with money they borrowed from these friends, so they owed money not to smugglers, but to friends.) Costs for the majority of the Chinese mothers we recruited were more than double what Ling and Wei paid; Ling was in our initial qualitative sample and so was not one of the parents in our later birth cohort who arrived in the mid-1990s to early 2000s. For many Fujianese immigrants, especially those who have no friends already in the States, debts are owed directly to the snakeheads who helped bring them over and are accompanied by threats of violence if they are not paid back.[7]

The magnitude of these debts make it virtually impossible for families with no relatives close by to provide child care, like a grandparent, to afford the high cost of infant child care. In paying their debts, both parents must work very long hours, generally in Chinese businesses, until the debts are paid off. In our birth cohort sample, the majority of this work was in Chinese restaurants. By the time we recruited our sample, the other historical mainstay of Chinese low-wage employment in New York—the garment industry—had declined in importance because of both the growing presence of the mainland Chinese garment industry in the United States and the collapse after 9/11 of the Chinese garment industry in New York City.[8] These exigencies—crushing debt, lack of grandparents in the United States, and the hours of low-wage work in Chinese businesses—compelled parents in our sample to send their infants who were born in the United States back to China very soon after their birth. They sent them back to Fujian province to be raised by grandparents until they were old enough to enter preschool or formal schooling. These several years of free child care saved families an enormous amount of money.

Breast-feeding provided the first hint of the infant sending in our sample. We discovered that very few of the Chinese mothers we recruited were planning to breast-feed their children. This puzzled us, as the benefits of breast-feeding are relatively well known among a range of immigrant communities and are communicated consistently in New York City public hospitals. Breast-feeding is also near-universal in China.[9] When our team made calls to schedule the six-month phone survey, we discovered that many of the infants in our Chinese sample had already been sent back to China. It turned out that a whopping 72 percent of that sample— forty of fifty-six mothers—had sent their babies back within the first months of life. We stopped recruiting midway to our projected goal of one hundred mothers.

How did these Chinese parents send their infants back if they themselves were not documented? One mother told us about "travel agents" who travel with the babies and deliver them to grandparents in Fujian province (usually Changle County). The parents pay these "travel agents" $1,000 plus the cost of the plane ticket for this service. On some flights to China (typically the least expensive ones, such as those that fly first through other countries in East and Southeast Asia), entire rows are nearly full of these intermediaries carrying babies back to China. Since the babies were born in the United States, they have valid passports.

This very high rate of parent-infant separation among Chinese low-income immigrants provides a strong contrast to the parent-child separations that scholars have identified among Latino immigrant populations. For example, Carola Suárez-Orozco and Cecilia Menjivar have written about the high rates of temporary returns among older children and youth to countries of origin like the Dominican Republic, Mexico, and South American countries.[10] These studies have been of older children and adolescents. For a variety of reasons, these trips often occur during the summer; the family may want the child to develop or maintain relationships with relatives back in the home country, or they may see the trip as a way of setting a child straight who has developed problem behaviors in U.S. peer or school contexts. The Chinese sending-back phenomenon, which has been noted in news media but never quantified as a proportion of low-income Chinese births, is unique in that it is driven almost entirely by the economic reality of huge debts.

At their child's birth, the Chinese, Mexican, and Dominican mothers reported very different plans for returning their babies to the home country. Although the groups did not differ substantially in their plans for the child to return (the vast majority indicated that their child would return at some point), the timing and reasons differed dramatically. The Chinese on average indicated that their child would return to China at seven months of age, while the Dominicans reported an average of twelve months, and the Mexicans an average of fifty-four months.[11] The early and late planned returns of the Chinese and Mexicans may be an indicator of the relatively high rates of undocumented status in these groups. That is, the Chinese, with no grandparents nearby to look after their infant and with high levels of debt, felt an urgency to send their infants back. The Mexicans, many of whom, as pioneer undocumented immigrants in their families, had few grandparents in the United States, may have thought that getting residency status was not likely in the short term and that therefore their children could not go and return with them for a long time. (Few "travel agents" exist for the risky prospect of bringing an infant or toddler back across the border on foot.) The Dominicans, with the highest proportions of family members with legal status, appear to have simply been thinking about the age at which it becomes easier for infants to travel; their answers were clustered around the twelve-month point.

Reasons for the planned return also differed dramatically among the ethnic groups. The vast majority of Chinese mothers (80 percent) mentioned financial constraints as a reason for their children's travel, compared to fewer than 2 percent of Dominican and Mexican mothers. And far more Latina mothers (50 percent and 45 percent for Dominican and Mexican mothers, respectively) than Chinese mothers (3 percent) reported meeting family members as a reason for their child to travel to the homeland. Similar and relatively high percentages (40, 43, and 40 percent for Chinese, Dominican, and Mexican mothers, respectively) of mothers across the three ethnic groups stated that their child would travel "to see grandparents." Overall, these data suggest that a large proportion of the Chinese intended to return their infants to China to be taken care of by their grandparents largely for economic reasons, not simply to get to know their relatives.

Being sent back to China as an infant may have a delayed effect on children's development. The disruption of infant and early childhood attachment can occur twice—first at the initial separation and then later when the child returns and experiences both the loss of the caregivers in China and adjustment to new caregivers in the United States. Such disruptions can be associated with later behavior problems, both of the acting-out kind and the withdrawn and depressed kind.[12] Later in childhood, as cognitive capacities increase, many children with this early history resent the fact that their biological parents sent them away. This reaction was reported by Ling: her son Guang had been sent back, returned as a four-year-old, and as an eleven-year-old expressed hostility toward his parents for having sent him back. Other studies have shown that children of migrant parents who were "left behind" or "sent back" express such feelings of abandonment or rejection by middle childhood and adolescence, even those whose parent was in touch with them frequently during the separation.[13] There has not been a systematic study to date, however, comparing "returning" Chinese American children to their peers who were not sent back to China in the first years of life.

In contrast to the Chinese, the undocumented Mexicans in our sample did not report high levels of debt to smugglers. Almost none of the Mexican children had returned to Mexico by the thirty-six-month point. Coyotes required payment immediately upon arrival in the United States. The amounts (a reported maximum of about $2,000 in the early 2000s) were also quite small relative to those paid by the Chinese, although even these small sums were significant for the Mexicans at the time of their crossings. Several Mexican mothers mentioned debts to relatives that they had to pay back. Patterns of exploitation, though few, were troubling. Nalda's mother Narunda, for example, had migrated with people who treated her like a prisoner, making her clean and cook for them in the months after her arrival until her debt was paid. She was told not to leave their house in order to avoid deportation.

For the relatively few undocumented Dominicans, who had primarily entered on a tourist or work visa that they subsequently overstayed, debts were not a big part of the picture after arrival. More Dominican children had been taken to the Dominican Republic by thirty-six months than Mexican children had returned to Mexico, though in nowhere near the numbers we found among the Chinese. These were short-term visits conducted so that grandparents could see their grandchildren. In sum, the economic structure of smuggling and unauthorized entry differed greatly for our three immigrant groups and determined the large differences we saw between the Mexicans and Dominicans, on the one hand, and the Chinese, on the other, in the impact of economic pressures on infant travel.

THE POLICY PARADOX: INELIGIBLE PARENTS, ELIGIBLE CHILDREN

Undocumented parents in the United States are eligible for virtually no public benefits for themselves aside from emergency health care. In many states (although not New York), they are also not eligible for Medicaid-funded prenatal or postnatal care. Not providing prenatal care to undocumented immigrants results in greater costs to the government in postnatal and emergency care.[14] However, there has been no political support recently to provide public funding for health insurance for undocumented immigrants. The undocumented are also not eligible for federally funded programs that would provide them with job skills and education or with work-based tax credits to lift them out of poverty. For example, they are ineligible for the Workforce Investment Act (WIA) dollars that fund nearly all job training programs in the United States. They are ineligible to sit for a general equivalency diploma (GED) test. They are ineligible for the federal Earned Income Tax Credit (EITC), which can provide up to several thousand dollars in extra income to working-poor families. The undocumented are cut off from these paths to social mobility that the United States provides for other workers with low levels of skills, education, or income.

On the other hand, citizen children of the undocumented, such as those in our study, are eligible for a wide range of benefits and programs, including welfare, or Temporary Assistance for Needy Families (TANF); child care subsidies, either through the Child Care Development Fund (CCDF) or TANF funding for child care; health care, under Medicaid and the State Children's Health Insurance Program (SCHIP); WIC (Women, Infants, and Children), a nutritional program that covers the prenatal period to age five; food stamps; and preschool (Early Head Start, Head Start, or New York state and city prekindergarten). Research suggests that many of these programs benefit family and child well-being. For example, the formula, food, and nutritional counseling that WIC provides leads to fewer perinatal difficulties, lower rates of preterm birth, and higher levels of very early cognitive abilities.[15] Child care subsidy receipt increases center care participation relative to informal home-based care.[16] Center-based care leads, in turn, to higher levels of early child language and cognitive skills than other types of care.[17] Receiving food stamps brings about lower household food insecurity.[18] But children in the first years of life cannot walk into government offices or community agencies and enroll themselves. Parents are powerful gatekeepers to these resources, and when they are afraid of receiving government help, their children cannot benefit.[19]

Legal immigrant parents, in contrast to the undocumented, are eligible for some programs and not others, particularly if they came after the 1996 welfare reform, which denied legal immigrants many means-tested benefits for their first five years of residence in the United States. For example, they are not eligible for federal Medicaid for themselves or cash welfare for the first five years. States vary a great deal in the extent to which they "fill in" for these intentional gaps in the federal safety net.[20]

For legal immigrants, taking up programs they are eligible for can have consequences for their transition to permanent resident status. The most recent federal guidance of 1999 stated that, except for two very unusual circumstances, immigrants who are legal permanent residents seeking to become citizens are not subject to "public charge" tests based on use of federal means-tested benefit programs.[21] For tourists, students, and other legal immigrants who are not LPRs, in contrast, the ICE can take into account receipt of SSI (Supplemental Security Income), TANF, and general assistance as evidence contributing to an assessment of "public charge" when considering a transition to LPR status. But the agency cannot take into account other forms of benefit receipt, including food stamps, child care benefits, health-related benefits such as Medicaid or SCHIP, school lunch, or housing benefits. As for mixed-status families—those with a noncitizen parent and a citizen child—the INS guidance states that receipt of cash benefits by an immigrant's citizen family member does not influence public charge determination unless the family is reliant on the benefits as its sole financial means of support. This situation is highly unlikely given the low levels of benefits and the high levels of work effort among undocumented parents. So overall the picture for noncitizen parents with citizen children suggests some risk in receiving cash welfare or SSI benefits for their child, but not other program benefits.

Parents of different legal statuses in our study had dramatically different information and attitudes about the programs for which their citizen children were eligible. For example, Adelina, the undocumented mother whose story opened this chapter, received WIC benefits for her son Federico, who was also covered by Medicaid. The application processes for these programs were very easy and had been facilitated at the hospital at the time of Federico's birth. She said that WIC was very helpful. "I have learned a lot with WIC. I almost did not know anybody here, and even if I tell myself what to give him [to eat] and what not to give him, I didn't know much." Her WIC nutrition counselor advised her not to give Federico too much sweet food, soda, or juice. The counselor also gave her recipes for healthy snacks to feed him.

Nalda, a Mexican mother who made the transition from LPR to citizen, was the sole mother among the Mexicans in our qualitative sample who was not undocumented. In contrast to Adelina, she knew a lot of details about government supports for children and families, most of which she had heard from a coworker. She herself used food stamps as well as WIC and Medicaid. While she was applying for citizenship, she knew about the differences between certain kinds of public programs—receiving some might be taken into account in her application for citizenship, while receiving others could not. She knew that receiving food stamps would not affect her application, while receiving cash welfare might.

With only one exception, the Dominicans in our qualitative sample had LPR or citizenship status. Beatriz was typical of the LPR parents. She received only Medicaid and WIC benefits, but she knew quite a lot about the other programs she did not participate in. When asked how she knew about them, she said that people just happened to talk about them or told her about them—"uno escucha, uno se entera" (one hears, one learns). The citizens among the Dominicans, like Sofia, knew the most, from both their networks and personal experience. Sofia had used welfare, general assistance, Head Start, housing subsidies, and WIC in addition to Medicaid. She explained that an individual has to have the right attitude and mood when asking for assistance. For example, to get fast service, she recommended being very cooperative and patient. She understood why workers in government agencies are often rude or mean; a lot of people, she explained, are trying to take advantage of the system.

Chun, a Chinese mother who lived in the suburbs, had a brother who was a citizen. (She herself had overstayed a tourist visa, coming from Hong Kong after going there first from Fujian province.) She heard about Medicaid through him. She faced an interesting choice when she was pregnant with her son Ming Sheng. Should she go to the hospital in suburban New Jersey or the one in a Manhattan Chinatown? Because the doctors in Manhattan spoke Mandarin and Cantonese, she decided to go there, using a former nanny's address. She referred to Medicaid in New Jersey (which provided health coverage for her brother's children) as "foreigners' Medicaid"—"foreigner" here meaning non-Chinese. She was very happy with the medical care in Manhattan's Chinatown. Midway through our study, her son was injured in a Chinese restaurant in a terrifying incident. In the middle of a bustling banquet at a large Chinese restaurant, a guest walked by their table and accidentally knocked over a pot of hot tea. Ming Sheng, who was next to the table, was burned when he was splashed with the hot liquid. All of his treatment after this accident occurred in Manhattan. Chun was amazed that, unlike China or Hong Kong, all of it was free. Like the undocumented and LPR parents in our other ethnic groups, Chun received only WIC and Medicaid benefits for Ming Sheng.

Fear of using benefits was widespread among our families, whether they were undocumented or legal residents. (Citizen parents expressed none of these fears.) One of our Mexican mothers told us about the "ladies in the park" who told her about welfare. Finding out that she was not working, a Puerto Rican woman advised her to apply for her children. She said that she and the other ladies in the park had applied for welfare for almost all their children: "Children born here not only could but should get that help." But this mother's husband did not want her to receive welfare for their child. "He says no because, according to a guy who was telling him, when they are older they send them to war." She felt that if the government helped her family, they would later require them to pay it back.

Other parents felt that enrolling their children in programs would make it harder for the children to get benefits like student loans later in life. One belief we heard multiple times was that benefits for a child come out of an account that is kept for their lifetime and that any "withdrawals" early in life require deposits later. One mother thought, for example, that if a family took advantage of the aid that was available, "there isn't much left [for student loans] because it's like their savings that the government is going to lend them." We heard these beliefs among both the undocumented and legal permanent residents in our study.

ENROLLMENT RATES OF CITIZEN CHILDREN: THE ROLES OF LEGAL STATUS, INFORMATION, STIGMA, AND PERCEIVED BENEFIT TO CHILDREN

The actual enrollment rates of the parents in our study, from the larger survey sample data, showed that the safety net provided by U.S. programs and policies for citizen children in poor families was being used unevenly. In these analyses, I compared the Mexicans and Dominicans not only to each other but also to African Americans. This group of parents, all U.S.-born, are fully eligible themselves as well as through their children. (Recall that the Chinese infants were sent back to China, so we have no survey data on that group after our baseline assessment.) As table 3.1 shows, there is one program in which all children in our study were enrolled at very high rates, regardless of ethnicity or parental documentation status: WIC. The hospitals from which we recruited appeared to do a very good job of enrolling these families in this nutritional program. A nurse at the hospital where Aurora, one of the Mexican mothers, gave birth helped her fill out Spanish-language forms that enrolled her in WIC. Aurora found the fifteen-minute process easy and was happy with what the program provided. Other mothers specifically mentioned the information (nutrition counseling, advice concerning formula) that WIC counselors gave them. One noted that her local "vivero" (butcher store where one can buy live chickens) accepted WIC coupons, so she did not have to buy inferior packaged chicken meat. This reflects recent revisions to the regulations governing WIC to allow for coverage of culturally appropriate foods, many of which are sold in small storefronts serving immigrant communities, not in the chain stores that have historically accepted WIC.[22]

Rates of enrolling children in food stamps (now renamed the Supplemental Nutrition Assistance Program, or SNAP) varied more, though less than twenty percentage points overall across our ethnic and immigrant groups. Mexican families made use of this benefit at rates similar to those of Dominicans (59 and 52 percent, respectively), though lower than African Americans' (69 percent). Food may be particularly acceptable as a form of public assistance to immigrants from Mexico and the Dominican Republic—most mothers from these countries mentioned that, when they were growing up, meat was a rare treat at the family table. In contrast,

Table 3.1   Use of Public Assistance for Children and Families, at Fourteen Months

	Full Sample	Mexicans	Dominicans	African Americans
WIC	98%	98%	100%	95%
Food stamps	60	59	52	69
Child care subsidies	21	2	17	35
TANF	28	12	20	46
Public housing/Section 8	27	15	21	39
SSI	6	7	0	11
Unemployment benefits	5	0	6	6

Source: Author's compilation based on data from the Early Childhood Cohort Study (Center for Research on Culture, Development, and Education 2009).

they greatly appreciated the range and affordability of food in the United States, and most of them noted that they could now serve meat every day to their children. Perhaps owing to the near-universal receipt of WIC and relatively high rates of food stamps use, across the twenty-four- and thirty-six-month surveys there was virtually no report of food insecurity (defined as not being able to buy the foods one would like to buy for one's family) among the mothers in our sample.

Mexicans, Dominicans, and African Americans differed in their use of other programs. For example, public housing or Section 8 subsidy use was much lower among the Mexican sample (12 percent) than the African American sample (39 percent). Rates of welfare use also showed large differences, with 12 percent of the Mexican group reporting it and 46 percent of African Americans. Child care subsidy use was also lower among Mexicans, at 2 percent, than African Americans (35 percent) or Dominicans (17 percent) at 14 months. (Similarly, at twenty-four months, these rates were 7, 39, and 22 percent, respectively, and at thirty-six months they were 6, 47, and 36 percent.)

Why these differences in program use for public housing, welfare, and child care subsidies? For public housing, the answer is simple—having a citizen child does not give you access to housing subsidies if you are undocumented. In addition, public housing and welfare were the programs viewed most negatively by our undocumented mothers. Many of them made disapproving faces when asked about these programs. They also looked down on groups that they thought used these programs. Mexican mothers tended to associate these programs with Dominicans and Puerto Ricans, the Dominicans associated them with Puerto Ricans, and the Fujianese associated them with the Cantonese. Virtually all of these mothers associated welfare and public housing with African Americans. The American public as a whole equates welfare use with African Americans and holds racialized stereotypes about them—for instance, that they are lazy[23]—despite the fact that the majority of mothers on welfare work.[24] The undocumented and recently arrived immigrant mothers shared these perceptions, but also applied them to immigrant groups that have not only longer histories in New York but higher parental citizenship and eligibility rates.

As for child care subsidies, a mix of information, eligibility requirements, and parents' preferences emerged in our data. The specificity of information about child care benefits was dramatically lower among the largely undocumented Mexican mothers and one undocumented Dominican mother compared to the documented Mexican and Dominican and all the African American mothers. The documented and U.S.-born mothers, when asked how they had heard about benefits such as child care subsidies or the other federal programs, reported having heard from so many people that they could not identify specific sources. ("On the street" or "news gets around" was a typical response.) When immigrant mothers knew about the eligibility requirements for child care, which typically include showing proof of employment, these were seen as barriers. Emiliana, for example, reported that her sister-in-law had tried to obtain child care subsidies for her daughter. The agency required a social security number or employer confirmation of her employment. However, Emiliana's sister-in-law did not have a social security number, and her employer "didn't want to confirm and then pay more taxes" for that one employee.

In addition, our Mexican mothers reported greater reluctance to use nonrelative child care than the African American mothers, with the Dominican mothers in between in their preference.[25] Other studies have found a preference for relative or informal care among Latinos.[26] But these studies have usually lumped all Latina mothers together; our data showed differences between the Mexicans and Dominicans. As the rates of child care subsidies across our groups showed, the Mexicans were consistently by far the lowest in their use of child care subsidies, with virtually no increases across fourteen to thirty-six months (a tiny increase from 2 percent to 6 percent). In contrast, across those two years, use of child care subsidies increased from 17 percent to 36 percent among the Dominicans, and from 35 percent to 47 percent among the African Americans. The Mexicans in our sample were more likely than the Dominicans to state a mistrust of out-of-home care and express fears of abuse.[27] Trusting only relatives with their children was also more common among our Mexican mothers than among the Dominican and African American mothers. And not surprisingly, Mexican mothers were returning to work across the first three years of their children's lives at lower rates than Dominican and African American mothers.[28] Partners and husbands also played a role in this: the Mexican mothers were more likely than the Dominican or African American mothers to mention that their husbands or male partners did not want them to work while their children were infants or toddlers. Pierrette Hondagneu-Sotelo and Patricia Pessar, as well as other researchers, have shown that traditional gender roles in the household, with women responsible for caregiving and men for breadwinning, break down with increasing time in the United States among immigrants from Mexico and the Dominican Republic.[29] The Mexican mothers in our sample, having come to the United States on average at an older age than the Dominicans, and with more recent arrivals as well in their networks, experienced more traditionally gendered divisions of labor in their households.

The preferences of mothers in our study for preschool differed from those for child care: by thirty-six months, the vast majority of mothers who had preferred caring for their children at home felt that they should enter preschool. Other studies also find no differences across immigrant groups and the native-born in preference for preschool education.[30] The barrier here was more starkly one of information. Our ethnographic study ended before children had the opportunity to enter preschool. (The final visit typically occurred prior to thirty months.) However, we did ask the mothers in our ethnography questions about their knowledge of preschool. A few of them did not know that the U.S. government provides free preschool to children from low-income families. The field-worker in these cases had been the first person to tell them about the availability of such programs. Others remembered exactly who told them about preschool. For example, one Mexican mother recalled that a friend told her about Head Start, took her to sign up, and told her it was a program for children whose parents might not know where to take them. Here they would be taught certain things like colors and names of fruits. In our study, the children are not yet old enough to provide a comprehensive picture of how many enrolled in preschool at the age of four.

Our data suggest that the undocumented majority of the Mexican mothers were well aware of the discrepancy between their own eligibility for public programs and their children's eligibility. Public health insurance, for instance, is a program for which eligibility and even funding streams are traditionally distinct for parents and children. In our survey sample, we asked about perceived eligibility for self and for child separately. For Dominican and African American mothers, rates of perceived ineligibility for self and children were almost the same—25 percent for self and 23 percent for children among the Dominicans, and 12 percent for self and 15 percent for children among the African Americans. However, among the Mexicans, there was a large difference in perceived ineligibility: 49 percent of the mothers considered themselves ineligible, but only 4 percent felt that their child was ineligible. These numbers support, from the standpoint of our larger survey sample, the qualitative evidence that the Mexicans have a much higher rate of undocumented status than the Dominicans.

When mothers did enroll their children in public programs, their experiences ranged from positive to feeling denigrated. For example, Alma, a Dominican mother, described good experiences with "el social security," "el daycare," and "la tarjeta para comprar comida" (food stamps). When she was hospitalized for severe depression, a social worker informed her of everything she should do and helped her complete all the necessary applications. Alma had only positive things to say about these benefits and reported no problems with them. Others described rude treatment by case workers, as is often reported by the working poor.[31] One Mexican mother, Victoria, was accompanied by her field-worker, Clarissa, to the welfare (one-stop) office at a recertification visit. Clarissa was horrified to see the poor treatment of the clients. At one point, a Guatemalan woman sitting next to Victoria and Clarissa was denied service after hours of waiting, despite her respiratory condition. Clarissa helped advocate for her, and then overheard the receptionist telling another worker, "You are being too nice to her." Although Clarissa was outraged, Victoria showed a surprising level of equanimity: "Nada es de gratis" (nothing is for free), because "está aquí de arrimada" (she is here as an unwanted guest). "She is like a charity case," she said. "This is not her country; she does feel entitled, yet she knows her rights. She seems to be well informed. Her conscience is clean; she feels at ease. She has nothing to hide; she doesn't lie."

Victoria's high tolerance for the treatment of mothers in welfare offices might be informed by comparisons to the social safety net in her home country. Mothers from Mexico, the Dominican Republic, and China in our ethnography unanimously reported that the United States is more generous than their countries of origin in the help it provides children and families. This was true regardless of the mother's documentation or citizenship status. Countries of origin were reported as corrupt and uneven in the implementation or offer of support to poor families. The Mexican mothers mentioned most often the serious consequences of the lack of quality health care. They said that public hospitals and doctors in their home country were overwhelmed, with often devastating consequences for the health of the patients they served. According to them, the wealthy in Mexico were able to purchase good care, but the poor received low-quality care that threatened their health. They cited programs for the poor like Mexico's milk assistance program, but still compared them unfavorably to U.S. programs like WIC. National data show in fact that the milk assistance programs for the poor in Mexico in the 1980s and early 1990s had uneven coverage and were subject to local corruption; they have since been replaced by a more comprehensive antipoverty program in which the central government provides assistance directly to parents to support their children's early health and nutrition.[32]

Both Mexican and Dominican mothers mentioned the corruption of politicians. Aurora thought that politicians in both the United States and Mexico were corrupt, but that things were probably worse in Mexico: "The money they are supposed to use for improving roads or schools often goes in their pockets." The Dominican mothers mentioned "big bosses" as sources of corruption. Julio, Mercedes' husband, said that government officials in the Dominican Republic, from the city council to mayors to senators, used their position to make money. They did it, he said, by engaging in unethical business practices or receiving bribes from unethical businesspeople. He also emphasized their involvement in the drug trade. One Mexican mother reported that people farther away from Mexico City got less help; a Dominican mother thought that the government regularly took taxes and paid themselves, with the net effect that the country was poor.

CONCLUSION

The avoidance of legal authorities and policies for which U.S. citizen children are eligible affects many of the infants and toddlers in our study. For legal and illegal authorities specific to immigration, the story is a simple one of avoidance and fear. From their first days in the United States, the undocumented in our sample experienced the uncertainty and anxiety felt by any new immigrant compounded by warnings and fears about encounters with strangers. Learning the ropes and finding out where the greatest dangers lay takes time, and so the initial hosts of these undocumented women often forbade them to leave their apartments. Moreover, as in many other studies in the developmental literature, the depressive symptoms of our mothers were related to lower levels of cognitive skills in their children.

Access to the range of policies that can help families make ends meet and improve children's early cognitive development and health—particularly WIC, food stamps, center-based child care, and health insurance coverage—varied among our sample for several reasons. All of these programs were experienced differently by the documented and the undocumented. The first and most basic difference among them was the wide variation in eligibility requirements, particularly the extent to which different forms of identification and proof of employment were required of the parent. For example, child care subsidies and welfare typically require information regarding employment. Proof of employment is a form of information that the undocumented did not wish to share, in order to protect themselves (and by extension their employers). The mothers also differed in whether they thought they were eligible for particular services. The Mexican mothers were more likely than the Dominicans or African Americans to report a difference in eligibility between themselves and their citizen children.

Second, the amount and quality of information differed by type of program. For example, information about WIC and food stamps was fairly consistent, and through its easy enrollment (a fifteen-minute visit by a social worker on the maternity ward), WIC had provided near-universal assistance in our sample. In contrast, the amount and quality of information about housing, child care, and preschool was inconsistent across our groups, with the undocumented knowing little about the details or even existence of many programs. The only cases in the qualitative study of mothers not knowing about free preschool, for example, were among the undocumented.

Third, the fear of consequences, such as "public charge" assessments in transitions to residency status and citizenship, was cited by some mothers in our qualitative study. These perceived consequences, however, often went far beyond current U.S. law. Several of the immigrant mothers thought that their citizen children would have to "pay back" the value of the benefits and programs they have used when they later seek financial aid for higher education, or that they would even be sent to war.

Finally, some forms of help were mistrusted or stigmatized. Mexicans were most likely to report concerns about child abuse or mistrust of non-relative child care providers. Cash welfare and public housing were stigmatized by the group least likely to be eligible for these benefits—the undocumented. Like other U.S. parents in poverty,[33] the undocumented in our study found programs that provide in-kind assistance, such as food stamps and WIC, more acceptable than those that provide cash assistance. The former were more likely to be perceived as helping children directly.

Rates of enrollment of the citizen children of the undocumented were highest when all of these factors lined up. For example, information about WIC was provided consistently in the public hospitals where our mothers gave birth, with immediate enrollment facilitated by on-site social workers and no proof of employment required. No stigma was reported about this program by any of the parents; it seemed to them a more successful and well-run version of the milk and nutrition programs in their home countries. In contrast, fear of consequences, negative attitudes and stigma, and eligibility requirements, including proof of employment, all converged for undocumented parents who decided not to enroll their children in cash welfare programs.

Chapter 4

Documentation Status and Social Ties: Households, Networks, and Organizations in the Lives of Undocumented Parents and Their Children

In the United States, we take for granted our access to institutions and resources that help children and families. These include features of everyday family life such as public libraries, neighborhood and civic organizations, banks, and parks, as well as forms of identification that provide access to some of these, such as driver's licenses or other photo identification. These resources offer families financial flexibility, freedom to travel, and an array of programs and enrichment activities for young children. In addition, parents rely on more informal networks such as extended family or friends for important information that concerns their children, such as the quality of child care programs and the good or bad features of neighborhoods. Why might these kinds of resources and information—more informal than the policies and programs discussed in the previous chapter and often termed "social capital" in the academic literature—matter for immigrant families? They can help in the post-immigration task of building human capital, in the form of child learning as well as adult education and job skills. For example, "weak ties" are social network ties that are relatively low in emotional and intimate confiding, time spent together, and exchange of resources, but that can nevertheless be powerful in enhancing social mobility and child development through mechanisms like job referrals or information about preschools or schools.[1] Some social organizations and settings provide wide access to these ties, including neighborhood organizations, libraries, and settings where parents of young children congregate, such as child care centers and playgrounds.[2]

Studies of how social capital—the resources, information, and norms of behavior that are conveyed through social networks—can build human capital have not considered the impact of documentation status in immigrant families on social capital. Data from our study show that households, social networks external to households, and neighborhood organizations are experienced differently by the undocumented. The undocumented mothers in our qualitative sample generally lived in households in which virtually every other adult was also undocumented. This high concentration of undocumented at the household level limited the extent to which information about the city's resources for children and families could be shared within the household. These mothers also experienced less social support from their networks outside the household. Most of those who had friends they saw regularly reported having no more than one friend who served as a link to information about programs and resources; many reported having no such friend or contact at all. Finally, our Mexican undocumented mothers resided in neighborhoods with very low proportions of other Mexicans. Only a fraction lived near the few large community-based organizations in New York that serve the growing population of Mexican families in the city. For those who did live close by, access to the expertise of these organizations made a difference in their lives in terms of mental health, advocacy, organizing, and supports for raising children. In contrast, the Chinese mothers lived primarily in one of the Chinatowns of the city and thus were generally much closer to the organizations and businesses that served Chinese of prior waves (the Cantonese) as well as the Fujianese.

The array of resources that can enhance children's development affects children most directly at the household level. At that level, resources that could not be accessed without identification proved to be a powerful variable in both distinguishing the documented from the undocumented in our sample and predicting children's early cognitive skills. Undocumented parents were less likely to utilize resources that required submitting multiple sources of identification, like checking and savings accounts and driver's licenses. The household-level absence of these resources was related to mothers' economic hardship, their depressive symptoms, and in turn their children's cognitive skills at twenty-four months.

UNIDENTIFIED LIVES: HOUSEHOLD NETWORKS, SOCIAL SUPPORT, AND RESOURCES THAT REQUIRE IDENTIFICATION

Flor, a Mexican mother who, uniquely in our ethnographic sample of this group, lived in a suburban neighborhood upstate from New York City, yearned for a driver's license. Although her husband had one, she did not, and she was therefore stuck in the house while he worked in a soda factory. Sometimes, Flor explained, "I feel that I am suffocating here—I could asphyxiate—but I have my three children." She was fed up and bored to death being stuck indoors ("Ya me fastidie de estar aquí adentro"); there was nothing but routine in her life. At the end of one visit, Flor burst into tears and shared her frustration about how dependent she felt because she did not have a driver's license.

The undocumented parents in our sample lived in households that were different from the households of the documented parents in several ways: in the concentration and number of both related and unrelated undocumented adults; in the likelihood of grandparent presence; in levels of social support; in the kinds of information that was shared; and finally, in resources that required identification to access.

First, the concentration of undocumented adults in households was higher among our undocumented mothers' households. This is not surprising in and of itself. But the degree of concentration was astonishingly high. In the qualitative study, all but two of the undocumented mothers appeared to live in a household in which all the adults were undocumented. I come to this conclusion based on details from stories about these other adults that included both recent arrival and crossing the border on foot. The first exception to this pattern was a mother who came to the United States very early compared to other Mexican mothers in our sample (around 1990). She had brothers who came before her and had become legal residents through IRCA. However, these brothers lived in other cities. The second exception was a Dominican undocumented mother whose husband became a citizen during the course of the study and by the end of it had started the sponsorship process for his wife.

The Mexicans, with higher concentrations of undocumented in their households, also had a higher number of adults living at home. In our survey sample, the average number of people in the household for this group officially met the definition of "overcrowded"—more than two people per bedroom. None of the other immigrant groups had such high levels of crowding in their apartments. The sharing of rent expenses with boarders is a well-known survival strategy among low-income immigrant households.[3] It is particularly common when the main family occupying a residence is undocumented, because they are ineligible for any public housing subsidies. What this doubling up means for the development of children has not often been explored.

A qualitative analysis of who lived in which room in each of the apartments in the ethnographic sample showed that, from a child's perspective, extra boarders meant that there was no living room. Each of the Mexican families had someone living in the "living room" of the apartment. Most often a couple was staying there, and in some cases a full family with children. Although over half of the boarding adults or families were related, many were not. In one case, a boarder was living in the kitchen of an apartment, sleeping right next to the refrigerator.

The story of Arturo was typical of the single boarders among the Mexican sample, who were generally young men who had recently arrived from Mexico. Arturo, who came from a very humble background, was a boarder in the household of Blanca and her husband Gerardo. He had been raised by his grandparents, whom Blanca described as very poor friends of Gerardo's family. Arturo never knew his father; his mother had remarried and rarely came to visit him when he was a child. When he was still in Mexico, Arturo would call up Gerardo a lot, asking him to help him out since they were from the same pueblo. Gerardo and Blanca agreed to help him out and paid $1,500 to have him brought up to New York. At the time of our study, Arturo had been living there for a few months. He was a very quiet young man who hardly spoke to anyone in the apartment when they are all there and rarely interacted with Blanca and Gerardo's son Miguel. At one visit, Blanca's field-worker, Francisca, observed Arturo coming into the apartment, putting down his things, and going to the backroom to watch TV. Blanca got up to serve him the tostadas she had just made. As she did, she whispered to Francisca that she did not like doing this. She was tired of Arturo being in her home all the time. It had started to make her uncomfortable, and she wished he would serve himself the food she made. She acknowledged that Arturo had been out of work for two months and it had been difficult for him to find a new job. But he was not contributing at all to household chores.

When boarders were entire families, not single adults, they often had just had a baby themselves and were looking for a place to stay where they would not be limited to a living room. Emiliana, for example, had a sister who lived in her living room at the beginning of the study. The sister was with her husband and their newborn infant. They subsequently moved out to the Bronx. However, that new living arrangement did not work out, and they returned. Emiliana described her sister as having a "difficult" personality; the atmosphere was tense when the two families shared their small one-bedroom apartment. During the period when her sister's family was not in the household, the brother of Emiliana's husband stayed with them.

In striking contrast to the Mexican families, none of the Dominican or Chinese families in our qualitative sample had someone living in their living rooms. This is why it was much more common for our field-workers to conduct their in-home interviews on a bed when interviewing the Mexican families (as with Ana's interviews with Emiliana) than when interviewing members of our other groups. Overcrowded living conditions can have important consequences for children's development: a quiet, individual study space is much less available to children living in housing this crowded, and there is evidence that such conditions not only lower academic achievement among children but also raise children's blood pressure and the likelihood of behavior problems at school.[4] Overcrowding in the home can increase the levels of household stress and chaos experienced by children and affect their biological stress processes.

A household with boarders has more adults, and we wondered whether these adults might be a resource to households with young children—by providing free child care, for example. Paradoxically, the opposite was true. Our Mexican mothers reported lower levels of available support, despite greater numbers of adults in the household, than the Dominican and African American mothers. We asked questions about three forms of support in our survey measures at fourteen and twenty-four months: help taking care of children if she had to go away for a few days; help making ends meet, such as paying bills; and help finding a job. For each kind of support, the mother was asked to name up to three sources of this support in her life (she could name people or organizations, such as agencies). For all three kinds of support, and at both time points, the Mexican mothers in our survey sample reported significantly lower levels than the Dominican and African American mothers. This paradox might be explained by the fact that the boarders, being undocumented themselves, generally worked very long hours and were not around the children very much. Those who had children themselves were often looking for another place to stay, given the discomfort of sleeping in a secondary room in someone else's apartment, and were therefore not stable sources of child care. The housing narratives of our Mexican households, much more so than those of the other groups, were filled with stories of boarders' moves in and out.

When undocumented status, crowding, and physical problems with housing coincided, the consequences were sometimes horrific. Alejandra, a Mexican mother, lived in a one-bedroom walk-up apartment. Boarders typically lived with her, her husband Mauricio, their daughter Elisa (the focal child in our study), and their older children, nine-year-old Bernardo and eleven-year-old Leon. The apartment was quite crowded, and it was difficult for Bernardo and Leon to have a quiet time to study in the evenings. Their apartment was on the ground floor, and the garbage cans for their walk-up were directly outside their living room. With cracks in the wall, rats came in and out of their apartment. Things got even worse when the bedroom ceiling caved in. As both Mauricio and Alejandra were undocumented, they did not have an official lease, and the landlord would not give them one. Thus, they had no legal recourse for repairs to their apartment. No matter how much Alejandra cleaned and disinfected the apartment, rats, cockroaches, and mold infested it. The landlord continued to refuse to repair the ceiling. Finally some workers working on other parts of the building took pity on the family and left some bricks and materials so that Mauricio and Alejandra could repair it themselves.

The households of the undocumented also differed from those of the documented in the likelihood of including grandparents. Dolores, for example, a citizen who had come to the United States from the Dominican Republic in early childhood, and her son Gilberto had daily contact with her parents. Each night after work, Dolores took Gilberto to her parents' apartment, where they ate dinner. There they usually saw Dolores's sister Irene and her son Emilio before they headed home to Brooklyn. Gilberto thus saw his cousin and grandparents every day. And recall from chapter 1 the story of the Dominican mother Elena and her mother, Maria Graciela. The grandmother of Elena's children provided that family with a link to documented status, child care, and job referrals for Elena. She came by Elena's apartment every evening after work to spend time with her daughter and grandchildren. She also read to Alberto. The Dominican infants in our study were more likely to have access to a grandmother residing in the household than the Mexican infants. In our survey sample, one-third of our Dominican families (33 percent) reported a grandparent in the household when the infant was fourteen months old, compared to 12 percent of the Mexican families.

As in many societies around the world, grandparents in the Dominican Republic, Mexico, and China typically provide extraordinarily dedicated love, attention, and care to newborns and young children. A recent national study in the United States found that, on average, grandparent presence in the household is beneficial to children's development if at least one parent is also present.[5] In contrast, grandparent-only care leads to lower levels of educational achievement and child well-being. Reasons for the benefits of supplemental grandparent care include the close blood ties, the significance of the transition to grandparenthood in life-course development in many cultures, and the lower likelihood that grandparents are working full-time. In our study, the two groups with the highest rates of undocumented parents (Mexicans and Chinese) were also the least likely to have access to grandparents in the United States, owing to their being pioneer migrants in their families. This had some dramatic consequences. As we saw in the previous chapter, because of their debts to the snakehead smugglers and the cost of infant child care, the Chinese parents with no one from the grandparent generation in the United States sent their infants back to Fujian province, where the grandparents lived.

As in the United States, grandparent-only care in China may have mixed consequences for children. Studies by Lian Rong, a professor of psychology at Fuzhou Normal University in Fujian province, and his students show that U.S.-born children in Changle County (Fujian) preschools being raised only by their grandparents are faring less well on local cognitive and social assessments than children being raised by their parents or those being raised by both parents and grandparents.[6] Although these findings have not been replicated, they suggest that despite having more privilege in China owing to their status as U.S. citizens, these children may not be faring that well in the first years of life. A variety of reasons may be responsible. First, the contrast between the grandparents' generation and the parents' generation in levels of education is particularly stark at the current historical moment in China. The grandparents' generation lived through much of the Cultural Revolution, including the experiences of having their education interrupted, being sent to the countryside for "re-education," and enduring the more general economic and political hardships of the Great Leap Forward of the late 1960s and 1970s. In addition, with the rapid growth in China's economy and primary and secondary education enrollment throughout the 1970s, 1980s, and 1990s, the current generation of parents has on average 2.9 more years of education than their parents' generation. (This analysis compares 1982 to 2005 census data from China.[7]) Over the course of these years, the gender gap in average years of education in China also declined, from men having an average of two more years of education than women to one year, suggesting a particularly large gap between grandmothers and mothers in education. So, in addition to the emotional consequences of a transition back to the United States to parents whom the child had never known, the returned children experienced a particularly large education gap between their caregivers in China and those in the United States.

Why is grandparent presence so correlated with undocumented status across the immigrant groups in this study? Simply put, an undocumented immigrant has no access to family reunification provisions in U.S. immigration policy. Once one person in a family is a legal permanent resident, and especially once citizenship is achieved, federal law states that parents (as well as spouses) can be sponsored to come to the United States. Across the changes in immigrant exclusion and other U.S. immigration policies, one relatively constant principle across the twentieth and twenty-first centuries has been that of family reunification.

Family reunification is also an important building block in the development of immigrant enclave neighborhoods in gateway cities like New York. As families with one LPR or citizen member bring additional relatives into the United States, the newcomers can progress rapidly toward citizenship and sponsor their own relatives. Over time, new arrivals settle near their relatives already in the United States, and certain neighborhoods become concentrated areas of residence for particular immigrant groups. The Dominican community in Washington Heights developed family by family, with the proportion of undocumented most likely declining gradually over the years (and plunging in the late 1980s after IRCA) as each family acquired more and more members with LPR and then citizenship status. More recent low-income arrivals, like the Mexicans from the Mixteca region and the Chinese from Fujian province, have been much less likely to have access to members of the older generation. Many more have been like Ling and Emiliana, the first in their families to arrive. And these pioneers in the most recent waves of migration generally came after IRCA and thus have had no pathway to residency or citizenship. When additional members of family or friendship networks have arrived, they were likely to be undocumented themselves. The result has been households with very high concentrations of undocumented adults in neighborhoods with as-yet low concentrations of coethnic members, as was the case with many of the Mexican households in our study. This double whammy resulted in the relative paucity of network connections among the Mexicans to documented, older, or long-term residents of the United States and probably explains the lower levels of support availability reported by this group. Other researchers have also found lower network support reported early in their waves of migration among groups with high proportions of undocumented (for example, Salvadoreans in San Francisco in the early 1990s).[8]

ACCESS TO RESOURCES AND THEIR ASSOCIATIONS WITH CHILDREN'S EARLY COGNITIVE DEVELOPMENT

How exactly might the lack of resources that require identification or the concentration of undocumented adults in households affect children's development? In this study, the answer to this question came from a realization that the undocumented may be less willing to access resources that require them to show identification. For example, to acquire a public library card, enroll in a GED class, apply for credit, open a savings or checking account at a bank, or apply for a driver's license, one typically has to show photo ID or multiple forms of identification. In many states, these resources are not accessible to undocumented parents unless they are willing to risk using fake forms of identification. Of these, the driver's license is a particularly important and common master resource in most U.S. states that opens up access to the others. There is little research about how access to these community resources differs for undocumented immigrants compared to documented ones.

In many public library systems, unless you have a school-aged child with a report card, getting a library card requires multiple forms of identification or a photo ID. Undocumented parents with only young children are therefore less likely than their documented counterparts to be able to get a library card. Although some states provide photo ID for noncitizens, undocumented immigrants have been reluctant to obtain these forms of identification for fear that they could be used to facilitate deportation. In

New York City, the public library system is relatively accessible to undocumented immigrants—for example, the Mexican "matricula consular" (Mexican government–issued ID that can be obtained by legal or illegal immigrants to the United States) counts as one of two forms of ID that meet the requirements. Although most of the others are forms of photo ID, also on the list of acceptable forms of ID is a rent bill, which is relatively easy for the undocumented to produce.

Similarly, in many states enrollment in GED classes requires a state-issued photo ID card. Undocumented parents in our sample, like many low-income immigrant parents, were highly motivated to pursue their education.[9] However, this pathway to higher job skills and social mobility was also largely closed off to them. In New York State, as in the majority of states, GED classes and diplomas are offered only to those who can establish proof of residency through such documentation as social security numbers or state-issued photo IDs.

Of the different forms of resources requiring identification, a central one is the driver's license. Driver's licenses are at the center of raging policy debates, with most states having moved in recent years to either separate forms of identification for the undocumented or completely prohibit this most common form of state-issued ID. Many of our undocumented parents reported a strong desire for a driver's license and difficulty obtaining one. For example, Mauricio, Alejandra's husband, had had a delivery job for years, riding a bike to deliver for a deli. He hurt his knees through repeated wintertime falls on the ice making deliveries. As his sons, Bernardo and Leon, became older (they were nine and eleven years old, respectively, at the time of the study), he became increasingly ashamed that he continued to work as a "delivery boy." He desperately wanted to be able to tell them that he had made more of his life than delivering food to strangers. His dream was to become a taxi driver; however, he did not have a license and so could not become one. And obtaining a New York City taxi medallion, including the lifetime right to lease it for income, now costs upward of $500,000.

Mauricio finally quit his job midway through our study and left New York State to find another job and get a license. He went to one of the few states left that was still providing driver's licenses to undocumented immigrants. He was unable to find either a job or a license, however, and ended up returning to New York and sharing a livery cab that a friend had. He drove during the twelve hours that his friend was not driving it. It cost Mauricio $40 a day to rent the car, and he had to pay for gas and car washes. Alejandra reported to her field-worker Francisca at one of the final visits that the $40 that day had come out of their savings. Mauricio had driven around in the hope that people would stop his car, but he had had no customers.

Table 4.1   Household-Level Access to Resources That Require
Identification (at Fourteen Months)

	Full Sample	Mexicans	Dominicans	African Americans
Checking account	61%	37%	79%	66%
Savings account	56	36	73	58
Credit card	46	27	63	47
Driver's license	54	31	76	51

Source: Author's compilation based on data from the Early Childhood Cohort Study (Center for Research on Culture, Development, and Education 2009).

With a working car, life in the suburbs for the very few immigrant parents in our qualitative sample who lived outside the city was close to the American dream. Chun was an undocumented Chinese mother in our qualitative sample whose sister-in-law was a citizen. Chun lived in a leafy suburb of New York City. Without a car, it took Qiu, Chun's field-worker, three hours to get to her house (taking the subway from upper Manhattan, then a bus to the suburbs, changing to another bus, and then walking half a mile in the blistering July sun). After this first visit, when Chun was shocked to see this doctoral student show up sweaty and out of breath at her front door, she made sure to pick Qiu up at the bus stop. On the second visit, Chun and her family took Qiu along on a merry suburban ride in their SUV, stopping at a lavish suburban supermarket. The family regularly went there, not to shop (the prices were far too high), but to watch the life-size, animatronic cow and farmer dolls sing about shopping. Chun's house, shared with her mother, was palatial by the standards of the other undocumented mothers in the qualitative study. It had a front porch, a bedroom for each of the children, and a spacious kitchen, all features that none of the New York City Chinese families from our study enjoyed.

Because they lacked driver's licenses and other forms of identification, our undocumented parents also had less access to financial services such as formal banking (checking or savings accounts). Table 4.1 shows that Mexicans were twenty to forty percentage points less likely than Dominicans or African Americans to have anyone in their household with a savings or checking account. These important paths to building assets and to financial flexibility in the United States were not being accessed for the most part among our group with the highest proportions of undocumented. The children of the undocumented in our study therefore had less access to the economic buffers that can shield a family from financial shocks and stresses.[10]

Not only did the Mexican mothers have much lower levels of household access to these resources, but they also reported dramatically lower perceived access. At thirty-six months, we asked mothers who did not have a savings account whether they could get one if they wanted to. Over one-third (37 percent) of the Mexican mothers without a savings account reported that they did not feel that they could get a savings account if they wanted to, compared to 9 percent of the Dominicans and 3 percent of the African Americans.

Lack of household access to these resources appeared to have consequences for children's development. In work that I conducted with Erin Godfrey and Ann Rivera, we found that lower levels of access to these resources were associated with lower scores on our standardized assessment of children's cognitive skills at twenty-four months.[11] We hypothesized that this association could occur in two ways. First, these resources could affect parents' ability to support their children's learning with resources and interactions. We therefore tested a pathway through the cognitively stimulating materials provided by parents, such as toys and books, and the stimulating activities they provided, such as reading, telling stories, and playing with the children. We also hypothesized an economic and psychological stress pathway: Do lower levels of resources in the household result in higher levels of economic hardship, such as difficulty paying rent and other bills or having the phone disconnected? And do lower levels of household resources also lead to higher levels of psychological distress and depression? Mothers in this sample did not always reveal their feelings of sadness, depression, or worry to the field-workers, although sometimes the field-workers noticed these feelings in a mother's facial expressions or body language. Structured questions can be valid measures of psychological distress, so we added a well-validated measure of distress and depressive symptoms to the fourteen- and twenty-four-month surveys.[12]

The results from this quantitative study showed more support for the hardship and stress pathway than the cognitive stimulation pathway. That is, undocumented status (as reflected in the proxy variable of lack of access to resources requiring identification) was more sensitive to mothers' reports of hardship and stress than their reported parenting behaviors. Greater economic hardship in turn was related to mothers' distress and depressive symptoms, and distress lowered children's cognitive skills. These results were not explained away by family background characteristics, such as differences in parental education, family structure, or employment. Other studies have shown that hardship and distress can affect children's early learning.[13]

How did the undocumented parents in this study experience economic hardship? First and foremost, they were generally paying a larger proportion of their incomes on rent than documented parents, many of whom were eligible for public housing or Section 8 subsidies—a lifeline for the poor in the most expensive city in the nation. Undocumented households, with no access to housing support and most members earning particularly low wages, found that every penny was accounted for even before each month began. Hardship arose when unexpected expenses came up. Emiliana, for example, told Ana at one visit that she and Victor Sr. had had to send $400 back to Mexico to cover the surgery of one of their family members. Because this expense threw off their carefully balanced budget, they were ten days late in paying their rent. There was simply no wiggle room in their budget. In addition, like most other households of the undocumented, Emiliana's family was unbanked and had no financial cushion or savings upon which to draw for this unforeseen expense. When unavoidable but unpredicted expenses came up, the impact on the budgets and well-being of the undocumented parents was greater than it was for their documented peers. With this kind of experience happening repeatedly during children's first two years of life, one consequence was lower cognitive skills in the children. Greater hardship among parents—both economic and psychological—can harm children's learning by lowering parents' active engagement with their children, the quantity or quality of their language, or their warmth and responsiveness.

Overall, these data showed that our best survey marker of undocumented status—lack of resources that require identification—was indeed related to children's learning at the very early age of two years and that this occurred through the intervening pathway of economic hardship and psychological distress. In chapter 6, I show how a different pathway explained the influence of parent undocumented status on children's cognitive skills at three years of age.

BROADER SOCIAL NETWORKS AND THE ROLE OF DOCUMENTED BROKERS

Up to this point, the picture at the household level of social capital—access to resources and information—has seemed bleak for the children of the undocumented in this study. Living in overcrowded conditions, with many adults but few who are permanent residents or citizens or who have had experience raising children in New York City, rarely having grandparents nearby, having less access to resources and social support—these all seem like powerful strikes against the life chances of children of undocumented parents. Less access to resources, in particular, is associated with lower cognitive skills in children. However, networks beyond the household can also play a role in parents' well-being and their ability to parent well. Friendship support networks, far from being the "weak ties" that we might expect in comparison to blood ties, predict health and mental health across the life span, from childhood to adulthood.[14] Friendship support appears to affect parents' ability to provide nurturing parenting by increasing their psychological well-being.[15] In several cases among our undocumented mothers, relatively sparse information support from family or household members was countered by the rich informational and emotional support provided by a friend or neighbor.

Two stories from Mexican undocumented mothers illustrate the role of friends as brokers who provide information about resources for families in New York City. Perhaps not by coincidence, in both stories the friend was called "la Dominicana." These stories provide a window into the relationship between newer and older immigrant groups in a city of constant immigrant succession. One of the Mexican mothers, Adelina, lived in an area of the South Bronx that has become increasingly Dominican in recent years as rising rents in Washington Heights have led to flight from there into adjacent areas of the Bronx. (The South Bronx is directly across the East River from the northern end of Washington Heights.) Adelina had lived in the Bronx since she arrived in the United States three years earlier at the age of twenty. She did not like the Bronx and felt her neighborhood was dirty compared to those she knew in Manhattan, like Washington Heights, or parts of Queens that she had seen. Her husband worked at a grocery store in the Heights. He became acquaintances with an older Dominican woman who was a regular customer there. He explained to her that his wife had become pregnant, was at home much of the day alone, and would appreciate companionship. Adelina began to go to "la Dominicana's" home in Manhattan regularly—they would talk while doing household chores together. The Dominican woman gave her advice on the pregnancy and told her what to expect. She also told Adelina to apply for WIC, Medicaid, and welfare. At the point when our ethnographic study began, Adelina was still visiting "la Dominicana" regularly, and her son got along very well with her friend's three-year-old grandson.

Alfreda was a Mexican mother of three who had been in the United States for seven years. Her field-worker, Patricia, noted that she had few friends and no one to talk to. The interviews that Patricia conducted with her seemed almost therapeutic. Her household included several older children and two male boarders working very long hours—thus fitting the pattern among our Mexican families of additional adults living in the household who had little freedom or ability to help with child care. Alfreda lived in Fort Greene, Brooklyn, a neighborhood with very few Mexicans. Like many of our relatively recently arrived mothers, she had not acculturated to the U.S. notion of "neighborhood." When presented with a map and asked to define the boundaries of her neighborhood, she could not do so.

Alfreda met her Dominican friend, Claudia, in a restaurant. As Alfreda's family ordered their food and struck up a conversation with the waitress, the waitress asked how much Alfreda would charge for taking care of her children. Alfreda agreed to become her babysitter for a time, but after that period was over they became friends and "la Dominicana" returned the favor, babysitting for Alfreda for free. Claudia was Alfreda's only friend. When Alfreda's son was in the hospital, Patricia observed that he was comfortable with Claudia holding him. Alfreda and Claudia shared the food they got in the hospital, watched out for each other's belongings, and talked like they had seen each other yesterday. Importantly, Claudia also translated for Alfreda what the doctor said about her son's condition.

Tellingly, these cross-ethnic contacts were particularly important in the lives of these two Mexican women because both of them lived in neighborhoods with low concentrations of Mexicans. The settings in which these mothers met their future friends were the workplace or the neighborhood. In addition, as the previous chapter and other research have shown, playgrounds and other places where parents and young children congregate were a useful source of support for many of our mothers.[16] In those cases too, the support provided to Mexican mothers typically came from members of migrant or immigrant groups with longer histories in the city, like Puerto Ricans or Dominicans.

These two stories in particular show how friendship support develops across ethnic lines in cases where neighborhoods do not provide a high concentration of coethnic networks. In both cases, the friends were older and came from an immigrant group—the Dominicans—with a longer history in New York. With their prior experience in child-rearing and greater fluency in English, these women offered companionship to the undocumented Mexican mothers, but also advice to these younger women who had few supports in their own households and no coethnic friends. They provided links to other social networks and organizations and thus served as what Ronald Burt has called "brokers"—people who fill the gaps or holes between social networks that would otherwise have no contact.[17] These stories suggest that brokers from a prior wave of immigration act as crucial bridges in the sequence of immigrant succession and can play an important role in the gradual integration of a new and largely undocumented group into the fabric of American life.

NEIGHBORHOODS AND PROXIMITY TO COMMUNITY ORGANIZATIONS

Flor's field-worker, Isidora, was asking her and her husband, Rafael, if they knew of any organizations that provided help to children and families. Flor knew of none. Rafael thought he had heard of one—"I believe in Manhattan . . . I believe that it's Manhattan or the Bronx." He thought it was a Mexican organization that helped with children's education. Isidora asked how he had found out about this organization. He said, "A friend, a colleague from work that has friends from there." However, Rafael could not name this organization. Emiliana told her field-worker Ana that many people had come from her village to New York City but that they were "scattered" across the city, so she had little contact with them.

Community organizations can provide a brokering function beyond the individual level—that is, beyond a "Dominicana" here and there. They provide sustained opportunities for contact among residents, the building of social networks, the exchange of information, and the opportunity to mobilize resources such as services, advocacy, and community organizing.[18] Access to community resources is associated with more positive parenting practices and early childhood development among low-income populations.[19] The few stories among our Mexican families of community organizations providing support for raising children came from those parents who happened to live near one of the large organizations that serve the Mexican community. (Little Sisters of the Assumption and Asociación Tepeyac are the largest and best known.) But because the majority of Mexicans in our sample lived in other neighborhoods of New York City and were relatively isolated from networks of other Mexicans, they either did not know of these organizations or, like Flor and Rafael, had heard about them but only in a distant way. In contrast, most of the Fujianese, like the bulk of Chinese in the city, lived in or near one of New York's Chinatowns and so lived closer to long-standing organizations serving the Chinese.

In their relatively low neighborhood concentrations, Mexicans have much in common with other very recently arrived low-income immigrant groups in the United States who do not yet have a large ethnic enclave to call their own and live scattered across their host cities or towns. Let us turn to a bird's-eye demographic view of the neighborhoods of the three immigrant groups in our sample at the beginning of our study. On the basic socioeconomic variable of median neighborhood income, our groups did not differ very much. (For these analyses, neighborhoods are defined as U.S. census tracts, with data from 2000, the closest decennial census to the birth of the children in our sample.) The median income of the neighborhoods where the Dominicans lived was $25,282, for Mexicans $28,943, and for Chinese $26,053, with no significant differences among these three. (For African Americans in our sample, the median neighborhood income was $20,962, which was significantly lower than the other groups.)

However, the story that concerns us more in this chapter is the story of coethnic concentration, or the percentage of residents of one's own ethnicity in the neighborhood. Much attention has been focused on whether living in an ethnic enclave (a neighborhood with a high concentration of one's own immigrant group) is good or bad. Some argue that ethnic enclave residence can be good for both adults and children because it provides employment opportunities that can make up for the disadvantages of not speaking English, as well as coethnic support organizations that give children opportunities to learn in the form of study programs and out-of-school activities.[20] Others argue that ethnic enclaves concentrate adults with low levels of English ability and isolate them from mainstream society.[21] Whichever argument they make, most of these studies examine adult outcomes like employment or wages; a few examine outcomes for children and youth, but primarily educational progress or attainment and not outcomes in early childhood.

Most of these studies do not consider the particular challenges to incorporation following transitions to the United States among the undocumented, or the role played by ethnic enclaves for these most marginalized of immigrants. The studies that do look at these issues find that, with more time spent in the United States, ties to legal residents or citizens and to English-speaking residents increase (assuming that the immigrant has not returned to the homeland).[22] Over time, both households and neighborhoods with high concentrations of immigrant groups tend to increase in proportions of citizens and associated resources, most clearly when a sizable cohort of second-generation, U.S.-born children comes of age.

The data on the coethnic concentration of the families in our survey sample highlight the relative isolation of Mexican families at this point in time in New York City. The Mexicans in our sample lived in neighborhoods that averaged only 7 percent Mexican, with a range from 0 to 27 percent, while the Dominicans lived in neighborhoods that were on average 35 percent Dominican, with a range from 3 to 80 percent (the high end representing central areas of Washington Heights). This contrast is striking—the average concentration of fellow Dominicans for the Dominican survey group (35 percent) was higher than the maximum concentration of fellow Mexicans for the Mexican survey group (27 percent). The Chinese lived in neighborhoods that were on average one-quarter Chinese, ranging from 6 to 94 percent.

These numbers suggest that the Chinese, Mexican, and Dominican families in our study experience different New York City neighborhoods, but they do not show the strikingly different geographic concentrations of the three groups in New York City. For example, the Fujianese have tended to settle in established Chinatowns in Manhattan, Brooklyn, and Queens. If we examine a map of our study families arrayed against the ethnic concentration of their groups in 2000 in New York City, we see that the Chinese in New York were concentrated in the Chinatowns of lower

Manhattan; Sunset Park, Brooklyn; and Flushing, Queens (see figure 4.1). The Chinese infants we recruited lived primarily in the Manhattan and Sunset Park Chinatowns.

In contrast, Mexicans in New York, according to the 2000 census numbers, lived in a much more scattered fashion across the city. No single neighborhood achieved the density of Mexicans that any of the Chinatowns did for the Chinese. The neighborhood with the highest concentration of Mexicans was East Harlem in Manhattan, where the barrio of Spanish Harlem, the long-standing enclave for Puerto Ricans in New York, was gradually becoming a Mexican enclave in 2000. The Mexican families in our sample, like Mexicans as a whole in the city in 2000, were spread across Manhattan, Brooklyn, and Queens in neighborhoods with very low concentrations of their ethnic group (see figure 4.2).

The Dominicans represent a stark contrast to Mexicans in New York neighborhoods. As figure 4.3 shows, Dominicans in New York City were concentrated in 2000 in Washington Heights as well as in the South Bronx. Our Dominican study families were representative of Dominicans as a whole, residing for the most part in one of these two areas of the city.

In contrast to the relative isolation reported by many of the Mexican families, who lived in neighborhoods with very low proportions of fellow Mexicans, the few mothers who lived in the emerging ethnic enclave of East Harlem in Manhattan reported a very different set of resources. These mothers came from networks that were neighborhood-based, bridged many families, and were enriched by a large social service and advocacy organization serving Mexican families in the neighborhood. In the story of East Harlem and its networks and organizations, we see the potential future of Mexican New York. This is a chapter currently being written in the ongoing narrative of neighborhood succession: East Harlem was known for decades as Spanish Harlem when it was initially an enclave for Puerto Ricans and then, increasingly, Dominicans. The story is a powerful one of social integration that might counteract the social exclusion that can accompany undocumented status. Consider Victoria, one of the mothers from our first qualitative study (and thus recruited not from a public hospital but from one of the two largest social service organizations devoted nearly entirely to serving Mexicans in New York). In addition to her infant son Ruben, she had a nine-year-old daughter, Carlota, who lived with her and her husband Tito. One of Tito's brothers and his daughter lived with them as well in their small East Harlem apartment.

Victoria's neighborhood of East Harlem was anchored by East 116th Street. As the lifeline of a new ethnic enclave, this street had much in common with Broadway in Washington Heights. It was filled with small-box stores, such as music stores with signs advertising Latin American singers (Shakira, Cheyenne, Solis), clothing and shoe stores (big discount stores

Figure 4.1   Census Tracts of Residences of Chinese Families in
Sample Relative to Concentration of Chinese in New
York City, 2000

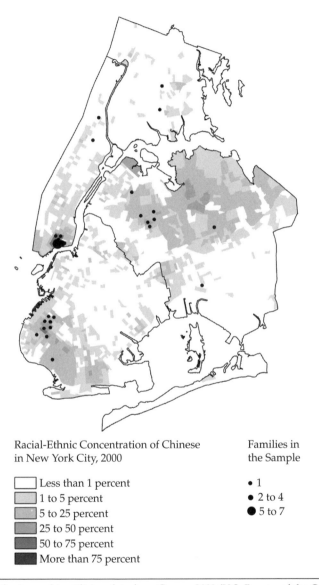

Racial-Ethnic Concentration of Chinese   Families in
in New York City, 2000   the Sample

☐ Less than 1 percent   • 1
☐ 1 to 5 percent   • 2 to 4
☐ 5 to 25 percent   ● 5 to 7
☐ 25 to 50 percent
☐ 50 to 75 percent
☐ More than 75 percent

Source: Author's graphic utilizing data from Census 2000 (U.S. Bureau of the Census 2000)
and the Early Childhood Cohort Study (Center for Research on Culture, Development, and
Education 2009).

Figure 4.2   Census Tracts of Residence of Mexican Families in Sample Relative to Concentration of Mexicans in New York City, 2000

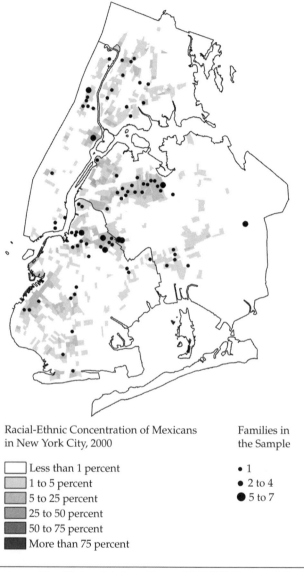

Racial-Ethnic Concentration of Mexicans
in New York City, 2000

Families in
the Sample

☐ Less than 1 percent
▨ 1 to 5 percent
▨ 5 to 25 percent
▨ 25 to 50 percent
▨ 50 to 75 percent
▨ More than 75 percent

• 1
● 2 to 4
● 5 to 7

Source: Author's graphic utilizing data from Census 2000 (U.S. Bureau of the Census 2000) and the Early Childhood Cohort Study (Center for Research on Culture, Development, and Education 2009).

Figure 4.3   Census Tracts of Residence of Dominican Families in Sample Relative to Concentration of Dominicans in New York City, 2000

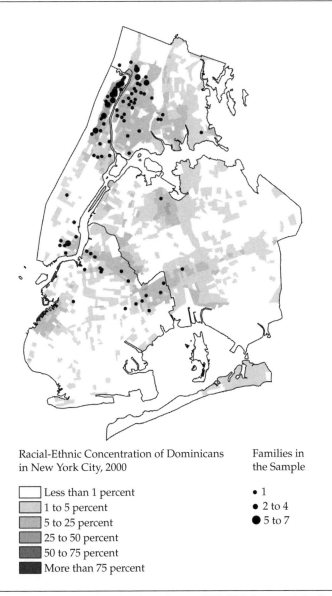

Racial-Ethnic Concentration of Dominicans in New York City, 2000

Families in the Sample

- [ ] Less than 1 percent
- [ ] 1 to 5 percent
- [ ] 5 to 25 percent
- [ ] 25 to 50 percent
- [ ] 50 to 75 percent
- [ ] More than 75 percent

• 1
● 2 to 4
● 5 to 7

Source: Author's graphic utilizing data from Census 2000 (U.S. Bureau of the Census 2000) and the Early Childhood Cohort Study (Center for Research on Culture, Development, and Education 2009).

and others such as Azteca Shoes), travel agencies (with signs in Spanish such as PASAJES PARA ECUADOR Y MÉXICO), money transfer agencies ("envíos de dinero"), banks with strong links to Latin America (Banco Popular), and an array of restaurants that vividly illustrated the immigrant succession and incorporation process (Wendy's, Mexican restaurants, and some Puerto Rican places that sell "mojo frío" and "chichifrutas"). Similarly, although there were no American flags in storefront windows, a few Puerto Rican and Dominican flags and a slew of Mexican flags signaled the ownership and target clientele of some stores. Tensions in community and local politics between the Mexicans and the longer-standing groups in the neighborhood—the Puerto Ricans and Dominicans—have emerged as a result of the succession process.[23] Changes in neighborhood political representation—following a long New York tradition—tend to follow changes in demographics only after a long and reluctant delay.

A variety of community and cultural events served regularly to draw together networks among East Harlem's Mexican families. Some were part of Victoria and Tito's daily routines. Every Sunday at a neighborhood park, for instance, they and other Mexican families got together and cooked, making a hole in the ground, filling it with hot coals, and roasting goat meat in a covered clay pot until it was done. Men played soccer and children played as their dinner cooked "under earth."

More dramatic than these weekly events is the "Mudanza de la Virgen" (Moving of the Virgin), which occurs every December around the feast day of the Virgin of Guadalupe, the patron saint of Mexico. When Victoria came to the United States, she thought she would forget the rituals she knew, but she soon realized that "it is the same here as it is in Mexico." In the Mudanza, the Virgin of Guadalupe is taken to houses in East Harlem by twenty to fifty believers (including women, men, and children). During the period leading up to the feast day, the statue is carried across a series of apartments in the neighborhood, staying in each apartment for three days. At the time of each move, groups of neighbors and community residents gather to celebrate and pray in the first apartment, then move the statue to the new one and pray again there. Throughout this process, money is collected for the Feast of the Virgin of Guadalupe, which occurs on December 12.

Clarissa, Victoria's field-worker, accompanied her one of the evenings when the statue was moved from one apartment to another in the neighborhood. As they walked into the first brownstone, they were greeted by two teenage girls who spoke English with each other without any Spanish accent (a sign of an emerging ethnic enclave when children of the second generation enter adolescence at that level of fluency). Clarissa and Victoria entered the kitchen, where ten or twelve chairs were arranged around the wall. The Virgin was in a corner, on a homemade altar with flowers and candles and an "alcancía" (kitty for donations). The statue of the Virgin had the colors of the Mexican flag—green, red, and white. On her were numerous rosaries, one of which was painted in the Mexican colors. Victoria explained to their host, "We have come to learn how to pray Mexican," explaining that Clarissa was from Peru. The group talked about a variety of things and shared stories about their passages to the United States. After prayers, they walked with the group of ten adults and seven children outside as the Virgin was carried to the next house. Children went first, carrying baskets with petals. They threw petals on the street in front of the statue (carried by a brother-in-law of the host), and a procession of adults with candles and flowers followed. The women sang as they walked down 117th Street. Mexican men passing by made the sign of the cross and took off their hats as the small procession passed by. Other people were curious, respectful, stopping and allowing the group to take over the sidewalk. The procession arrived at the house where the Virgin was going to stay for the next three days. The Virgin, like many New Yorkers, had to deal with a walk-up, ascending five flights of stairs to her new home.

The women continued singing as the Virgin was placed on a small table that had been arranged for her with a clean cloth on top and fresh pink roses in a vase. They set the Virgin down with the candles they had brought from the other house. This was a small one-bedroom apartment; the only sitting area was the kitchen. Like all the Mexican households in our qualitative study, what otherwise would have been the living room was occupied by a bunk bed. Some women sat down; the children sat on the bunk bed, close to the Virgin. The group sang another song and began praying the rosary. After the rosary was completed, the hosts set out food, a mix of Mexican and American—tamales, arroz con leche, champurrado, pan dulce, doughnuts, cookies, and coffee.

Multiple aspects of this event signaled how East Harlem has begun to develop the rich extended networks that have existed for years among the Dominicans in neighborhoods like Washington Heights. The children who greeted Clarissa and Victoria in English were a sign that networks in this neighborhood were multigenerational and multilingual. The visits to multiple households and apartment buildings via public procession through the streets and incorporation of the community provided visible and welcoming networks for newcomers and long-standing residents alike. The ritual itself was familiar from Puebla, where the Virgin is also taken from house to house on the day before her feast day.[24]

A ritual similar to the Mudanza de la Virgen in its religious and transnational aspects is the Antorcha. This annual event, described by both Robert Smith and Alyshia Galvez in her ethnographic study of the worship of the Virgin among Mexicans in New York, is somewhat similar to the Mudanza, but celebrates another patron saint, Padre Jesús.[25] Like the Mudanza, the Antorcha is a ritual that has roots in Mexico but has been transplanted to New York. The torch pilgrimage, in which runners from a town in Puebla carry a torch for Padre Jesús to Mexico City and back during the feast of the saint, has been replicated in New York since 1997. Runners travel with the torch from a church in downtown Manhattan to one in Brooklyn.

Behind every cultural and religious festival like the Mudanza or the Antorcha lies an organizational story. Such events, after all, do not organize themselves. The Mudanza that Clarissa observed was organized by a church in the southern end of East Harlem. Churches function as powerful brokers in the building of social capital for immigrant communities, drawing together social networks of Catholics from Puebla and the Mixteca region, who represent the majority of Mexican immigrants to New York City.[26] Many of these families had taken the same routes to the United States, and sharing the stories of their crossing was part of a community-building process encouraged by the churches. When we asked at thirty-six months whether they had attended church with their child, the Mexican mothers in our sample reported a higher rate of attendance (75 percent) than the Dominican mothers (49 percent).

Another powerful organizational force in the emerging Mexican enclave of East Harlem is a social service organization located on one of the main thoroughfares, Little Sisters of the Assumption). This organization provides a range of social services, including supports for parents of young children and resources for parental mental health care. The Mexican mothers in our first qualitative study, recruited from this organization, told many stories of how the services made a difference in their lives. Victoria's son Ruben, for example, was visited at home by a social worker from the organization who came to assess his development. She said that he was on target, but that Victoria should allow him to move around the house more freely. The social worker also suggested that Victoria buy some toys appropriate for his age. Another mother from our first study, Blanca, was referred to a therapist by the organization, as she suffered from abuse by her husband. She reported that through the therapy she learned to stand up for herself and to think of herself as an independent person who had value. During the course of our study, Blanca, tired of the drunken rages of her husband Gerardo, kicked him out of the house. He eventually came back when he agreed to a condition that she had set—that they attend therapy together.

Little Sisters not only provided social services but served as a hub for organizing and for the economic empowerment of Mexican women in East Harlem. On one visit, Blanca and her field-worker, Francisca, went to a meeting at Little Sisters to discuss the creation of a co-op business that would start by selling homemade wreaths. The agency volunteer who had organized the meeting told everyone about the immigrant workers' march that was going to be held the next day in Flushing Meadows Park in Queens. Little Sisters was providing bus transportation to the march from East Harlem. Blanca was the only one who raised her hand to say that she was going. Francisca observed that the other women were not too enthusiastic about it. The meeting shifted to discussion of the roles required to organize the co-op business.

The example of Little Sisters reminds us that not all organizations serving immigrant communities are alike. Scholars of social capital have highlighted the expertise of organizations that serve particular immigrant communities. For example, Min Zhou, among others, has written about the long history of Chinese organizations serving the Chinatowns of the United States by providing economic, educational, and child-rearing supports.[27] The specialization of organizations that serve groups with high proportions of undocumented may be especially important for the recent waves of Mexicans and Fujianese to New York City, since the needs of many of these undocumented call for changes in traditional social service approaches. Providing information about and referrals to means-tested programs is an entirely different enterprise, depending on whether the service is being offered to an undocumented adolescent, an undocumented parent with a citizen child, a legal permanent resident, a refugee, or a citizen parent with a citizen child. Staff who can provide such specialized expertise in the language of the particular immigrant group are in rare supply in many community-based organizations that do not focus on serving particular immigrant groups.

For the Chinese in our sample, we unfortunately have little data on how community organizations support them as parents because we did not follow up this sample after they sent most of their infants back to China. The few Chinese cases in the qualitative study were not very involved in community organizations. Ling did not mention community organizations during any of her visits. Chun had gone to a local Chinese church a few times, but did not know of other community organizations. She explained that in China most parents associated with others in their work unit or their family, but that there were few activities for residents of the same neighborhood.

The geographic concentration of Chinese in our sample in the Manhattan and Sunset Park Chinatowns did put them in close proximity to a large array of Chinese businesses and organizations. The organizations serving the Fujianese included a large group of long-established organizations providing social, economic, child care, advocacy, and other supports to families in Chinatown. The largest Chinese social service agency in New York, for example, the Chinese-American Planning Council (CPC), was founded in 1965 to serve mainly Cantonese-speaking immigrants from Hong Kong and Guangdong (Canton) province, then the largest sending province in China. Because Mandarin is the nationwide language of schooling in China, many Fujianese immigrants to New York can communicate with Mandarin-speaking staff at CPC and other agencies in the Chinatowns of the city. Staff at the hospitals and other agencies we contacted during the study reported, however, that serving those who spoke only Fujianese was difficult—few social service providers or health professionals in New York speak that language.

Among non–social service organizations, faith-based organizations play an important role in the new Fujianese community, as they have with prior waves of Chinese migration. Chun's contact with a Chinese church reflects the importance of a variety of religious organizations in the Fujianese community in New York. Other research has shown that a range of faiths, including Taoism, Buddhism, Protestanism, and Catholicism, are represented among the churches in the Fujianese community.[28] Such faith-based organizations can be important sources of social capital—including advice about immigration issues—for the undocumented among the Chinese.

The history of organizations specifically serving Mexicans in New York is more recent than that of the Chinatown organizations. Asociación Tepeyac, for example, was founded in 1997 by a group of church leaders aiming to support the new wave of Mexican migration to the city. It has links to many of the churches and church-based societies serving Mexicans in the city. Little Sisters of the Assumption, founded as a visiting nurse service in 1958, began serving Puerto Rican families in East Harlem and then followed the immigrant succession of the neighborhood. It now serves primarily Mexican families. Mixteca, an organization founded by a physician in 2000, serves the Mexican and larger Latin American immigrant community in South Brooklyn.

Organizations like these play a unique role in community organizing and advocacy for the undocumented, whether the advocacy is about work conditions, a route to citizenship, or political representation. We heard very few stories about these functions of organizations from Mexican parents in our hospital-recruited sample. Only one organization (Asociación Tepeyac) was mentioned by name. Most parents, like Flor and Rafael, could not name a single organization that served Mexicans. Although most of the Chinese in our sample lived near organizations that provided support for the undocumented, the Mexican sample did not.

Nevertheless, with its links to churches serving Mexicans in other neighborhoods, Tepeyac can mobilize for immigrant rights or advocacy across neighborhoods. It has the potential to reach those in our sample, particularly through churches and other religious organizations.[29] The very high rate of church attendance among Mexican parents of young children in our sample indicates that this may be a promising route to citywide community organizing and advocacy for Mexicans in New York. Such citywide reach is more difficult for an organization with a social service base, like Little Sisters, to accomplish. Only the largest social service organizations in the city (such as the original settlement house in the United States, University Settlement, founded in 1886) have had the resources to place satellite agencies across the city.

CONCLUSION

The promise of social ties to build human capital—education and work skills in the second generation—was present for our sample, but it was not equally distributed among the documented and undocumented families. For the undocumented Mexicans, lower availability of information and support in household and external networks and lower concentrations of fellow Mexicans in their neighborhoods were accompanied by lower access to the brokering organizations trying to serve the needs of this new wave of immigrants. For the undocumented Chinese, we had little data owing to the high rates at which they sent their infants back to China, but these families generally lived in close proximity to the Chinatowns of New York City and their long-standing organizational resources. In the longitudinal survey sample, lower household-level access to the resources most likely to differ among the documented and undocumented—those that require identification to access—was related to economic hardship and depressive symptoms among parents, which in turn were associated with lower cognitive skills among their children.

The differences between Mexicans in our pilot qualitative study, who were recruited in East Harlem from the central social services organization serving the emerging enclave, and Mexicans in our hospital-based birth cohort, who lived scattered in many neighborhoods across the city, were striking. It was the difference between knowing about the immigrant workers' march and not knowing about it; between being offered the opportunity to have children developmentally assessed and not receiving this offer; between hearing about the existence of Head Start and public libraries and not learning about them; between being referred for therapy in situations of domestic abuse and not being offered such a referral. Nobody in our hospital-recruited sample said, like Victoria, that although she had expected things to be entirely different in New York, some things turned out to be "the same here as it is in Mexico." In this respect, our Mexican sample was unlike those in recent studies of Mexicans in New York who have been recruited through social networks connected to religious or civic organizations.[30] In this study's more population-based sample, there was a distressing lack of access to social capital.

In the survey sample, our Mexican mothers reported significantly lower levels of social support for child care, financial help, and help finding a job than was reported by Dominicans and African Americans. Despite having the largest numbers of adults in the household among these three groups, the Mexicans experienced lower levels of support for raising children and for family life. Organizations that could make a powerful difference, like Little Sisters, are unavoidably neighborhood-based and thus hard to access for families living in distant parts of the city, like Emiliana in Far Rockaway. Networks of churches and religious organizations, like those of Asociación Tepeyac, may be in a better position to provide support—whether religious, social, legal, or political—across the city. In our data, some of the key bridging connections to networks that provided a wider range of information and resources came from women like "las Dominicanas," whom Alfreda and Adelina met in neighborhood settings. Through such connections, forged in seemingly chance meetings in restaurants and stores or on playgrounds, the incorporation of new undocumented groups into the larger eddies of New York City and American life begins.

Chapter 5

The Worst Jobs in Urban America: Undocumented Working Parents in the New York Economy

A good-paying job with opportunities for wage growth and advancement over time sits at the heart of the American dream. Such a job trajectory embodies hopes for one's own future and the future of one's children. For low-income parents, jobs characterized by stability and wage growth over time are in fact linked to more positive cognitive and behavioral development among their children.[1] Undocumented workers, however, fill jobs that are another rung below the typical urban low-wage job held by some U.S. citizens. The undocumented are overrepresented in the lowest-skilled jobs in the country. Despite representing about 6 percent of the U.S. workforce, they make up 25 percent of farmworkers, 28 percent of dishwashers, 27 percent of maids, and 21 percent of parking lot attendants. They constitute 17 percent of those working in construction, up from only 10 percent in 2003.[2] Construction can provide relatively well-paid jobs, but among construction occupations, the undocumented occupy the highest share of the lowest-ranking jobs, such as bricklayers (40 percent) and drywall installers (37 percent). These jobs are less likely than other low-wage jobs to lead to wage growth. Workers can get stuck with low, stagnant wages over the long term, a pattern that harms children's academic and behavioral outcomes.[3] This pattern is exacerbated by both employers' knowledge that undocumented workers will continue to work (in many cases, for years) at very low wages and the reluctance of workers themselves, who fear asking for a raise owing to the potential consequences, such as being fired. This combination of exploitation and dependence is toxic for family life and, as we will see in chapter 6, for children's learning and cognitive skills.

In telling the stories of their experiences working in New York, undocumented parents—in our study, principally Mexican and Chinese parents—showed us the dregs of the U.S. labor market. In this chapter, I demonstrate that many aspects of the jobs of undocumented parents—wages, rates of wage growth, benefits, nature of the duties—are substantially worse than is the case in the jobs of the documented. Most disturbingly, the likelihood of working jobs for wages that are below minimum wage is high among the Chinese and even higher among the Mexicans. I begin with the stories of three couples—Camila and Marcelo, Beatriz and Leandro, and Ling and Wei—whose jobs are representative of those generally held by the Mexican, Dominican, and Chinese mothers and fathers in our study.

CAMILA AND MARCELO

A dark-haired, heavyset woman from Mexico, Camila had a soft voice and seemed depressed at her first meeting with her field-worker, Isidora. She had had three children prior to giving birth to Natalia and being recruited into our study. At that point, Camila stopped working. Her grueling work schedule at a Laundromat was simply too much with four children.

Camila had grown up in San Gregorio, a small town in the state of Puebla. Her family raised chickens. They also had a donkey, a cat, a dog, and some cows. Camila, as the eldest in the family, was responsible for helping to raise her two siblings, a younger brother and younger sister. After finishing "primaria" (school up to sixth grade), she had to commute to a town one hour away to attend "secundaria," since her town did not have such a school. After finishing secundaria, she moved to Mexico City because there were no jobs in her town and the family's farming did not bring in enough income to pay for her sisters' education. She sent money back from Mexico City to help her family and support her sisters' education. During the two years she lived in the city, she worked two jobs every day: in the morning she was a nanny, and in the afternoon she did filing work in an office near her apartment. Subject to the complex calculations of rural-urban migrants working in the majority world, her salary was divided into three parts: paying rent to her aunt for a tiny room in her apartment; sending money back to San Gregorio to support her sisters; and saving money to use to travel eventually to the United States.

She first made the decision to go to the United States in conversations with friends from her hometown. When she then told her father in San Gregorio, he was understanding and wanted to make sure that migrating to the United States was what she really wanted to do: "You are leaving because you want to, not because you have to." Camila reassured him that she was going of her own volition. After a trip to New York that took twenty days, accompanied by a friend from San Gregorio and his sister, she arrived in New York. Camila remembered being struck by how old the buildings in New York were, as well as by the noise and pollution. She preferred the open spaces and fields of San Gregorio.

Camila's first job in New York was selling flowers on the street. In finding work as a street vendor, she became the latest in a centuries-old tradition in which thousands of new immigrants have literally colored the fabric of New York City. Whatever one is selling, street vending is a job that is not legal in the city except for the lucky few who have a license. The city has granted a total of 853 licenses since 1988; the current waiting list is twenty-five years long.[4]

Street vending in New York City has a long history, most of it outside the law and associated with immigrants. The nineteenth-century practice of pushcart vending on the streets of the Lower East Side, for example, stemmed from a 1761 law designed to protect farmers. This law allowed sales of goods in the street as long as sellers did not stay in one place for more than thirty minutes.[5] At that point, eastern European Jews were the largest immigrant group engaging in street vending; now, in twenty-first-century New York, new arrays of immigrants sell goods on the street, with flower selling a niche specific to Mexicans. Flower vending on the street was very common among our Mexican mothers and fathers as a first job.

Camila described her daily routine at this job: A friend would bring flowers from New Jersey. They would sell them along Fourteenth Street, a street bordering Union Square, Greenwich Village, and the East Village that for decades was a commercial center for low-priced goods in Manhattan. Some days she sold all her flowers, and other days she sold only half of what she had brought with her. Camila would clean and wrap her own packs of flowers: twenty packs of roses, ten packs of "claveles" (carnations), and twenty packs of other kinds. She worked from Wednesday to Sunday. In her best weeks, she would make $200 to $250, but some weeks she grossed much less. (Her best income works out, at even a conservative thirty hours a week, to far below minimum wage at that time in New York.) In her own words, flower selling was a "very uncertain" job. She soon left it.

Camila's second job was at least indoors, but it also had much in common with the jobs typically held by the Mexican parents in our study. She worked in a twenty-four-hour Laundromat, on the 9:00 AM to 9:00 PM shift, six days a week. She worked until she was eight months pregnant with her first child, Humberto (who was seven years old at the beginning of our study). The work was physically hard. Although loading the washing machines, transferring clothes to the dryers, and folding clothes were relatively easy tasks, the large laundry bags that she had to pack and put away sometimes weighed 80 to 150 pounds and required two people to heave.

At the Laundromat, Camila and her friend worked for a Brazilian manager. She and her friend would often be in charge of opening and closing the place. Since they had no other coworkers, it was only Camila and her Mexican friend in the Laundromat. Camila reported that their boss was usually nice to them. But one day she did something that was unfair to Camila's friend. A customer came into the Laundromat saying that a very expensive shirt was missing from his laundry bag. The customer claimed that it was a shirt that had cost him hundreds of dollars. After a while, the Brazilian woman told Camila's friend, who was still working that day, that she had to pay for the shirt. She was told that an installment payment would be taken out of her weekly salary. The following day, Camila's friend did not return to work. Later, the Brazilian woman kept calling her on the phone and even called Camila to find out if she could convince her friend to go back to work. Camila's friend eventually got another job at another Laundromat nearby.

Camila's hopes for her career, after her kids have grown up, were very different depending on whether she was thinking of New York or Puebla. In New York, she felt that she could perhaps get a job making jewelry. In Mexico, in contrast, she felt that she would want to have "un negocio para mi"—to own her own business selling a variety of goods, perhaps a convenience store.

Camila's husband Marcelo was also from Puebla and had come to the United States three years before Camila. In fact, he was one of the friends who had convinced Camila to come to the United States. In Mexico, Marcelo had had several jobs. He was a schoolteacher and taught math in a small private school in his town. At the same time, he held another part-time job and sometimes ran errands for the local church. After working in his town for some years, he moved to Mexico City and started working a pretty easy job in a hardware store that paid better. He was eventually promoted and moved to a larger warehouse of the hardware store, where he supervised people loading merchandise. He had a very good relationship with the manager, who once lent Marcelo some money when he needed it. When he told his boss that he was planning to go to the United States, his boss told him that he had a good job and a good salary—why leave that to go to the United States, where the future was uncertain? Eventually the manager told Marcelo that if he could not complete the crossing, he could come back to his job. That was the last job Marcelo had in Mexico.

Marcelo, like Camila, began work in the United States as a flower seller. He would buy flower bouquets on the western edge of the historic flower district of Manhattan, around Eighteenth Street and Eleventh Avenue. Then he would go around the city selling flowers he carried in a shopping cart. Marcelo did not have a permit to sell flowers, and not surprisingly, he was arrested eight or nine times. Isidora gasped when she heard this, but Marcelo, smiling, quickly turned his tale into an adventure story. He said that things were not really that bad, that the jail stays were usually only a day or two. Marcelo also said that his friends all knew that if someone did not return to the streets, he had probably been arrested. He had this job for almost a year. He made about $150 per week (an income that, again, works out to far below the minimum wage at the time). As we will see later in this chapter, the Mexicans in our sample were much more likely to work below the minimum wage than the Dominican, Chinese, or African Americans.

After Marcelo had sold flowers for several months, a friend came to him to say that the restaurant where he worked in Hoboken was hiring. Marcelo could make $80 for the weekend (Saturday and Sunday) shift. Marcelo thought that was a good deal. It was much more than what he was making by selling flowers, and it would probably involve less hassle from the police. He took that job. The restaurant was a twenty-four-hour restaurant, and Marcelo worked the night shift. Working twelve-hour shifts, six days a week, he brought home $250 a week. This pay worked out to an hourly wage of about $3.47 (again, below minimum wage). His wage stayed the same for six years. He felt that he should have been paid more, but he never asked for a raise. After six years, his boss doubled his salary. During the next ten years, Marcelo received one more small wage increase. By the time of our study, however, he was still making under $10 an hour at a job he had had for sixteen years.

He spoke with Isidora at length about this restaurant job. One of his stories illustrates the peculiar and toxic mix of exploitation and mutual dependence that often characterizes the undocumented and their employers. In a defiant tone, Marcelo told her that, from the beginning, he had known that he would not accept being abused by his boss at the restaurant. One time he and his mostly Mexican coworkers were cleaning the grill, and a couple of customers walked in and left because there was no service. The owner became angry and frustrated and started to yell at everyone. He yelled at Marcelo, "Get the fuck out of there," which Marcelo interpreted to mean that the boss wanted him to leave the restaurant. Marcelo got angry and said he was not going back. He went to the train station, fuming. While he was there on the platform waiting for his train, his boss came looking for him and explained that there had been a misunderstanding. He had not in fact asked Marcelo to leave. But Marcelo insisted that he had understood what the boss meant. Finally, he agreed to go back. He continued to earn around $250 a week, but after this incident he was allowed to work not just in the deli section of the restaurant but in the full-service section as well. This change was what led to the doubling of his salary.

By the end of the ethnographic study, Isidora no longer thought that Camila was depressed. She was instead impressed by how stoically Camila coped with the household's limited economic resources. Isidora wrote, "She seems calm overall and takes her life day by day. What I found admirable is her patience as she fills in her days with the thousand things she must accomplish all by herself while taking care of four kids."

BEATRIZ AND LEANDRO

Beatriz, a tall woman with a gentle demeanor, had come to the United States, like many of the Dominican mothers, on a work visa (in her case, a three-month visa). At the point when she stayed in the United States past three months, she became undocumented. By the end of the ethnographic period, however, she was waiting to be considered for a green card, sponsored by a relative. She grew up in the capital of Santo Domingo; her mother raised her for most of her childhood as a single mother. Her father, a campesino, would visit from time to time from the countryside. Since Beatriz was an only child, she always got everything she wanted, whether a nice dress or a pair of shoes. Beatriz's father made a decent living, enough to send money and food, such as big bags of rice, to her and her mother on a regular basis. Sometimes, when he visited them in Santo Domingo, she would experience the treat of her father buying her a pair of nice shoes.

Beatriz had earned a B.A. degree in computer engineering. Her first job following her undergraduate education was an office job in which she could use her computer skills. This job made it possible for her to get a work visa to come to the States; the company had a branch there, so it was able to send her to New York City to work for three months. She came and stayed on past the three-month point, living with a friend for a year. When that friend moved to California, Beatriz had to find her own apartment.

When she overstayed her visa, she began looking for a job. Her work experience in Santo Domingo had involved clerical work and filing, but she could not find anything related to that in New York. She ended up working for Payless, the shoe store, then at a "factoría" (garment sweatshop), and after that, in a clothing store. She felt that she was exploited in these jobs. As she told Isidora, her field-worker in our study, she knew all too well the disadvantages of "not speaking English and having to take jobs as janitors."

In fact, her first relatively well-paid job in New York was cleaning offices in midtown. She was hired through an agency that paid $12 to $15 an hour. She worked five to six hours, five days a week. During that time, Beatriz was working a night shift, starting when people left the office, around 6:00 PM, until 11:00 or 12:00 at night. Taking into account her commuting time, she would sometimes not make it home until 1:00 AM. Beatriz worked cleaning offices for five years, until shortly after 9/11.

Most of the people who cleaned offices for the corporate world of midtown Manhattan were women, from a range of nationalities. Beatriz worked alongside some men—most of them were assigned to cleaning bathrooms. Her supervisor was a Yugoslavian man who sometimes screamed and yelled at people, she reported, but who for the most part created a friendly environment. Some offices had large kitchens, and the workers assigned to cleaning only those kitchens were paid more money. At the beginning of each shift, all the cleaners went to a locker area where they left personal items; then they picked up their cleaning carts and were dispatched to their floors. Each floor was made up of roughly three hundred cubicles and some kitchenettes and took two to three hours to complete. After the first floor was cleaned, the cleaners got a break, then went on to another two-to-three-hour floor. At the end of the night shift, the cleaners returned to the locker area, after which they were free to leave.

Beatriz started making $10 an hour at this job, with benefits. (Compare this wage to Marcelo's: he made under $10 an hour after sixteen years at his restaurant job, with no benefits.) Her first raise was to $13.45, and by the time she quit the job six years later when her first child, Olivia, was born, she was making $27 an hour. Her benefits included health insurance and paid vacations, and the cleaners were well represented by a union. Some of the things that Beatriz liked about the cleaning job were the schedule and the benefits. But one thing she disliked about the job was how "inferior" she felt when she walked into the office wearing a uniform that designated her as cleaning staff. In explaining those feelings, Beatriz said that it felt bad to be cleaning the very same offices in which, with her B.A. in computer skills, she could have been working during the day. She disliked the thought of people looking at her as "the cleaning lady." She worked for one year on the morning shift, but preferred working the late shift, when there was almost no one left but a few people working late.

Beatriz met her husband, Leandro, at a dance club. They flirted but did not begin dating until she saw him again at the same club several months later. In between, he had returned to his home country of Mexico. Unlike most of our Mexican parents, Leandro was from the area surrounding the cosmopolitan city of Guadalajara, capital of the state of Jalisco. At the beginning of our ethnographic study, Leandro was working as a landscape gardener, six days a week, Monday to Saturday. Each day he left home at 6:00 AM and was driven with a group of other workers to suburban, affluent Westchester County (a reverse-commute drive of about an hour). He got off work at 4:30 PM. If there was heavy traffic, he would not arrive home until 6:00 or sometimes 7:00 PM. He explained that in the Westchester area most of the Mexicans were from Puebla.

Leandro said that Mexicans in construction or landscaping were often supervised by Italians who owned the houses or hired cheap labor—an instance of the classic succession pattern of the immigrant job ladder. Latinos (mainly Mexicans and other Central Americans) generally did the landscaping, construction, and house cleaning for the residents of Westchester County.

Leandro also reported very low pay. Despite the reputation of construction as a relatively good entry-level job, the Mexican immigrant laborers on Leandro's team received little. The Italian contractor on Leandro's construction site, he said, paid little more than $5 per hour, even to people who had worked for him for more than fifteen years. This wage is comparable to Marcelo's and shows that even in what is considered the stable and well-paid sector of construction, undocumented workers are paid bottom-of-the-barrel wages and experience extreme wage stagnation.

Leandro and two other Mexican men met up at their work site every day and were assigned by their employer to the houses they would work on that day. In a day they could do approximately ten houses, and sometimes as many as twenty. Leandro reported getting along well with the other two men he worked with, but Beatriz said that many days he returned home exhausted. She called the job "desgastante" (draining) and said that she would prefer that he not work so hard, but at the same time she knew he liked the job. In a joking way, he told Isidora that if she knew of any job offers, she should send them to him. Every winter, when there was little landscaping work, represented a lean period for Leandro and therefore for his and Beatriz's family. He looked for temporary work during the cold months. By the advent of the wet, cold New York spring, he was usually rehired in landscaping.

LING AND WEI

Ling's job trajectory once she arrived in New York was quite typical of the pre-9/11 jobs of the Fujianese in New York. She first worked in the garment industry in a sweatshop and then shifted to working at home, beading jewelry. The sweatshop was oddly located—in Brooklyn under the Manhattan Bridge (an area called Dumbo [Down Under the Manhattan Bridge] that has since filled up with hip artists and galleries). She reported that her boss liked her "because I worked really hard." Her son Guang, at that time an infant, was the only child at the work site. He slept until 9:00 at night, and then Ling would take him home. The work hours were a grueling 9:00 AM until as late as midnight. She was doing piecework, what she called "breaking pieces of fabric." That is, every worker in the sweatshop would work on a particular part of a garment (for example, only doing collars). As Margaret Chin notes in her book on Chinese firms in the garment industry, this form of assembly-line work gives parents with children no flexibility.[6] To take even a five-minute break is to risk holding up the line of workers laboring over other parts of the garment. The pay (typically per piece) also tends to be lower than pay for the alternative mode of sweatshop work—what Ling called "pulling bones"—in which each worker sews entire garments. With greater control over the pace of the work, workers with very young children, like Ling, had greater flexibility and "more freedom" working this way; however, she was not allowed to switch to that mode in this particular sweatshop. Ling usually made about $400 a week, working six days a week, fourteen hours a day (which works out to $4.76 an hour). This pay was above the minimum wage at the time, though barely.

Ling reported that conditions in the Chinatown garment sweatshops were worse than in the one she worked at in Brooklyn. In the Chinatown sweatshop where she worked for a brief period, she said that, "if you were a little bit late, they would blame you; if you come earlier, they would also blame you. I'm afraid I don't have time to pick up my child from school, so I come earlier. Like this, they would still blame." She also told Yong, her field-worker, that the Chinatown sweatshop paid less than the one where she ended up working. The bulk of the Chinese garment industry was devastated by 9/11, after which only portions of the industry remained in the city. At first some of the firms moved to Sunset Park and other nearby neighborhoods in Brooklyn, but most of the Chinese garment industry—after more than one hundred years of history in Manhattan—collapsed and disappeared. Also contributing to the industry's demise was the powerhouse of the ever-growing Chinese mainland economy.[7] By this period, however, Ling and Wei's debts had been paid off, and there was less pressure on them to work fourteen-hour days, six days a week. Ling shifted to jewelry making, which may sound like being paid to do a hobby activity but was far from that.

Most people in New York City assume that all of the beaded jewelry sold at the city's discount stores is made in China. This is not the case. Some of it is made by Fujianese immigrants in New York. By the beginning of our qualitative study, Ling was working at home stringing beads for jewelry. The pay was fifty cents for making something simple like an earring made up of two linked rings; for more complex jewelry, the pay ended up being quite a bit higher, and so she typically held out for this kind of work. The jewelry was destined for Manhattan discount storefronts. Ling reported making a "few hundred" dollars a month with this work. She liked it because she could work at home and have flexible hours. "I do it at home, can't really earn that much money. But I can watch the children." However, the pay was not steady. "Like last year, had to wait from November until April until I had something to do, I was really worried waiting at home." She went to other jewelry dealers and worked making the simpler pieces for "bad pay" until her usual boss informed her that she had more work for her.

Ling was paid only every month or two. When we interviewed her, she was owed two or three thousand dollars. She said she was afraid that the woman she worked for would just run off with the jewelry, but "see, it has good pay. So there's no use, even though I'm afraid, if I go to the others, with bad pay, also can't earn a lot."

Ling's husband Wei worked in his brother's Chinese restaurant in Queens. It took over an hour to commute to the restaurant from their apartment. He left around 9:00 AM and returned around 1:00 AM, usually getting Tuesdays off. More than 90 percent of our Chinese fathers reported working in Chinese restaurants. (They were surveyed once at baseline about their current or most recent job.) By the time our study began, restaurant work was the dominant occupational niche for Fujianese immigrants, owing to the disappearance of much of the Chinese garment industry from the city.

Chinese restaurants provide an extremely defined career trajectory for aspiring Fujianese immigrants without papers, built on millions upon millions of orders of Chinese food adapted for American tastes, like General Tso's chicken or beef with oyster sauce. Ling told Yong how the progression works. First, most newly arrived Fujianese immigrants without a relative already in the restaurant business go to one of the employment agencies on Forsyth Street, near Division Street in lower Manhattan. A nerve center of the Fujianese community, these agencies field requests for jobs from storefront and buffet restaurants all over the eastern half of the United States. On bulletin boards at these agencies, slips of paper are posted citing the positions available—cook, fryer, cashier, waiter, or waitress—and their area codes. Buses are waiting outside to transport workers immediately after a phone call to their new employer. The "Chinatown" buses, so well known to East Coast budget travelers, that travel between the cities of Washington, D.C., Philadelphia, New York, and Boston also ply the highways to South Carolina, Illinois, and Florida. Not coincidentally, they tend to stop along the way at gas stations with adjacent buffet restaurants owned or managed by Fujianese immigrants.

A Fujianese immigrant's first restaurant job is usually in one of the thousands of storefront Chinese restaurants in the eastern United States. These are very familiar to tourists and locals alike, with their rows of light-box photographs of dishes above the ordering counter and larger light boxes on the walls with photos of the Temple of Heaven in Beijing, the spiny mountains of Guilin, or the Great Wall.[8] A typical goal is ownership of one of these storefronts, and then working one's way up to owning a buffet restaurant, where the profit margins are higher. "If you want to open a regular takeout Chinese restaurant," Ling explained, "you need to have $60,000 to $70,000. And if you could have business of $30,000 a month, then you could survive. But if you want to open a buffet restaurant, you need to have $400,000." Yong noted that that was a lot of money—how could a recent immigrant get that kind of money? Ling said that one could always borrow from one's friends; she described the social networks of the Fujianese as "small circles" that were nevertheless "very generous." A few years earlier, her sister had managed to open a regular restaurant with no more than $10,000 of her own; the rest came from personal loans. Ling said that her sister had paid back the loans in three years. Ling really wanted to open her own restaurant. She told Yong almost every time he visited her that one of her friends in Chicago had five restaurants and was thinking of opening a sixth. She envied her friend very much.

Restaurant work itself, however, can be crushingly repetitive and tedious. As Fen, one of the Chinese mothers in our study, told Qiu, her fieldworker, her job as a cashier in a restaurant was very dull and boring. "That is just the life I am living now," she conceded. Fen told Qiu that her English was adequate for taking orders at a restaurant but still not very good. When Qiu asked her if she had any plans to learn more English, Fen shook her head with an embarrassed smile, saying, "I am not a person of smart brain. I am not good at learning. It is fine as long as it is enough to make a living. I hope my kid will do better than me."

THE WORK CONDITIONS OF
UNDOCUMENTED PARENTS

On several dimensions—hours, wages, benefits, nature of job duties, opportunities for advancement and wage growth, and risk for exploitation and wage violations—our quantitative data support the ethnographic evidence, which suggested that groups with high proportions of undocumented have drastically worse jobs. Like Camila, Marcelo, and Wei, the majority of undocumented parents in our study worked in small businesses such as Laundromats, groceries, and restaurants, or did cleaning work.

We coded each of the mothers' and fathers' current or most recent jobs from the larger survey sample using the current U.S. Department of Labor codes for 949 U.S. occupations.[9] In reporting these data, I again supplement data from Mexicans and Dominicans with data from the African American mothers in our sample as a comparison group of low-income working mothers who were U.S. citizens. The most common occupational categories for fathers from the Mexican families were food preparation or service and office or administrative; for fathers from the Dominican families, construction and driving were the most common occupations, and fathers from the African American families mainly worked in office or administrative and maintenance or repair. The most common occupations for Mexican mothers were building cleaning and production (largely garments); for Dominican mothers they were food preparation or service and personal care or service, and African American mothers commonly worked in sales and office or administrative jobs.

Unlike the shifts worked by many low-wage urban workers in the United States—which can spill over into evening and weekend hours, but often still conform to day, swing, and night shift structures with long shifts of eight hours—many small workplaces with high proportions of undocumented workers in New York function on twelve-hour shifts.[10] With one-hour commutes on average, our undocumented, full-time working parents were often away from home for fourteen hours a day, six days a week. Workweeks for the undocumented in our sample were as likely to be six days a week as five. This made average work hours extraordinarily long for the Chinese and Mexican workers in our study (see table 5.1). Fathers' work hours (which are less affected by child care decisions than mothers' hours) averaged 54.5 hours for the Mexican fathers when their children were fourteen months old and 52.5 hours two years later, when the children were thirty-six months old. The hours for Dominicans and African Americans, respectively, were 40.2 and 40.2 hours at fourteen months and 41.9 and 37.9 hours at thirty-six months. So average weekly hours were almost two full days greater for the Mexican fathers compared to their Dominican and African American counterparts (whose averages working full-time hours were already high, indicating that many were working more than a forty-hour week). And the Chinese fathers, for whom we have data only at the one-month survey, had even higher work hours—an astonishing average of 64.5 hours per week.

When I examined the hourly wages of the men in the sample, average wages for Dominicans and African Americans were generally between $10 and $15 an hour, depending on the wave of assessment. Wages for Mexican men, in contrast, were between $8 and $10 an hour. In the only assessment we have, at one month, of the Chinese fathers, the average was also very low—about $7 an hour. How do these wages compare to national estimates of wages? The national median wage for men in 2006 was $16.66 an hour. Men in all three of our groups had average wages below this level. The definition of a poverty wage used most often by researchers—the wage at which working full-time (forty hours a week for fifty-two weeks a year) leaves a worker at the federal poverty threshold for a family of two adults and two children—was $9.83 for 2006.[11] In our data, 59 percent of the Mexican fathers had wages below this level, compared to 48 percent of the Dominican fathers and 26 percent of the African American fathers, at the thirty-six-month point in time.

Table 5.1   **Fathers' Hours and Wages, Percentages Below Minimum Wage, and Wage Change over Two Years, by Ethnicity (Means and Standard Deviations)**

	Chinese	Mexican	Dominican	African American
Weekly Hours				
At one month[a]	64.50 (12.11)	50.23 (15.10)	45.83 (13.77)	38.84 (12.32)
	$N = 40$	$N = 80$	$N = 65$	$N = 58$
At fourteen months		54.54 (17.18)	40.20 (14.97)	40.18 (15.81)
	n/a	$N = 62$	$N = 49$	$N = 46$
At thirty-six months		52.47 (16.37)	41.88 (19.23)	37.89 (14.67)
	n/a	$N = 59$	$N = 51$	$N = 38$
Hourly wages				
At one month	7.03 (2.44)	8.54 (5.11)	10.59 (4.28)	12.35 (10.24)
	$N = 37$	$N = 64$	$N = 43$	$N = 31$
At fourteen months		8.08 (3.71)	14.64 (12.61)	12.35 (7.35)
	n/a	$N = 57$	$N = 43$	$N = 37$
At thirty-six months		9.30 (4.86)	14.04 (7.30)	15.47 (12.20)
	n/a	$N = 55$	$N = 37$	$N = 23$
Percentage working below minimum wage				
At one month[b]	16%	22%	9%	0%
At fourteen months[c]	n/a	30	9	5
At thirty-six months[d]	n/a	31	11	5
Wage change				
Average change in wages between fourteen and thirty-six months	n/a	+$1.08 (5.58)	+$3.21 (8.04)	+$7.04 (12.06)

Source: Author's compilation based on data from the Early Childhood Cohort Study (Center for Research on Culture, Development, and Education 2009).
[a] At one month, questions about wages and hours in the current or last job were asked. At fourteen and thirty-six months, the questions were only asked about the current job.
[b] Minimum wage in New York State in 2004 of $5.15 an hour.
[c] Minimum wage in New York State in 2005 of $6.00 an hour.
[d] Minimum wage in New York State in 2007 of $7.15 an hour.

The data for the mothers are harder to interpret because smaller percentages of mothers than fathers went back to work after giving birth, and because the percentages of those who did return to work were so different, with larger percentages among the Dominican and African American mothers than the Mexican mothers (see the numbers reported in table 5.2). This difference was due in part to differences in family structure: rates of marriage and cohabitation were much higher among the Mexicans than among the Dominicans and African Americans (as found in other studies).[12] The differences may also have been due to different degrees of gendered division of labor in households. Divisions of labor between male breadwinners and female caregivers appear to weaken after migration from Mexico and the Dominican Republic to the United States, driven primarily by higher rates of women's employment after migration.[13] We found more evidence of a traditionally gendered division of labor among the Mexican households than among the Dominican ones. Those who had gone back to work among the Mexican mothers were therefore less representative of their group as a whole than Dominican and African American mothers. Average thirty-six-month wages did not differ across the groups, but the different rates of return to work made this difficult to interpret.

The depth of wage poverty experienced by the Mexicans in our sample is most striking if we examine the percentage of those working below the minimum wage. In New York State, the minimum wage as of April 2006 was $7.15 an hour. All of our thirty-six-month data were collected after this point, with the majority collected in 2007. The percentage of fathers who were earning below minimum wage was nearly one-third (31 percent) of the Mexican sample, compared to 11 percent of the Dominican fathers and 5 percent of the African American fathers. Similarly, the percentage of working mothers earning below the minimum wage was 38 percent for the Mexicans compared to 14 percent among the Dominicans and 13 percent among the African Americans. These disparities are similar at the one-month and fourteen-month time points. At the one-month time point, the comparison to Chinese mothers and fathers is also possible—this group earned wages below the minimum wage at rates higher than those for the Dominicans and African Americans but lower than the rates for the Mexicans. The rates across groups of wages below the legal minimum were similar whether I included or excluded those who reported that their wages were after taxes or those who worked in restaurants. (Although we asked mothers to report their earnings including both wages and tips, some in restaurant jobs might have reported only wages.) Wage violation rates in this study are also comparable to those in a large recent survey study of low-wage workers.[14] In that study of three

Table 5.2 **Mothers' Hours and Wages and Percentages Below Minimum Wage, by Ethnicity (Means and Standard Deviations)**

	Chinese	Mexican	Dominican	African American
Hours				
At one month	59.26 (17.21)	42.44 (16.70)	35.26 (16.05)	32.66 (12.42)
	$N = 39$	$N = 81$	$N = 89$	$N = 80$
At fourteen months		25.55 (19.50)	29.55 (14.33)	25.41 (17.11)
	n/a	$N = 26$	$N = 50$	$N = 38$
At thirty-six months		30.23 (16.81)	32.56 (11.80)	31.15 (12.15)
	n/a	$N = 35$	$N = 54$	$N = 42$
Hourly wages				
At one month	7.45 (2.43)	8.17 (6.61)	8.58 (5.29)	9.66 (7.32)
	$N = 40$	$N = 74$	$N = 84$	$N = 80$
At fourteen months		9.29 (8.28)	11.57 (7.62)	10.29 (4.57)
	n/a	$N = 26$	$N = 49$	$N = 31$
At thirty-six months		12.11 (12.02)	11.35 (5.99)	14.23 (15.91)
	n/a	$N = 34$	$N = 50$	$N = 40$
Percentage working below minimum wage				
At one month	13%	32%	10%	4%
At fourteen months	n/a	31	12	3
At thirty-six months	n/a	38	14	13

Source: Author's compilation based on data from the Early Childhood Cohort Study (Center for Research on Culture, Development, and Education 2009).

cities, 37 percent of undocumented workers reported earnings and hours that worked out to under the minimum wage.

A measure of hope in the work lives of all parents is the degree to which wages rise over time. Wage growth for parents has been linked to both higher levels of school achievement in children and lower levels of behavior problems. Parents who experience wage growth appear to hold higher levels of academic expectations for their children and report lower levels of parenting stress and fewer depressive symptoms.[15] The levels of wage growth in our sample were a powerful indicator of the very poor work conditions of the Mexican parents. During years of historic economic growth in the United States and in New York City, Mexican fathers experienced an average increase in wages of just over $1 an hour between the fourteen- and thirty-six-month assessments ($1.08), with Dominican fathers experiencing average increases of $3.21 and African American fathers $7.04. This statistic was not calculated for the mothers, owing to the very different rates of early maternal returns to work between fourteen and thirty-six months among the three ethnic groups.

Another measure of job quality is the nature of job duties. Day in and day out, lower-quality jobs are more automated and repetitious, more physically demanding, and less likely to offer opportunities for self-direction and autonomous decisions.[16] These characteristics are also associated with harsher, more authoritarian parenting, higher parental stress, lower levels of cognitive stimulation, and more focus on obedience in children.[17] The Department of Labor, in addition to classifying all the occupations in the United States, characterizes them according to a large number of qualities of the job duties, with ratings developed for each occupation on each characteristic. Of these, following the work of Ann Crouter and her colleagues, we developed scales representing self-direction, physical demands, and automated or repetitious jobs.[18]

These job quality indicators showed group differences similar to those I found with wages. Recall that the vast majority of the fathers (though not all) were of the same ethnic group as the mothers. Fathers in Mexican families had jobs with significantly lower self-direction opportunities than did the fathers in both Dominican and African American families. Mexican mothers had jobs with significantly lower self-direction than was true of the jobs of African American mothers. The jobs of Mexican mothers were also significantly more physically demanding, automatized, and repetitious than the jobs of both Dominican and African American mothers. The Mexicans, the group in our study with by far the highest proportions of undocumented, were more likely in their jobs to obey orders and not make autonomous decisions, to serve others with little discretion, and to be limited to repetitive, physically demanding tasks. At baseline only, we had the Chinese sample data as well. Almost all of this group worked in restaurants. Interestingly, despite the equally long hours of restaurant work put in by our Chinese parents, their restaurant work was more likely to involve some supervision than that of the Mexican group. This is because the Chinese occasionally worked as front managers or cashiers. The restaurants and service establishments in which our Mexican parents worked were typically multiethnic workplaces, with Mexicans occupying the bottom rung. Their positions—dishwasher, delivery person, or, at best, line cook—were less likely to include the possibility of advancement to restaurant manager.

Finally, one last part of the job quality picture—benefits—showed disparities in our sample that were just as large as those for wages and job duties, if not larger. At fourteen months, we asked about four types of

Table 5.3   Rates of Overtime, Paid Sick and Vacation Days, and Health Benefits at Job, at Fourteen Months

	Mexican	Dominican	African American
Mothers			
Overtime	35%	47%	55%
Paid sick days	15	40	46
Paid vacation days	9	45	41
Health insurance			
benefits	9	34	31
Fathers			
Overtime	31	60	71
Paid sick or vacation			
days[a]	30	46	66
Health insurance			
benefits	15	40	63

Source: Author's compilation based on data from the Early Childhood Cohort Study (Center for Research on Culture, Development, and Education 2009).
[a] These two types of benefits were not separated out in the questions on fathers.

benefits: paid overtime, paid sick days, paid vacation days, and health insurance benefits. Dominican and African American fathers and mothers were two to four times more likely to have these benefits at work compared to their Mexican counterparts (see table 5.3).

Are these poor work conditions simply a reflection of low levels of parental education? Our data suggest that they are not. For example, all of the group differences in self-direction, physically demanding tasks, and automatized or repetitive job duties held up after controlling for levels of mothers' and fathers' education. A national study supports this finding as well—what economists call the return to education, or the gain in earnings that an increase in education can buy, is lower for undocumented Mexican workers compared to documented Mexican workers.[19] Thus, undocumented workers have lower wages than documented workers even when we compare those with the same levels of education.

We might expect that these poor work conditions translate into higher perceptions of discrimination in the workplace. Discrimination overall against undocumented immigrants is rising in the United States. Violence against illegal immigrants has surged, including in communities in and around New York City. Most notoriously, the murder in November 2008 of Marcelo Lucero, an Ecuadorean immigrant living in suburban Patchogue, New York, drew headlines because the group of high school students who killed him set out that day with the goal of "killing a Mexican."[20] The influx of Latin American workers into low-paying jobs in U.S. suburbs has been accompanied in some communities by such hate crimes. Rates of bias crimes against Latinos grew nationwide, despite overall decreases in crime, during the recent surge in undocumented migration to the United States.[21]

In our survey, we measured experiences of discrimination by asking mothers whether they had experienced unfair treatment in the workplace. In their answers to these questions, the three ethnic groups differed very little in their perceptions of unfair treatment. In fact, for several possible reasons, the Mexican mothers reported lower levels of perceived discrimination across these measures than the other two groups. As immigrants who arrived more recently on average than the Dominicans, our Mexican sample might have been less accustomed to the patterns of discrimination in the United States based on immigration status, race, or ethnicity. In fact, studies show that with more years in the United States, perceptions of racial-ethnic discrimination increase among immigrant populations.[22] The lower levels of English-language ability among the more recent immigrants in our sample may have limited their ability to understand whether comments in English were derogatory. Finally, the well-known phenomenon of "immigrant optimism"—the perception of opportunities and hope that is part of the American dream for recent immigrants to the United States—could also be responsible for lower perceptions of discrimination among more recent immigrants.[23]

Why do undocumented immigrants stay in such poor-quality jobs, often years into their residence in the United States? One common argument is that this population is willing to take poorer jobs than other low-income groups in the United States, such as immigrant groups with higher rates of residency or citizenship (such as Dominicans) or U.S. citizens with low incomes (for example, African Americans). The evidence on this question is mixed. Some studies find little evidence in U.S. cities that low-skilled immigrants "take away" jobs from low-skilled native-born workers.[24] Other studies show that such a pattern does indeed exist. One recent twenty-year analysis showed that rises in immigration between 1980 and 2000 were associated with reduced employment among low-skilled African American males.[25] My study cannot answer this question of whether low-skilled immigrants' jobs are substituting for those that the U.S.-born would otherwise take. The job sectors of the three groups of parents did not overlap very much; Mexicans and African Americans showed the least overlap, and Dominicans were in the middle. For example, office and administrative support was the most common job sector for African American women (21 percent), but rare among the Mexicans (4 percent), with Dominicans in between (14 percent). In contrast, cleaning homes or offices was most common among the Mexican women (23 percent), rare among the African Americans (3 percent), and also relatively rare among the Dominican women (8 percent). It is difficult to interpret these data as the result of competition for the same jobs on the part of undocumented immigrants, documented immigrants, and the native-born.

Research does show that employers in the lowest-wage sectors prefer workers from groups with high proportions of undocumented. They may perceive that such workers are less likely to complain to bosses for fear of being deported, and this may be one reason why rates of wage violations seemed high among undocumented parents in our qualitative sample as well as the survey sample. Employers consistently report, for example, that immigrant workers are more likely to put up with subordination than U.S.-born workers.[26] Racial stereotypes also bolster perceptions that U.S.-born African Americans are more disobedient or disloyal in the workplace than immigrants.[27]

Undocumented employees often feel "locked into" their jobs and are reluctant to ask for a raise or leave a job for a new employer. The hallmark of what economists call job mobility—moving to a new job with a higher wage—requires a basic level of trust (in other words, assurance that the employer will not call "la migra"). This makes the low-wage job market a very different one for the undocumented compared to the documented. Fears of being deported may be precisely why employers prefer the undocumented, and why wage growth rates are so stubbornly low among this group. Consider Gustavo, a father in one of our Mexican families who had worked at the same pizzeria since he arrived in the United States at age fourteen. At the time of our ethnographic study, he was twenty-six, so he had been working at the same place for twelve years. He worked six days a week, typically twelve hours a day, and brought home $600 a week. That worked out to a wage of $8.33 an hour. His wife, Aurora, said that she thought one reason Gustavo did not look for another job was because he was fearful of what might happen with a new employer. She thought he should at least ask his boss for a raise or ask him to help him achieve legal residency. Gustavo refused to do this, however, because then he would be indebted to his boss and he would feel like a slave. Besides, he thought that his boss would not want to make the investment in his residency because if Gustavo was a legal resident, he could get a better job. Gustavo's experience, like Marcelo's interaction with his boss on the train station platform, suggests a complex mix of indebtedness to and frustration with employers. At the same time, workers can experience support from their bosses. By the end of the ethnographic study, Gustavo's boss had agreed to try to sponsor him for legal residency. However, this has been almost impossible for employers to do since the 1986 IRCA law, owing to penalties for employers who knowingly hire undocumented immigrants.

The qualitative and quantitative data together suggest that wage violations occur much more frequently in undocumented parents' jobs than in those of documented parents. The ethnography also shows that the period immediately after arriving in New York is a particularly risky time for labor exploitation among the undocumented. Flor, a Mexican mother in the sample, said that "when you first come to the U.S., people take advantage." When Flor first came to New York, she worked in a clothing factory. In this sweatshop, the workers were not paid on any day when there was no work. Flor would therefore arrive at 6:00 AM to get more work assigned. There was a supervisor, a Cuban woman, "who hated me." "She would not give me work and would yell at me, 'Espera tu turno'" (wait for your turn). Flor had very low self-esteem and was feeling miserable. One day "la Cubana called me 'Mexicana Ilegal,' and I jumped." She knew that this woman called her "illegal Mexican" in order to offend her and that she used the phrase as a derogatory way to signify that Mexicans were at the bottom of the ladder. Flor argued back so forcefully that she even made the Cuban woman cry. Her coworkers' initial reaction was shock; they were very surprised that someone had confronted the boss. Flor felt more confident and secure about herself at work from then on.

As we saw from Camila and Marcelo's story, flower selling on the streets was a particularly risky unauthorized job. Other goods were sold on the street as well by Mexican undocumented migrants. Our earliest narrative chronologically of an immigrant to New York from Puebla was that of Larunda, the mother of Nalda. Larunda, the pioneer in her family, arrived in the mid-1980s. She sold sheets and bedding sets on the street after arrival in New York.

As found in other studies of recently arrived undocumented migrants, another particularly risky job for work violations immediately after arrival was full-time, in-home child care.[28] Mercedes, a young Dominican mother in our study, arrived in the United States at the age of fifteen. She worked as a live-in housekeeper for over a year, when she was sixteen and seventeen. Toward the end of that period she was not being paid, and she was not allowed to leave her employers' apartment to see family except on Sundays. Larunda (Nalda's mother) also worked there for a time soon after her arrival. She was told to stay in the house to avoid deportation; in her words, she was kept "prisoner" in the apartment, cooking and cleaning.

CONCLUSION

The combined ethnographic and survey data from this study show that undocumented parents are at particular risk of encountering the worst working conditions in New York City: low wages and wage growth, low rates of benefits, particularly repetitive and physically demanding jobs with low levels of autonomy, and high rates of minimum wage violations. All of these work conditions are risks for low school achievement and more behavior problems in children.[29]

Our data suggest that the rates of wage violations—working below the legal minimum wage—were extraordinarily high for undocumented workers. Between one-quarter and one-third of Mexican fathers were working below the minimum wage, as were between 30 and 40 percent of Mexican mothers at different points during the study. The comparable percentages were much lower (between 5 and 15 percent) for Dominican and African American mothers and fathers, and they were in between for Chinese mothers and fathers. The jobs of the group with high proportions of undocumented—the Mexicans—were worse than we would predict after taking into account their lower levels of parental education. As we saw in a prior chapter, our qualitative data provides evidence suggesting that the fathers in the Mexican families were generally undocumented if the mother was undocumented. Thus, the combination of poor working conditions among families where both parents are undocumented is of particular concern.

The period immediately after immigration is a particularly risky time for poor job conditions. In New York City, there are not only niche occupations for particular low-income immigrant groups but an entirely different and particularly exploitative set of jobs for recently arrived undocumented immigrants, such as flower-selling on the street, in-home, full-time child care, and garment sweatshop work. The more stable jobs that undocumented workers find later are not much better; the hours for many of them, like the restaurant jobs of the Chinese and the deli, grocery, and restaurant work of many of the Mexicans, are twelve hours a day, six days a week. These jobs raised the average number of hours for Mexicans and Chinese in our sample far above those of the Dominicans and African Americans.

How might these work conditions affect children's early learning? The several pathways that lead from poor parental work quality to compromised child learning and cognition can be summarized as time, money, and values. First, parents' work can take time away from opportunities to interact with their children. Interestingly, however, the literature does not support a strong association of work hours with children's development. Some national studies of nonstandard work hours and children's development report some effects,[30] but others find smaller effects among low-income families.[31]

Second, higher wages and wage growth result in higher household income, which appears to have positive effects on children's learning. With more money, parents are better able to invest in their children's learning through materials like books or supports such as center-based child care, which is in general beneficial to children's early cognitive skills.[32] In this study, we might hypothesize an even tighter link between work and center-based child care because of the expense of center care. Low-income families often purchase this type of care with the help of child care subsidies. However, because the undocumented parents in this study were often unwilling or unable to provide proof of employment (required to get child care subsidies), the pathway to higher cognitive skills represented by center-based care was nearly completely closed to them.

Finally, jobs that involve more autonomy and complexity in their duties can affect parents' values and behaviors toward their children. Classic studies in the sociology of work have found, for example, that job duties fostering obedience to authority are associated with putting a greater value on obedience in children.[33] Higher self-direction and autonomy at work are associated with more responsive parenting as well as higher levels of child cognitive skills.[34]

The research on how low-wage work conditions affect children's development suggests that there may be a difference in even the very early learning of children whose parents experience different levels of job quality. Although we do not have data on any of the Chinese children's development in the first three years, we do have information on the children of Camila and Beatriz. How were their children faring in their learning? If these effects of work conditions on children hold—even among a low-income sample, as the research suggests—we might expect to see differences in the early language and learning of the children of these two mothers. Indeed, the ethnographic descriptions of their children's early language suggest a difference. Natalia (Camila and Marcelo's daughter), at twenty-two months, spoke only a few words that the field-worker, Isidora, could understand. She was obsessed with the Spanish word for cat, "gato," which she pronounced "tato." Isidora had shown her a picture of her own cat on her cell phone. Camila would slowly repeat the name of the cat, Lola ("Low-laaah"), but Natalia would not try to say the name; she would only continue to say, "Tato, tato." In contrast, the same field-worker noticed Beatriz and Leandro's son Raul using a larger vocabulary and putting words together in two-word phrases at twenty-four months. For example, Raul pointed out and repeated words from what he was watching on TV. He called out the names of animals as they appeared on a TV show. He said all of these words for animals—"cow," "dog," "cat," "donkey," "duck"—in Spanish.

The quantitative data from our measure of cognitive skills—the Mullen Scales of Early Learning—showed a difference between these two children as well, with our standardized assessment showing a higher score for Raul than for Natalia. Although the size of the difference was not large, the difference is suggestive of some validity to the hypothesis that work conditions matter for children's learning even in the first years of life. In chapter 6, I pursue this hypothesis using the full sample and show that poor work conditions do in fact predict children's early cognitive skills. As the current chapter's findings suggest, parent work conditions provide a key pathway through which their undocumented status can harm the development of their children.

Chapter 6

How Parents' Undocumented Status Matters for Children's Early Learning

How does having a parent who is undocumented affect a child's early development? In May 2010, the first ladies of the United States and Mexico were visiting a second-grade classroom in Silver Spring, Maryland. A session was caught on video in which children asked a variety of questions of Michelle Obama. One worried Latina girl raised her hand and talked about her mother. "My mom said, I think, she says that Barack Obama's taking everybody away that doesn't have papers." Obama, taken aback, replied, "Yeah, well, that's something we have to work on, right? To make sure that people can be here with the right kind of papers, right?" The girl responded, "But my mom doesn't have [papers]."[1] This incident gave the problem of undocumented immigration a new and intimate perspective—that of a child's anxiety that her mother will be taken away from her. The American public became aware that documentation status might influence the children of immigrants, not just the immigrants themselves.

By second grade, children of the undocumented, like the girl in Silver Spring, can have a powerful sense of the chaos that a parent's deportation could cause. Even in the absence of actual deportation, worries about its possibility may affect these children's development by increasing their parents' anxiety or distress or influencing their own worries and ability to concentrate in school. In this chapter, I show that parental undocumented status can have harmful consequences for children's learning even earlier in their lives, when they have barely begun walking. At the age of two or three years, children cannot understand that their parent is undocumented. They do not ask questions about their mother's or father's legal status. Thus, the effects of parental undocumented status on the development of toddlers must occur in other ways.

The data reported in chapters 3, 4, and 5 showed that citizen children of the undocumented have lower access to a variety of resources. These resources can be formal, such as public programs, or informal, such as social network supports; they can be material, such as the stable income that a good job at a living wage brings, or psychological, as reflected, for example, in parents' well-being, which is essential for the emotional development of children. Recall that at two years of age, economic hardship and parents' feelings of distress, depression, and worry transmitted the influence of undocumented status to their children's cognitive skills. In this chapter, I test a model of how parental undocumented status can affect cognitive skills at three years of age. I find that the two key factors that transmit the effects of being undocumented to children's learning at this age are parents' work conditions and their children's access to center-based child care.

The terrible jobs of the undocumented have consequences for their children's development. These factors are reflected in the daily routines and experiences of Alfreda, an undocumented mother, and Elena, a documented mother, and their two sons.

ALFREDA AND LUCIO: "SOMETIMES I FEEL LIKE GETTING THE HELL OUT OF HERE"

Alfreda, a Mexican woman in her midthirties, was frustrated by her husband Carlos's unwillingness to buy even basic things for his sons. She was generally quick to smile, but on occasion her interviews with Patricia revealed the depths of the desperation she felt from the many stressors in her life. "He never has money for anything" for the children, she said. The day before, their nine-year-old son, Javier, had asked Carlos for money to buy a folder for school. Carlos gave him two dollars before Alfreda told him that at the local store it would cost more. Carlos grudgingly gave his son three dollars. Javier then asked for some extra money to buy an illustrated book he wanted, but Carlos would not give him the money. Alfreda, in a despairing tone, said, "As they say, 'He doesn't love us.' I ask, 'Why?' and they say, 'Because he never gives us anything.'" She went back to work when Lucio was two years old because she could no longer stand not having enough money to provide her children with the basics.

Alfreda was an undocumented mother of four, three of whom were living with her in the United States: Javier, her seven-year-old daughter Anita, and Lucio, the focal child in our study. Like most of our Mexican mothers, Alfreda was from a small town in the state of Puebla. Her father was a carpenter and jack-of-all-trades. The town she grew up in was quite poor, and her parents depended for clothes on castoffs from the family of her father's boss. Her parents told her that education was a "waste of time." Soon after finishing secondary education, she left for Mexico City and worked cleaning houses, sending money back to support her family in Puebla. Her husband Carlos (and the father of her children) was also undocumented. He came to the United States three years prior to her arrival, but went back and forth a few times before summoning her to come to the States (leaving their oldest child in Mexico). She gave birth to Javier, Anita, and Lucio in New York City.

Alfreda had a busy daily routine that did not let up on the weekend. She worked during the weekdays taking care of three children of neighbors. They came early in the morning and stayed the full day. She would run errands after they left, in the afternoons. On Friday, Saturday, and Sunday nights, she worked the overnight shift as a waitress at a Mexican restaurant in Brooklyn, leaving home at 9:30 PM and arriving home around 5:30 or 6:00 in the morning. She would take a $7 taxi there and back because she was concerned about the dangers of the subway late at night. After 1:00 AM, the restaurant served only drinks, and the customers turned raucous and sometimes abusive. Her coworkers also often drank and would occasionally leave her with unpaid checks from their tables. Her return home on Mondays was the most difficult because the children in her care arrived at 7:30, only a couple of hours after she had come home from the restaurant exhausted. Her husband also often bickered with her when she came home, accusing her of flirting with customers at work.

Alfreda was committed to her son Lucio's learning. When Patricia, her field-worker, brought a book to one of the first visits, Alfreda immediately started to name some of the things that were in the book. But at other times she seemed tired. On these occasions, Patricia observed few interactions between Alfreda and Lucio that did not entail breast-feeding. For example, there appeared to be relatively few toys in the apartment; descriptions of interactive play were relatively rare in the field notes. When Patricia brought toys on a visit, however, she observed that Lucio's older brother Javier played with him in an unusually responsive and sensitive way—guiding his hands to play with a toy, for example.

Aside from "la Dominicana," described in chapter 4, who provided much-needed friendship and social support, Alfreda could not name any regular visitors to the home who interacted with Lucio. This relatively low level of support placed her at risk for depression.

Alfreda had several preferences for the kind of child care she wanted for Lucio. She thought he should understand both English and Spanish by the time he started preschool, so having a bilingual child care provider was important. She also wanted him to be in a child care setting where he would learn how to read. She was reluctant, however, to enroll her child in government-sponsored child care. Although she did not say that this was because of her undocumented status, it may have played a role in her reluctance to fill out the paperwork for a child care subsidy. Instead, she obtained a job on the night shift that would not require her to get child care. During her nights at work, however, she was worried about the quality of care that Carlos provided.

At twenty months, Lucio responded to commands or used words to get her attention, like "mira" (look) or "Lucio, ven" (Lucio, come). He was generally compliant with his mother's requests regarding his behavior. For example, when Lucio was once playing with a Q-tip and putting it in his ear, Alfreda told him no, and he stopped immediately. To request things, he pointed and vocalized, though not usually with an intelligible word; for example, he pointed at bananas and said, "Eh."

At twenty-four months, Patricia accompanied Alfreda and Lucio to a medical appointment. The only word that Patricia heard Lucio say during this visit of several hours was "mama," when his mother was lying down in the examination room and he pulled at her shirt. Lucio was still not talking very much—aside from frequently saying "mama" to call his mother, and when he wanted to be breast-fed, pulling on her shirt and saying "ah." By the last visit, at roughly two and a half years, he was naming his siblings and the children his mother took care of during the day.

At the twenty-six-month visit, Patricia brought a toy that played music when certain buttons were pressed. She observed Alfreda's teaching behavior with this toy. The mother held it by the handle and told Lucio, "Look, hold it like this." He held it that way and started to play it while sitting on the floor. He turned it around and looked at it from all angles. After Lucio had had a minute or two of exploration, Alfreda pressed one of the buttons and the toy started to play music. Lucio smiled and did it himself. His smile was even bigger when it started playing after he pressed it. He continued to play with the toy by pressing the different buttons, but there was one in particular that he kept pressing, perhaps because he liked the music. Alfreda also engaged in teaching with the toy, showing Lucio how to count when he started to move some balls on one side that simulated an abacus.

The low levels of social support, the stresses of her work life, and her difficulties in making ends meet sometimes overwhelmed Alfreda. At the last visit, she admitted to feeling "despairing": "Sometimes I feel like getting the hell out of here—to take the children and go where, I don't know, where I can be at peace. But it is very difficult. I have to keep on working hard. We'll see what God says." As we saw in chapter 4, such despairing and depressive feelings explained the influence of parents' undocumented status on children's cognitive skills at twenty-four months.

ELENA AND ALBERTO: LEARNING EMBEDDED
IN NETWORKS OF CARE

Elena and Alberto, the documented Dominican mother and her son whom we first met in chapter 1, were at the center of a rich network of relatives and friends, all documented like Elena. These people—cousins, aunts, uncles, grandparents—interacted with Alberto regularly, playing with him and reading books to him. One aunt and one grandmother in particular, Lola and Maria Graciela, visited several times a week. In contrast to Lucio's older brother Javier—who, aside from Lucio's parents, was the only person to play and interact regularly with him—Alberto was surrounded by adults who had had experience raising children themselves. They therefore not only interacted with Alberto but also provided a range of advice and information to Elena.

For example, Elena's mother had referred her for her job as a home care attendant. Unlike the jobs of the Mexican mothers, this was a unionized job. And unlike many of the Mexican parents' jobs, which were six days week, twelve hours a day, Elena's job was five days a week and more flexible in schedule. When Alberto was small, for example, Elena did not work weekends at all for seven months. Her bosses found out and told her that should not have happened and that she owed them and should work every day for six months. She called the union. Her representative intervened, saying, "You're right. That is not your problem if they didn't realize that you weren't working, that was theirs, that was, they should have checked the computer. And they can't make you work six months straight because you have children, and besides, it is against the law."

Elena took the bus to work, usually leaving around 8:30 in the morning for a twenty-minute commute to another part of Washington Heights. When she arrived at her client's apartment, she had to "punch in" on the phone, calling her boss with her ID number. Her client had some neurological problems and had had brain surgery, but was not very elderly—she was in her fifties. She could not hear very well, had persistent dizziness, and could not smell at all, so Elena did a mix of care and errands—cleaning the bathroom, washing clothes, preparing lunch, running errands, accompanying the woman to doctor's appointments. Elena worked five days a week from 9:00 AM to 5:00 PM, and 9:00 AM to 4:00 PM on Saturdays. Exhausted on Sundays, she still could not rest. Her children wanted to play on this one day they had with her, and she also had to do household chores. So she usually tried to get a head start on Sunday chores by doing laundry during the week and shopping on weekday evenings.

Elena's husband Ramon worked in a hotel, helping with banquet preparation. He worked a swing shift—starting in the early afternoons and going into the evenings—not a twelve-hour shift like those of many of the undocumented parents in our study. He usually took Alberto to child care—a babysitter who lived in Elena and Ramon's apartment building—for the afternoon hours until Elena came home. They paid a relatively princely sum of $100 a week for the child care. Elena thought it was worth the price because the babysitter was always teaching Alberto things. "I have gotten there and I have just stood there like that, before knocking, and I hear her: 'A, say it with me, say it with me.' Teaching him the vowels, like a game." Just like Alfreda, Elena wanted her child to learn both English and Spanish. Alberto's babysitter, a Dominican woman, spoke both languages. By the sixteen-month visit, Alberto recognized three words—"mama," "agua," and "sorry." He said "sorry" when Josefina, his sister, was talking about how he had hurt his dad's eyes (with his fingernails).

Patricia observed Elena interacting with Alberto and books when he was twenty months old. Elena told him, "Ven aca, Alberto—ensenale a Patricia lo inteligente que tu eres" (come here, Alberto—teach Patricia how intelligent you are). The book was in English and had thick cardboard pages, big pictures, and a little bit of text. Alberto flipped the pages and started "talking" as if he were reading. He held the book in the right position. He did not start "reading" until he had opened the book, just as his mother would do when she read to him. Elena was not the only one reading to Alberto; Patricia saw that Maria Graciela did this too. Patricia noticed that Alberto's vocabulary was larger in comparison to just four months before: now he said not only "agua" but "ica" for "galletica" (cookie) and "enta" for "mint." "Hello" was "eou," and "ya" stood for "it's done." Without looking at his feet or pointing to them, Elena asked him if he had seen how dirty his feet were—he looked down at them and laughed. He also complied with requests to throw things in the "basura," or trash.

At twenty-three months, Alberto was used to being around others playing with computers. He used the word "dora" for "computadora," and he would point out names of people on the screen when someone was flipping through photos. In one slide show that Patricia observed, he noticed faster than anyone gathered around the computer that the pictures had started to repeat. At this visit, Elena was having some trouble controlling Alberto's behavior. He threw a ball very hard at Elena and pinched Patricia hard in the back during this visit. Patricia told him to stop pinching her, but he did it again. Elena then took him, put him on her lap facing her, and told him to look at her. She used her index finger to point at him as she told him to look at her. Once they were making eye contact, she took him by the hand and patted him on the hand as she told him that he should not do that. He did not seem to take her seriously, however, and was smiling as she did this.

Patricia noticed that Alberto, at the age of twenty-four months, was saying more words in Spanish than in English and that both Elena and Ramon encouraged him to say words in English. It appeared that this was particularly true with language about regulating his behavior. For example, whenever Alberto interrupted by telling his mother "mami ven" as he grabbed her by the arm, Elena told him that she was talking to Patricia and that he had to say "excuse me." This was true even though all of Patricia and Elena's conversations were in Spanish.

At his second birthday party, Alberto was very well behaved and helped his mother distribute pieces of cake to his friends. Elena said that he was going to be like his father—always a good host. At the next visit, he was also quite cooperative and followed all of his mother's commands. He moved the digital voice recorder once, but slowly, knowing that it was a fragile object. He did not get upset that Patricia was getting his mother's attention, as he had done a couple of visits before. At the last visit, when he was twenty-nine months old, Alberto knew when he was being talked about in the interview; he smiled and looked at Patricia and Elena without moving his head, pretending not to be looking.

As the stories of Lucio and Alberto suggest, Lucio's cognitive development was delayed relative to Alberto's. At their thirty-six-month assessments, the two boys' scores on the Mullen Scales of Early Development—a general measure of cognitive skills that is like an early IQ test—were far apart, with Alberto's score over three standard deviations above Lucio's (a very large difference, statistically speaking).

The difference in their social behavior was just as large, but in the opposite direction, with Alfreda reporting Lucio to be better behaved. At the thirty-six-month home visit, when a large battery of structured questions were administered in person, she reported lower levels of aggression and more cooperation and empathy in Lucio's behavior than Elena reported about Alberto's behavior. These differences were also relatively large—over two standard deviations in magnitude.

Prior studies support the difference between Lucio's and Alberto's early cognitive development—the child of undocumented parents being at particular risk—but also point to the lack of this risk relationship for early social development. These studies show that children from groups that differ in rates of documentation status, like the ones in our sample (children of Mexican and Dominican immigrant parents and U.S.-born African American parents), also differ in their levels of cognitive school readiness. Nationally representative studies such as the Early Childhood Longitudinal Studies—Birth and Kindergarten Cohorts show that, beginning at twenty-four months and through the age of school entry, Mexican children have lower levels of cognitive skills than other Latino groups, such as Dominicans, as well as African American and white children.[2] In these studies, indicators of socioeconomic status (education or income), household factors, and even language use in the home do not fully explain this difference. So the large difference between Lucio and Carlos in their cognitive skills at thirty-six months is representative of children in their ethnic groups as a whole in the United States and is unlikely to be completely due to differences in their parents' education or work skills.

In contrast, in areas of early behavioral development and attention, Mexican children's skills are comparable to those of other groups. In national studies, their behavioral development, as measured by attention and acting-out behaviors, is indistinguishable at school entry from that of children from other Latino groups, as well as white and African American children.[3] Here again, Lucio's and Alberto's behavioral data (showing, if anything, more well-adjusted behavior on Lucio's part) are in agreement with the national data. And in our larger sample as a whole, on measures of behavior reported by parents, such as antisocial or cooperative and empathic behavior, there were no differences among Mexicans, Dominicans, and African Americans.[4]

LINKING THE EVERYDAY CONTEXTS OF UNDOCUMENTED PARENTS' LIVES TO THEIR CHILDREN'S EARLY LEARNING

How might Alfreda's undocumented status and Elena's documented status have played a role in the differences in early learning between their two children? Alfreda's level of social network support was dramatically lower than Elena's. The number of adults who could interact with Lucio was much lower than the number in Elena's household. As we saw in chapter 4, this was representative of our Mexican sample as a whole. As a recent immigrant group with few roots in the city, living primarily in neighborhoods with very few other families of their ethnic group, the Mexican mothers reported lower social support availability than the Dominicans in our study. Alberto had multiple figures in his life who would interact with him in both Spanish and English. In contrast, Patricia noted that Alfreda's isolation might have been partly responsible for her depression.

The difference in job quality between these two parents was also quite dramatic. Alfreda's waitress job, like those of most of the Mexicans in our sample, gave her very little opportunity for autonomy and self-direction—qualities predictive of more positive parenting in prior research.[5] There was very little to learn in this job, and it also paid very little. Coworker relationships were sources of stress rather than support during the late-night hours filled with drunken customers. These hours also left Alfreda exhausted during the weekend and early weekdays. In contrast, Elena's job was characterized by a relatively high degree of autonomy: she was alone with her client most of the day, and she only had to check in with her boss on arrival at her client's apartment. In addition, her union job (for which her mother had provided the referral) gave her support when she made choices like not working on weekends to be with her family. Although her work life was not easy (she had only Sundays off), the benefits and supports provided by the union made all the difference when her boss made requests like wanting her to work seven days a week for six months.

As in many families, jobs and child care were intimately intertwined in these two families. In part because of her reluctance to apply for government-sponsored child care subsidies, Alfreda found a job with overnight hours so that she and Carlos would not need to pay for child care. Lucio therefore did not experience the positive benefits that a stimulating out-of-home care setting can provide. Elena and her husband Ramon had a combined work schedule that required child care during the mid- to late afternoon hours. They found a child care provider who appeared to provide a rich language environment for the children in her care.

In addition to not experiencing stimulating child care outside the home, Lucio was also exposed to fewer cognitively stimulating materials in the home, such as books and toys, than Alberto during the first three years of his life, probably because Alfreda and Carlos earned less than Elena and Ramon. For example, Carlos's hourly wage during the ethnographic period of $4.17 an hour was less than half of Ramon's ($10.70). Elena and Ramon also received food stamps to help support Alberto. With this key support, which supplements the often meager earnings from low-wage jobs, they had more disposable income to spend on books and toys.[6] More learning materials, along with the interactions they can elicit, would have provided a stronger basis for Lucio's cognitive development. The toys that Patricia brought to the household were some of the few that she observed Lucio playing with during the qualitative study.

The contrast between Alfreda and Lucio, on the one hand, and Elena and Alberto, on the other, powerfully shows the disadvantages that children of the undocumented experience despite comparable investments in children's learning, as were reported by Alfreda and Elena. They were both mothers who wanted their children to have the best learning environments prior to school, including care providers who taught them how to read and exposure to both Spanish and English. But the cumulative strikes against Lucio were many, judging from the apparent impact of poor job quality, lower disposable income, and lack of access to quality child care interactions on his early learning. These are all *developmental contexts* for children's early development. The ethnographic and other evidence up to this point have suggested a range of influences not just in the home but also in child care, parental work, and parent social networks.

As the developmental psychologist Urie Bronfenbrenner hypothesized over thirty years ago in his classic book on the ecology of human development, the contexts that matter for children's early development include not only those that they themselves spend time in but also those that their parents experience, like workplaces and social support.[7]

I now turn to the survey and child assessment data to examine how undocumented status might affect children's cognitive skills through differences in their developmental contexts. The measure of cognitive skills we used in this study was the Mullen Scales of Early Development, an IQ test–like measure of fine motor skills, visual perception, and early language skills, both receptive (understanding of language) and expressive (verbalizations of language). These dimensions are quite highly intercorrelated, so I use the composite single measure. The measures of developmental contexts are the ones suggested by the evidence in chapters 3, 4, and 5 and in this chapter for which survey data were available.

To test the hypotheses posed by the stories of Lucio and Alberto, as well as by the evidence presented in chapters 3, 4 and 5, I analyze a conceptual model, developed from the qualitative data presented in the previous chapters, that relates undocumented status to the everyday experiences of parents in household, network, and work settings and to the experiences of children in the two main settings of early development—the home and child care. The general conceptual model was depicted in figure 1.1. Here I fill in the model with actual data from this study's longitudinal surveys and child assessments (see figure 6.1; for more details on the measures and approach to the analysis, see the appendix). In this figure, the arrows represent statistically significant associations, with the direction of the arrow representing prediction. Using standard two-tailed tests, I indicate the degree of statistical significance with asterisks: .05 with one asterisk, .01 with two, and .001 with three. The number itself can be interpreted like a correlation, with a potential range from −1.00 (for two variables that are perfectly negatively correlated) to +1.00 (for two variables that are perfectly positively correlated). For more details on all measures depicted in figure 6.1, including sources, reliability, and sample items, see the appendix.

Recall that there is no direct measure of documentation status in our survey data. Undocumented status is therefore represented by one variable that appeared in the qualitative data to distinguish the documented from the undocumented: utilization of resources that require identification (the index described in chapter 3 of household-level access to checking or savings accounts and driver's licenses). Undocumented parents are unlikely to use resources that require multiple forms of identification to obtain. Among the survey measures, this is the best stand-in for the unmeasured variable of documentation status. In figure 6.1, this variable is

Figure 6.1   Path Model Predicting Thirty-Six-Month Cognitive Skills

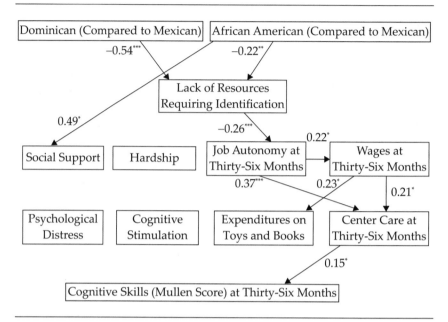

Source: Author's graphic.
Note: Controls: Fourteen-month Mullen score; mother education; married; number of children; mother foreign-born years in United States; primary language in home; mother employed; work hours; discomfort with out-of-home care
Fit Statistics:
    CFI = 0.991
    TLI = 0.980
    RMSEA = 0.018
$^*p < 0.05$; $^{**}p < 0.01$; $^{***}p < 0.001$

represented by the box labeled "Lack of Resources Requiring Identification." It was assessed when the child was fourteen months old.

The three groups analyzed in this figure—Mexicans, Dominicans, and African Americans—provide contrasts in citizenship rates and rates of documentation status. (Recall that the quantitative analysis cannot include the Chinese because of the very high proportions in that group of infants who were sent back to China.) All of the African American mothers were U.S.-born and therefore citizens. From the qualitative evidence, the Dominicans and Mexicans varied in their rates of being undocumented: rates were high among the Mexicans and low among the Dominicans. The top boxes in figure 6.1, labeled "Dominican" and "African American," represent the contrasts between each of these two groups and Mexicans. These ethnic contrasts are expected to predict the variable of lack of resources requiring identification—that is, levels of these resources are expected to differ significantly across ethnic groups.

The next row of variables in figure 6.1, labeled "Social Support," "Hardship," "Job Autonomy at Thirty-Six Months," and "Wages at Thirty-Six Months," includes some of the everyday experiences of being an undocumented parent that were discussed in chapters 4 and 5 and that are available in the surveys. These are experiences that undocumented parents may be more likely to encounter than their documented counterparts, even accounting for indicators of socioeconomic status; they include lower levels of social support for making ends meet and for help with child care, higher levels of economic hardship, and lower wages and autonomy on the job. Our measure of autonomy at work comes from the Department of Labor codes characterizing job duties described in chapter 5. Social support and hardship were measured at fourteen months; job autonomy and wages were measured at thirty-six months because that was the time by which most mothers in all of our groups had returned to work.

Finally, the next row in figure 6.1, with variables labeled "Psychological Distress," "Cognitive Stimulation," "Expenditures on Toys and Books," and "Center Care at Thirty-Six Months," reflects the immediate contexts in which children spend the most time in the first three years of life: the home and child care. These were all measured at thirty-six months. Center care is included here because in many studies this type of care, compared to informal settings like family child care homes, predicts higher levels of early language skills. Research shows that this is because center care is more likely than other types of care to be provided by trained and qualified caregivers and to involve a wider range of cognitively stimulating materials and activities.[8] Such child care features are important for the development of cognitive skills, such as motor and language skills, in early childhood.

Aside from center care, the other three variables in this part of figure 6.1 represent three kinds of factors that can explain links between low social support, high economic hardship, and poor work conditions, on the one hand, and lower levels of early language development and later achievement, on the other. First, these conditions of parents' lives can be stressful to them. Day in and day out, the stresses of jobs with poor work conditions and the need to live "under the radar" can bring about the psychological symptoms tapped in our questionnaire items, such as feelings of anxiety, low energy, depression, and hopelessness. Such feelings can reflect not just psychological processes but biological ones. Research shows that economic stress can get "under the skin" by affecting the body's immunological responses and nervous system functions that respond to stress. Some of the body's natural defenses can become chronically overactivated. Although we did not obtain the kind of physiological data that would test this hypothesis, research shows that elevated responses to the kinds of survey items we asked are related to these biological stress responses.[9]

Second, everyday experiences of being undocumented can reduce parents' ability to engage in stimulating learning activities with their children. Such activities include not only reading books but other activities that build early language, motor, and visual skills. For example, playing with a variety of toys can build fine and gross motor skills, and singing songs can build early language and working memory. Peek-a-boo games incorporate the kind of moment-to-moment, serve-and-return interactions—termed "responsiveness" in the parenting literature—that strengthen language skills in the first years of life.[10] Here I use a measure of daily cognitively stimulating activities that sums across a list that includes singing songs, reading books, telling stories, and playing interactive games like peek-a-boo.[11]

Third, poverty and economic hardship can reduce parents' ability to purchase learning materials for their children. Investments in children's learning are important across the life span; in infancy and toddlerhood, such investments include purchases of toys and books.[12] Expenditures on children were assessed in our survey using an extensive inventory that was developed from the initial qualitative work.[13] Here I use a variable that sums household expenditures on toys and books.

So what does figure 6.1 show regarding differences in the ethnic groups' rates of undocumented status? Starting at the top of the figure, the negative numbers for the arrows between "Dominican" and "Lack of Resources" (−.54***) and "African American" and "Lack of Resources" (−.22**) show that the rates at which Dominicans and African Americans reported a lack of resources requiring identification were lower than they were for Mexican parents. In other words, both of these groups had higher levels of these resources than Mexicans. This supports the ethnographic evidence, which suggested higher rates of undocumented status among the Mexicans than the Dominicans.

Turning to the next row of variables, African Americans reported higher levels of social support than Mexicans (0.49*). This again supports the qualitative data, this time from chapter 4. In that chapter, I showed that Mexican mothers in our sample experienced lower levels of social support, despite having more adults in the household than other groups.

The proxy for undocumented status—lack of resources requiring identification—predicted lower job autonomy, as shown by the negative coefficient linking these two variables (−.26***). This suggests that undocumented status is linked to lower job autonomy, as reflected in the chapter 5 accounts of Camila's and Marcelo's jobs and the account of Alfreda's job in this chapter. Job autonomy in turn was associated with wages, in an expected direction (higher job autonomy associated with higher wages).

Both job autonomy and wages are associated with higher rates of enrollment of children in center-based care (0.37*** and 0.21*). This suggests that those in better jobs are better able to enroll children in center care (and conversely, that children of parents in worse jobs are less likely to be in center care). Higher wages were also associated with higher expenditures on toys and books (0.23*), but higher expenditures were not associated with cognitive skills. Instead, center care enrollment is the ultimate link to cognitive skills (0.15*), with those enrolled in center care having higher scores on the Mullen assessment.

There is a clear overall story we can derive from the string of arrows linking the proxy for parent undocumented status to three-year-olds' cognitive abilities. That is, undocumented status appears to be associated with lower levels of child learning through poorer-quality jobs, as represented by lower wages and lower job autonomy, and lower enrollment in center care.

This pattern holds up adjusting for a variety of potentially confounding factors. All the significant associations in figure 6.1 controlled for a variety of family structure, acculturation, and maternal education factors; the primary language in the home; whether the mother was employed and her hours of work; her preferences regarding type of child care; and earlier child skills (the Mullen test, measured at fourteen months; see the box in figure 6.1 labeled "Controls"). I do this in order to examine whether the associations in the model hold up after adjusting for a range of potentially confounding family and child characteristics.

These results support the hypotheses outlined in chapters 3, 4, and 5—that undocumented status is reflected in everyday experiences such as avoidance of use of resources requiring identification, in lower levels of support, in greater economic hardship, and in worse work conditions. Compared to their Dominican and African American counterparts, Mexican mothers did report lower household-level access to resources requiring identification, such as savings accounts, checking accounts, and drivers' licenses. In turn, not having these resources was associated with lower job autonomy, lower rates of center care, and lower levels of cognitive skills in children as young as three years old. These patterns were not explained away by family characteristics that might have confounded the results—factors like mother's education, number of children, years in the United States, primary language in the home, marital status, or even children's earlier cognitive skills.

Recall that in chapter 4 I showed how undocumented status lowered children's cognitive skills at an earlier point—at twenty-four months of age—through greater economic hardship as well as psychological distress and depressive symptoms among their mothers. At age thirty-six months, parental undocumented status was linked to children's early cognitive development, not so much through higher psychological distress, lower cognitive stimulation, or lower expenditures on toys and books as through work conditions and exposure to center-based care. It is striking that parenting behaviors did not play an explanatory role in these results. The measure of cognitively stimulating parenting activities we used in this study did not differ across our ethnic groups. There do not appear to be culturally based differences in the frequency of these activities, such as reading books, telling stories, or playing with toys with children. And in other analyses from our study, we have found that rates of parents' endorsement of children's learning and cognitive development as primary developmental goals do not differ across our ethnic groups.[14] This suggests that a culturally based model does not explain differences across groups that differ in proportions undocumented in our study.

Instead, the combination of work conditions and child care was a powerful mechanism transmitting the effects of being undocumented to children's learning. The terrible jobs of the undocumented have consequences for their children's development. Two conditions made a difference—wages and job autonomy. As suggested in chapter 5, undocumented working parents are exposed to much higher rates of pay below minimum wage than their documented counterparts. In this quantitative analysis, lower wages were related to lower child cognitive skills. And as we also saw in chapter 5, the undocumented experience significantly fewer opportunities for autonomy and self-direction at their jobs. Their work experiences generally involve doing repetitive tasks, taking orders, and having no opportunity to develop new skills. Low job autonomy also linked the proxy for undocumented status to lower child cognitive ability in the current analysis. This is supported by prior research on the negative effects on children of lower wages and lower self-direction and autonomy in job duties.[15]

Why were there no associations through economic hardship or psychological distress? In previous work predicting cognitive skills one year prior to the thirty-six-month point, we found that lack of resources requiring identification predicts higher economic hardship and higher psychological distress.[16] Distress, in turn, predicts lower cognitive skills at twenty-four months. At that point very early in their children's development, not enough mothers had gone back to work or placed their children in center care to reliably test associations with these factors. At thirty-six months, the associations involving quality of work and center care swamped any associations between hardship, psychological distress, and children's early cognitive skills.

Enrollment in center-based child care provides the final link explaining how undocumented status affects child learning. Mexican mothers accessed child care subsidies—which are associated with higher center care use in our sample and in many other studies—at much lower levels than the Dominicans or African Americans: at thirty-six months, 36 percent of Dominicans and 47 percent of African Americans in our sample reported getting subsidies to help with child care, compared to 6 percent of Mexicans. These associations could be explained by other factors, such as children's earlier cognitive skills or cultural preferences for relative care. That is, Mexican mothers might simply prefer relative care, or perhaps some of these mothers place children with lower early cognitive skills in center care. However, all of the results in figure 6.1 adjusted for children's fourteen-month skills as well as for mothers' discomfort with out-of-home care. (We obtained information about this when the babies were one month old.) A national study by Robert Crosnoe has shown that lower rates of center care help explain the lower cognitive skills of Mexican children at school entry relative to those of children from other ethnic groups.[17] The data from this chapter support this finding and link center care with lower wages, lower job autonomy, and our proxy variable for undocumented status (lack of resources requiring identification).

Subsidies are often the only way in which low-income parents can access center care, the type of care that benefits children's early cognitive skills the most. But as we saw in chapter 3, subsidy programs typically require verification of employment. Undocumented parents are likely to be paid in cash and therefore to not have pay stubs. They may also be unwilling to identify their employers. As we saw in chapter 5, relationships between the undocumented and their bosses are complex, with some degree of mutual trust that neither the employer nor the employee will reveal the other's identity. The two largest federally funded sources of child care subsidies, the Child Care Development Fund (CCDF) and Temporary Assistance for Needy Families (TANF), also often require other documentation, such as tax returns, on which income is typically reported. These again are sources of information that the undocumented may not want to share or do not have. The end result is much lower exposure to center care among citizen children of the undocumented compared to their peers whose parents are documented. Lower access to center care among children of the undocumented has consequences for their cognitive skills.

CONCLUSION

The stories of Alfreda and Elena at the beginning of this chapter suggested that several aspects of being an undocumented parent in a new wave of low-income migration—sparse social networks, lower-quality jobs, less access to stimulating child care, fewer financial resources to invest in children—harm early development by increasing parental stress and reducing the amount of stimulation that parents can provide and purchase for young children. The scores of Lucio and Alberto on our omnibus measure of cognitive skills were indeed far apart, with Lucio at a much more disadvantaged level as early as thirty-six months. On socioemotional skills, in contrast, Lucio was, if anything, doing better than Alberto. The factors suggested by the stories of these two families, as well as the findings in chapters 3, 4, and 5 and the conceptual model in chapter 1, set up clear hypotheses about the everyday experiences of being an undocumented parent that might affect learning in the first years of life.

The quantitative results shown in figure 6.1, in fact, support these hypotheses. They provide confirmation that the experiences reported by undocumented mothers in the ethnography do indeed matter for children's early cognitive skills. Parenting behaviors such as cognitive stimulation were not as powerful in transmitting the influence of undocumented status as the terrible jobs they endured, as reflected in their low wages and low job autonomy and low levels of access to and enrollment in child care centers. This is largely a story about access to learning opportunities outside the home—for both parents and children—not about parenting quality. Through this pathway, parents' undocumented status affects outcomes as intimate, yet societally important, as a preschooler's vocabulary, motor, and perceptual skills.

Chapter 7

Providing Access to the American Dream for the Children of Undocumented Parents

E arly childhood is an especially important time to ensure that children have access to supports for their learning. The first years of life are foundational to the development of later skills. Cognition and learning as early as the first three years of life are associated with later school readiness, achievement, and even later earnings.[1] As the economist James Heckman has posited, early skills beget later skills.[2] Because the skills that children learn at each stage in their development build on those established in earlier stages, public investment in early childhood skills brings about larger economic benefits than supports later in development. Providing access to learning opportunities for all young children in the United States, particularly those exposed to social or economic disadvantage, is a good investment in children's future productivity as citizens and residents of the nation.

Despite the widely accepted importance of investments in early childhood learning and development, there is almost no recognition of the link between undocumented adults and young children. The undocumented are typically viewed as lawbreakers, not as parents of citizens. Yet 91 percent of children of the undocumented below the age of six are U.S. citizens. These children grow up to represent nearly one student in every public school classroom in the United States—a total of four million children in 2010. They share citizenship with the children of the native-born. Policy debates raging about undocumented immigrants in the United States fail to consider the effects on children of policies targeting the undocumented. This book has proceeded from the assumption that we should care about the early development and later productivity of the four million young citizen children of the undocumented in our country. I addressed the book's central question—how does parents' undocumented status affect their children's development?—with the longitudinal ethnographic and survey data from nearly four hundred infants recruited at birth and studied, along with their parents and families, during their first three years.

In this New York City study, we recruited immigrant parents of newborns from Chinese, Mexican, and Dominican backgrounds. All the infants were U.S. citizens by virtue of being born in the city. We did not expect that their parents would differ in their documentation status to the degree that they did. Among parents in the qualitative study, large differences emerged on this characteristic, with very high rates of undocumented status among Mexican mothers, moderate rates among the Chinese, and low rates among the Dominicans.

The qualitative evidence from this study showed that the undocumented immigrant experience in the United States takes on new meaning when we consider these immigrants as parents of young U.S. citizens. Living under the radar of public programs and institutions, these children, who were eligible for programs that could have enhanced their development, were very often not enrolled in the programs by their ineligible parents. Living as a new group in New York City with high rates of undocumented status and little access to coethnic networks, these undocumented families were exposing their children to fewer adults with knowledge of learning opportunities such as preschools, child care centers, and schools. And finally, working as undocumented immigrants in the city, these parents were exposed to the worst job conditions in urban America—high rates of wages below the legal minimum, low access to benefits, and few opportunities for learning new skills.

The quantitative data suggested that having an undocumented parent does indeed harm children's development, especially their early cognitive skills. Two sets of factors transmitted the influence of undocumented status to children's early language, motor, and perceptual skills. At twenty-four months, parents' economic hardship and feelings of depression, anxiety, and worry explained how their undocumented status lowered their children's cognitive skills. In contrast, the key mechanisms by the thirty-six-month point were disastrous work conditions—including low wages and job duties that came with little opportunity for self-direction or autonomy—and lower access to center-based child care. Together, these experiences predicted lower scores on a measure of vocabulary, motor, and perceptual skills in children at thirty-six months.

The developmental risk conferred by having an undocumented parent was specific to cognitive skills (as suggested by comparisons of the same immigrant groups in national data).[3] For example, Mexican children, with the highest rates of having an undocumented parent, did not differ in their antisocial or cooperative behavior from children in other groups. Although we had no data on Chinese children who had returned to the United States after being sent to China as infants, some limited evidence from both mainland China and New York City preschool programs suggests that these children may have experienced emotional and behavioral problems both while they were being raised by their grandparents in China and after they made the transition to living in the United States with their biological parent(s) for the first time.[4]

What can be done to improve access to learning opportunities among children of undocumented parents? Three paths to improving the contexts of development for the young children of the undocumented emerge from the findings of this book in the domains of immigration policy, employment, and community-based supports for young children in immigrant groups with high proportions of undocumented parents. Certainly a wider range of policy options exists to improve child development among disadvantaged families. I focus here on the ones that are directly implicated by the data from this book and are most specific to the experience of undocumented parents and their young children.

IMMIGRATION POLICY AND THE PATH TO CITIZENSHIP

Imagine Emiliana and Ling, the undocumented Mexican and Chinese mothers whose stories opened this book, with the status of legal permanent resident or citizen. What would be different about their lives? How would documented status affect their ability to provide resources and opportunities for their children? Their reluctance to use public programs would diminish, and they could enroll in a variety of programs to improve their job skills and education—GED classes, job training programs—for which they had previously been ineligible.

Like Elena and the other Dominican mothers in our study, Emiliana and Ling would almost certainly have better jobs. With employers who knew that their workers were documented, and workers who knew that their employers knew, Emiliana, Ling, and their husbands, Victor Sr. and Wei, would have more job options. Engaging as full participants in the labor market, they would be more willing to consider other job offers and ask for raises, and ultimately they would experience higher wage growth. They would be more likely to receive employer or public benefits such as sick days, overtime, and flexibility for parenting needs. Instead of the typical pattern we saw among the undocumented—working for years without getting or asking for a raise—their wage growth patterns might more closely approximate the mainstream of low-wage workers in the United States. These are not great work conditions, but they are far above the current plight of undocumented working parents, who, as I showed in chapter 5, suffer high rates of wages that are de facto below the minimum wage and labor in jobs with the lowest levels of self-direction and autonomy, benefits, and wage growth. Better jobs would provide more income to purchase center-based care by the time most parents, including Asian and Latino immigrant parents in the United States, want it (when their children reach preschool age, at around three or four years). With legal permanent resident status, Emiliana and Ling might feel comfortable showing the proof of employment that is generally required to be eligible for child care subsidies.

Would parenting improve with a transition to legal permanent resident status? I found relatively little evidence, using the available measures, that parenting behaviors important for children's learning, such as engaging in cognitively stimulating interactions or investing in children's books and toys, were related to undocumented status. As we saw in chapter 1, parents from the three immigrant groups in this study were equally invested in providing stimulating activities and materials in the home for their children. Their values and goals for their children's learning and later achievement also did not differ. The added learning opportunity of center-based care outside the home appeared to be more sensitive to variation in documentation status than these parenting behaviors and goals.

This exercise in imagining a different future for undocumented parents and their children in the United States is just that—an exercise. Under current law, a citizen child can sponsor an undocumented parent for residency only at the age of twenty-one. By this time, a child's development is complete, and the impact of parent undocumented status is irreversible. Can we afford to wait this long for incorporation when an immigrant group is new and has high rates of undocumented status, such as is the case with the current waves of Mexican and Fujianese migrants to New York? With no path to citizenship, entire generations of children may be "lost" in such cohorts, denied access, by virtue of having an undocumented parent, to learning opportunities for which they are otherwise eligible. As a society, we cannot afford to lose entire cohorts of millions of children in this way.

Policymakers have not considered the potential harm to citizen children of a lack of a path to citizenship for their parents. In this book, I have shown that having an undocumented parent results in lower levels of use of the public programs and resources that can help children in poverty, such as subsidized center-based child care. As in many other studies, I also found that center-based care predicts higher levels of cognitive skills in young children.[5] The lack of access to the primary learning opportunity for children ages zero to three in the United States—center-based care—appears to lower the cognitive skills of children of the undocumented as early as the age of three years.

A fundamental solution to improving the development of the young children of the undocumented rests in immigration policy. Arriving as they did in the late 1980s, after the last door to amnesty among the undocumented had closed, the undocumented parents in our sample had no access to a path to citizenship.[6] With access to such a path, parents would not feel the need to avoid using resources that might help them and their families—particularly resources that require identification. Perhaps one result would be higher take-up of formal programs that foster children's cognitive development, such as adult GED and education classes, libraries, center-based care, and preschools. With higher use of these organizations and programs, information traveling through the social networks of the formerly undocumented would change and become more likely to incorporate news about the quality of particular early childhood programs and schools.

A variety of approaches to providing a path to citizenship have been proposed in recent years in Congress and by the executive branch. For example, President George W. Bush in 2006 proposed providing undocumented immigrants in the United States with a path to citizenship if they demonstrated residence and employment in the United States for a certain number of years, paid a fine, and took a place in line behind others waiting for legal permanent residency.[7] Currently, a mix of policy elements—including tougher border enforcement, labor law enforcement, provision of a path to citizenship with steep requirements, and a secure national ID system to allow employers to know who they can and cannot hire—are under discussion.[8] These proposals strike familiar chords in American immigration policy, balancing the interests of labor, business, and policymakers on the left and right, advocacy and civil rights groups, and the growing Latino voter bloc. Although President Barack Obama has supported a variety of these approaches, he has not put forward a detailed proposal for immigration reform as of this writing. In the meantime, local and state legislation has been passed in both exclusionary and inclusionary directions. In Arizona, after passage of a bill that would require immigrants to have state-sponsored identification and would give the police the power to detain people they suspect of being undocumented immigrants, the governor introduced another bill to send citizen children of the undocumented to their parents' home countries. Proposals to revise the Fourteenth Amendment to deny citizenship to the U.S.-born children of the undocumented have been discussed.

Among the inclusionary local policies are local city identification cards, such as those recently implemented in San Francisco, Trenton, and New Haven.[9] Although these do not represent permits to work, they are intended to facilitate access to public libraries, service organizations, and public recreation facilities. Such local policies, in the absence of federal action, address one of the major barriers to inclusion and children's learning analyzed in this book—the reluctance of the undocumented to use any service that requires photo identification.

Local policies to encourage adult education among the undocumented would also address one of the most glaring and overlooked opportunities to improve the learning of children of the undocumented. These parents cannot sit for a GED examination or engage in any publicly funded basic education or job training activity. Recent research by Katherine Magnuson shows that even small increases in adult basic education can improve cognitive development in children growing up in poverty.[10] Without the opportunity to reach the first rung on the American educational ladder, many undocumented parents—with, on average, lower levels of education than their low-income counterparts in the United States—are denied the chance to become competitive in even the low-wage labor market. In the absence of federal action on this issue, local policies affording access to basic education for the undocumented—for example, by implementing state certification and accompanying classes—could begin to open the door to learning for undocumented parents.

REFORMING THE WORLD OF UNDOCUMENTED IMMIGRANT WORK TO IMPROVE CHILD DEVELOPMENT: LABOR LAW ENFORCEMENT AND UNIONIZATION

Near the end of the afternoon on March 25, 1911, 146 women, most of them immigrant teenagers, died at work when the three top floors of the ten-story building at the corner of Washington Place and Greene Street in downtown New York City became a charnel house. The owners of the Triangle Shirtwaist Company had locked the doors of 23 Washington Place from the outside to keep union organizers from entering. As a fire that started on the eighth floor spread to the ninth and tenth floors of the building, women trying desperately to escape were crushed against locked doors and burned to death. Many plunged to their deaths with sickening thuds directly onto Washington Place as firefighters and New Yorkers looked on helplessly. In the wake of the fire, the trial of the firm's owners for manslaughter ended in acquittal. There were at that time no laws ensuring adequate exits in the case of workplace fires. Many immigrant workers were working in industrial workplaces in New York City as much as twelve hours a day, six days a week, and churning out 10 percent of the U.S. economy's industrial production.

In the four years after the Triangle Shirtwaist Factory fire, Robert Wagner, Al Smith, and other legislators in Albany passed the most progressive set of labor laws in the United States, covering a vast array of work conditions: sanitation, drinking water, ventilation, safety, wages, and hours. Women could no longer work more than fifty-four hours a week. Frances Perkins, a labor organizer in this effort, went on to become the first female cabinet member in the United States under President Franklin Roosevelt. On her watch, his administration passed landmark labor legislation, including the Fair Labor Standards Act, which for the first time set a minimum wage and maximum hours.

Minimum wage, hours, and overtime pay standards such as those passed in the years following the Triangle Shirtwaist fire, first in New York State and later across the nation, do not exempt employers of the undocumented working parents in our sample. As far as the data in this study show, none of the undocumented workers in our sample had positions that were exempt from the laws. (The Fair Labor Standards Act exempts independent contractors and volunteers.) This historic body of legislation constituted one of the earliest and most comprehensive sets of labor laws in the industrialized world. One hundred years after the Triangle Shirtwaist calamity, with NYU students and professors now working quietly on the floors where the conflagration occurred, working conditions of the undocumented are on some dimensions indistinguishable from those of the women who toiled in the Triangle Shirtwaist Factory.

The data I report in chapter 5, as well as in another recent study,[11] show that about one-third of groups with high proportions of undocumented in New York City work below the minimum wage. Over one-third of these groups do not receive overtime pay. In contrast, for groups with lower rates of undocumented status (in our study, Dominican immigrant mothers and U.S.-born African American mothers), the likelihood of working below minimum wage, among those who work, is much lower, even controlling for parental education and other background factors. The work hours of undocumented parents are routinely far more than the fifty-four hours a week set as a maximum for women in New York State in 1914; for some of the groups in this study with the highest proportions of undocumented (mothers and fathers in the Chinese families and fathers in the Mexican families), the *average* hours of work per week were above this level.

Poor work conditions were the primary mechanisms through which parent undocumented status affected children's learning in this study. Low wages and lack of autonomy on the job were linked to our proxy of undocumented status. Both low wage and low job autonomy, in turn, were associated with lower child cognitive ability at thirty-six months, and this was explained by lower enrollment in center-based child care. These associations overall suggest that improving the terrible job conditions of undocumented parents would improve their children's learning as early as the first years of life.

One clear route to better jobs is tougher labor law enforcement. Between 1980 and 2007, the labor force of the United States increased by 52 percent, but the number of federal inspectors investigating minimum wage and overtime violations decreased by 31 percent.[12] Their research led Annette Bernhardt and her colleagues to recommend more investment in such inspectors, as well as more partnerships between government enforcement, on the one hand, and immigrant worker organizations and service providers, on the other. Providers and organizations have a major role to play when fear of consequences keeps undocumented workers from complaining or making public their work conditions. Tougher enforcement of IRCA's sanctions of employers who knowingly hire the undocumented has only recently begun under the Obama administration. Only through enforcement of such existing labor laws can work conditions begin to improve for this group.

Another route to better jobs is unionization, which provides a structure within which low-wage undocumented workers such as Emiliana and Ling could be assured basic legal work conditions through collective bargaining. For Elena, unionization made a difference in her ability to take care of Alberto. Once, when he was ill enough to be hospitalized for two days, Elena took two days off from her home attendant work, and her employer told her that they could not pay her because it was her son who had been sick, not she herself. Elena complained to her union representative, and she was eventually paid for the two days as sick days. And as mentioned in chapter 1, she received three paid months of maternity leave to recover from complications associated with her pregnancy.

Unionization of undocumented immigrant workers in nonfarm jobs has often been considered nearly impossible to accomplish. Many believe that undocumented immigrants are difficult to organize because of their fears of deportation. But this is not necessarily the case. Immigrant low-wage workers have in some contexts been more likely to support unionization than their native-born counterparts. Since the late 1990s, for example, Los Angeles has emerged as the somewhat unlikely success story in organizing undocumented workers.[13] A now-famous drive to organize janitors in Los Angeles, spearheaded by John Sweeney and the Service Employees International Union (SEIU), resulted in a collective bargaining contract. In its wake, other unionization campaigns succeeded in occupations with high concentrations of undocumented workers, such as drywall construction workers. When John Sweeney took over leadership of the AFL-CIO in 1995, he made organizing immigrants, including the undocumented, a new priority for that powerful union.

The successes in Los Angeles were made possible by the convergence of several factors. First, there was a new surge in Latino political strength and support for unionization in city politics in the late 1990s and 2000s. Spurred by the County Federation of Labor's efforts to register Latino voters as well as the surge in voter registration that followed the passage of restrictions on legal immigration through Proposition 187 in 1994, a new generation of labor-friendly political leadership was installed in the city. Second, political change coincided with a period of unusual strength in union leadership, with capacity for innovation. The SEIU janitors' strike in 2000 was supported by forty-eight local politicians, members of both houses of the state legislature, the entire city council, and even the Republican mayor, Richard Riordan. And finally, Latino immigrants proved to be open to unionization. Contrary to popular expectations, during this period documented and undocumented Latino workers alike were more receptive to unionizing than native-born workers.[14]

Could such a coalition be replicated in other cities and communities in the United States? Political unity among immigrant communities in New York is hard to come by, with previous immigrants' hard-won strength often in tension or conflict with the needs for representation of newer groups. Unlike Los Angeles, where generations of Mexicans have been arriving and providing a base for advocacy and representation for newer waves, New York's Mexican migration is so recent that no representative of the group holds a position in the city council. Even a group as well established as the Chinese has taken over a century to achieve citywide representation; only in 2000 did John Liu become the first Asian American elected to the city council. Although several class-action lawsuits have countered egregious labor law violations in Chinatown and some Asian restaurants, these have been conducted outside any unionization process. The Chinese Staff and Workers' Association helped to bring some of the most famous suits to successful conclusions, such as those involving the Silver Palace and Jing Fong restaurants in Manhattan's Chinatown.[15] In addition, recent efforts to unionize some low-wage sectors in the city, such as home-based child care workers who receive federal subsidies (though few of these workers are undocumented), have been successful. Notwithstanding these successes, widespread change in labor conditions for the undocumented has been difficult to achieve in the city. As the New York city council becomes more diverse, members may provide more political support to unions (such as the former AFL unions) that have been most active nationally in organizing immigrant workers.[16] The need for organizing and political advocacy to reform the disastrous work conditions of undocumented parents is urgent, not only in New York City but in communities nationwide.

COMMUNITY-BASED SUPPORTS FOR UNDOCUMENTED PARENTS AND THEIR YOUNG CHILDREN: THE PRINCIPLES OF PERCEIVED BENEFIT TO CHILDREN, TRUST, AND EASE OF INVOLVEMENT

A third pathway to improving the contexts of development for young children of undocumented parents lies in building community and policy supports for citizen children of the undocumented that are responsive to the particular needs and concerns of this population. As we saw in chapters 3 and 4, some policies and programs are more acceptable than others to undocumented Latino and Asian parents. Trustworthy supports that are responsive to these immigrants' roles as gatekeepers and parents of their citizen children can increase their children's access to learning opportunities in the first years of life.

Two success stories emerged in our study among the variety of policies, programs, and organizations that we asked mothers about. The first was WIC. Across our sample, regardless of the parents' legal status, virtually all children were enrolled in the nutritional program covering the prenatal to age five period (see table 3.1). This program is best known for providing vouchers for food and formula. However, it also provides counseling about early health and development, including nutrition and breast-feeding. In recent years, improvements in its implementation have encouraged healthy choices in food, and WIC vouchers now cover culturally appropriate foods that in prior years had not been eligible (and had created an underground market in WIC product exchange).[17]

The second success story was community organizations like Little Sisters, to which several of the Mexican undocumented parents had access by virtue of living in the budding ethnic enclave of East Harlem. This organization provides a range of services—from mental health services, child care, microenterprise investment, and help with public programs to advocacy and community organizing—that are tailored to the needs of the local Mexican population. With a long history in the emerging ethnic enclave, beginning when East Harlem was Spanish Harlem, a Puerto Rican enclave, the organization has adapted to the new immigrant influx and is perceived as a trusted community organization. For example, the only mothers in our study who enrolled in counseling for themselves were those who had connections with Little Sisters.

Community organizations that provide a range of services can also effectively organize undocumented immigrants. Recall from chapter 4 that the few stories in this study about involvement in the immigrant workers' marches of 2006 came from parents with connections to either Little Sisters or Asociación Tepeyac, the other large organization primarily serving Mexicans in New York. As the political scientist Janelle Wong has observed, community-based organizations have partially filled the void left by the decline of party-based efforts to recruit immigrants in the United States.[18] The goals of service provision and political incorporation need not be mutually exclusive.

Why were these two examples—WIC and Little Sisters—so successful? They adhered to three principles that could guide future efforts to improve the early development of children of undocumented parents. First, they provided services that parents felt were related directly to their children's development. WIC's provision of food rather than cash, for example, circumvented the disapproval that both Mexican and Fujianese undocumented parents expressed toward cash welfare. Food and nutritional counseling was perceived as directly helping children. Little Sisters and organizations like it that serve high concentrations of the undocumented provide help with child care and parenting.

Second, in both cases services were provided in settings that the parents trusted. The hospitals and associated clinics where children in our study were born earned the highest level of trust from the parents, who were generally very happy with the quality of medical care they received before, during, and after the birth of their child. Many families who subsequently moved far away from these hospitals—to another borough of the city or even outside the city—returned to these hospitals and clinics for well-child visits, a powerful behavioral statement of trust. Community organizations like Little Sisters or those in the Chinatowns of New York earn the trust of immigrant communities through neighborhood proximity and through the range of family support, child development, mental health, and cultural and advocacy supports they provide. At a more basic level, parents trusted these organizations not to turn them in to authorities that could deport them.

Third, enrolling in the services was easy. Most of the mothers reported that social workers in the hospital enrolled them in WIC in as little as fifteen minutes, helping them fill out forms in Spanish or Chinese. With this kind of hands-on help, which was often provided by fellow immigrants, benefits from the government for citizen children were perceived as helpful.

The principles of perceived help to children's development, settings that parents trusted, and ease of enrollment could be supplemented or applied to other programs. The high enrollment rates and acceptance that WIC enjoys in these communities could be transmitted to other programs that help children. For example, proven programs that address parenting and child development could be provided in the context of WIC and primary care clinics. Providing this service in this way could be particularly advantageous because, unlike most community organizations, WIC and primary care have nationwide reach into most communities. Two examples of such programs exist. One is the Family Check-Up, a three-session program that helps parents identify and act on their goals. The program provides a short, focused counseling approach—using motivational interviewing techniques that have proven successful in a variety of prevention and treatment programs—in WIC settings.[19] In the first session, data are gathered from the family about their needs and strengths. In the second, based on these data, parents are helped through a process that identifies their family goals (such as parenting, job, or educational progress) addresses immediate crises, and identifies other short- and long-term goals. A plan is set up for immediate action on the primary goal. For parents who identify improved child-rearing as a goal, a brief, empirically proven parent education program of six sessions is provided. For those who identify their goals as education- or job-related, a six-month action plan on that front is developed. In evaluations conducted by Thomas Dishion, Daniel Shaw, and their colleagues, the program has improved observed parenting practices and reduced young children's acting-out behaviors in two randomized evaluation studies conducted in several cities.[20]

Another program that has proven successful in improving parenting and children's development—this time with Mexican low-income parents in New York City—is the Video Interaction Project, led by the pediatrician Alan Mendelsohn and his colleagues.[21] This program provides a structured curriculum to help parents learn how to engage in the most productive reading approaches with their infants and toddlers. The curriculum is provided by trained facilitators at each well-child visit in the first two years. Videos are made of parents reading to their children, and these are reviewed with feedback during the sessions. The program, of higher intensity and effectiveness than the well-known Reach Out and Read program, has improved cognitive skills in the first four years of life for children with mothers who are most likely to be undocumented (Mexican mothers with low levels of education). The program has also improved parenting practices related to reading and responsiveness. Finally, the program has reduced these parents' depressive symptoms, which, as we saw in this book, can transmit the influence of documentation status to children's cognitive skills at twenty-four months.[22]

Both of these programs meet our three principles. Parents perceive the Family Check-Up and the Video Interaction Project as benefiting their children—in the first program, by identifying goals that improve parents' ability to raise their children, and in the second, by videotaping parents interacting with their children to help them engage in particular reading strategies. The programs also are provided in the trusted settings of WIC clinics and child primary care clinics. And finally, access to these programs is easy, largely because they are provided in service systems that reach a large percentage of parents in poverty, including low-income immigrant parents such as the undocumented in our sample. These programs could also be provided in community organization contexts as well.

In addition to such service-oriented programs, the examples of Little Sisters, Asociación Tepeyac, the Chinese American Planning Council, and the Chinese Staff and Workers' Association (chapter 4) highlight how community organizations can serve as trusted venues for advocacy and organizing. Our birth cohort sample of parents reported very low involvement in such activities, perhaps because they were not recruited through agencies or organizations. And many of our undocumented parents lived far from these organizations' offices. However, those organizations with networks capable of reaching across the city—such as Tepeyac's associated congregations—can link undocumented parents, like Emiliana, who live far from enclave neighborhoods to both services and advocacy. They can take such simple steps as inquiring about the work conditions of immigrant parents, about their children's access to child care of good quality, and about the levels of social support or isolation experienced by immigrant families. Practitioners and service providers thus have a major role to play in addressing the developmental contexts of children of the undocumented, not only in organizations that specialize in services for immigrants, such as Little Sisters, but in the much wider range of organizations that serve the increasingly diverse children and families of the United States. Such efforts can provide children of the undocumented with a better future as preschoolers, students, and citizens.

These three policy directions—providing a pathway to citizenship, reforming the work conditions of the undocumented, and increasing the responsiveness of community supports—could combine to have cumulative effects on early learning among children of the undocumented. By bringing these families out of the shadows and providing them with access to better work conditions and learning opportunities, we can ensure that the nation's most vulnerable young citizens have an equal chance to succeed in their early development, later schooling, and adulthood.

As the A train rolls through the New York night, we leave Emiliana, Elena, and Ling. We wonder how their children are faring now. As citizens of the United States, as three of the more than four million young children of undocumented parents in our nation, do they have equal access to learning opportunities compared to children of the documented? Their three mothers share a lifelong commitment to supporting their children's learning. On this they do not differ. They do differ in their documentation status. In this book, I have shown that this status matters for the work conditions they experience every day, for the programs they enroll their children in, and for the networks and organizations they have contact with. This status, invisible yet ever-present in the groceries, playgrounds, and middle-class homes of New York City, has consequences for the present and future citizens of the republic. We ignore these consequences at our peril.

Appendix

Overview of Study Design and Methods

All the data reported in this book are drawn from the early childhood studies of the Center for Research on Culture, Development, and Education. Data from two phases of the study were included: a first pilot qualitative study and the main birth cohort study. The center's mission is to examine how the contexts of home, peers, child care and school, parental work, and public policy affect the development of young children in the first years of life and of youth during adolescence. As a researcher in public policy, parental work, and child development, I was interested primarily in these topics as one of the center's principal investigators. The other principal investigators were Catherine Tamis-LeMonda, Diane Hughes, and Niobe Way, all professors of applied psychology at New York University. Co-investigators who directed the birth cohort and embedded qualitative study, which together form one of the center's two cohort studies, were Ronit Kahana-Kalman, Ajay Chaudry, and Diane Ruble.

As the data collection progressed in an initial qualitative study and in the subsequent first waves of a larger birth cohort study, my initial interest in economic hardship and survival strategies among the immigrant families in our sample gradually was overtaken by the realization that documentation status appeared to be a significant and substantial theme in the qualitative analysis. Two empirical puzzles led to the emergence of this theme. First, the Mexican mothers in the birth cohort, despite reporting lower incomes than the Dominicans and African Americans, also reported lower economic hardship (as measured by events such as not being able to make the rent or pay other bills). Something else must have been going on in these families, and as we collected the data on their immigration experiences, the very high rates of undocumented status among the Mexican population struck me and the qualitative team as important. The second puzzle occurred early in the birth cohort study, when the Chinese mothers told us that they were not planning on breast-feeding their infants. This was a puzzle given that knowledge of the benefits of breast-feeding is widespread. In the ensuing months, as we followed up our sample with six-month phone calls and interviews, we realized, to our surprise, that most of the Chinese infants had been sent back to China. The story of Ling from the pilot qualitative study, it turned out, was a much more common story than we had expected.

PILOT QUALITATIVE STUDY METHODS

As principal investigators of the Center for Research on Culture, Development, and Education, Catherine Tamis-LeMonda, Diane Hughes, Niobe Way, and I did not feel comfortable immediately engaging in hypothesis-confirming social science without initial exploratory work. Ajay Chaudry (at that time a professor of public policy at the New School) and I therefore led an initial, intensive qualitative study. In addition, two professors of applied psychology at New York University, Gigliana Melzi and Niobe Way, helped supervise subgroups of field-workers. Twenty-four mothers of Chinese, African American, Puerto Rican, Dominican, Mexican, and European American origin were recruited into this qualitative study with the assistance of New York City community agencies that served low-income families. These groups were chosen because together they represented over 80 percent of the New York City population and encompassed some of the largest immigrant groups in the city. We recruited a larger range of ethnic groups than is presented in this book because this pilot qualitative study informed not only the birth cohort study that is the focus of this book but also the adolescent study that included a much wider range of ethnic groups. In addition to ethnicity, we used the following eligibility criteria: resident of New York City; recruited from an agency that serves neighborhoods with high concentrations of the ethnic and immigrant groups included in our study; age eighteen or older; and household income below 250 percent of the federal poverty threshold for the prior year.

Children in the families were either between three months and three years old (an early childhood subsample) or between ten and thirteen years of age (an early adolescent subsample). From the subsample of families with young children, four Mexican families, two Dominican families, and one Chinese family were drawn for analyses in the book. (For the names of the mothers and focal children used in this book, which are all pseudonyms, see in the notes to table A.1.)

A combination of semistructured interview and participant-observation methods were employed in this study, which was conducted between the summer of 2003 and the summer of 2004. Each mother was visited between six and twelve times over periods ranging from six to nine months (See the acknowledgments for the list of field-workers and supervisors.) Visits alternated between semistructured interviews and participant-observation, and they lasted for the most part between two and three hours. Visits that included semistructured interviews were tape-recorded; two-thirds to three-quarters of the visits, depending on the family, included an interview component.

Semistructured Interviews

Trained qualitative field-workers, many of whom spoke Mandarin or Spanish, covered a range of topics in the six semistructured interview visits. All of the Mexican families spoke only Spanish, and all of the Chinese families spoke only Mandarin or Fuzhou. (They were interviewed only in Mandarin.) The majority of the Dominican mothers were interviewed in Spanish. Interview modules addressed (1) daily routines, immigration experiences, and childhood experiences; (2) relationships, including those with household members, extended family, and friends; (3) parents' work experience; (4) child learning, schooling, and child care experiences; (5) experiences of ethnicity and race, media, and peer relationships of the child; and (6) household expenditures and income, employment, and policy and program use. Data consist of field notes, written in English by the field-worker after each visit, and interview transcripts for the semistructured visits, which were first transcribed in the original language (English, Spanish, or Chinese) and then translated by bilingual graduate students.

Participant-Observation Visits

Although all visits included some participant observation, the same field-workers visited the families six times using only participant-observation methods. The field-workers engaged in unstructured conversation and interaction in a variety of settings. Although the majority of these visits occurred in the home, they also took place in child care settings, workplaces, welfare offices, health clinics, transportation settings, and the homes of various network members, including relatives and friends.

Training and Supervision

The training of all field-workers occurred in full-team meetings, across a period of several months. One series of trainings were devoted to interviewing techniques, with practice interviews recorded and reviewed by the whole team. A series was also devoted to fieldwork techniques, including multiple exercises for participant-observation and field-note writing. All of the training sessions were accompanied by a variety of readings in qualitative methods, as well as classic ethnographic studies of families and urban neighborhoods. During the data collection periods, all field-workers attended group supervision meetings. Full-team meetings were held once every several weeks. In between, subgroups of field-workers met that were ethnicity- and language-specific; these groups were led by Gigliana Melzi and Ann Rivera for the field-workers working with Latino families, by Ajay Chaudry for the field-workers working with African American families, and by Niobe Way and myself for the field-workers working with the Chinese and white families. In addition, each supervisor provided feedback both electronically and in individual supervision on every set of field notes and interview transcripts. Finally, each of the faculty supervisors carried at least one case in the qualitative study.

Qualitative Interview Protocols

The semistructured interview protocol included five modules, conducted in five separate visits. The first module covered the basic background information for the mothers, the important figures in the child's life, and the father, as well as the family's daily routine. The second covered child care, experiences of hardship and coping or survival strategies, and attitudes toward and experiences of community and government assistance programs. The third covered immigration experiences, educational goals for the child, and the mother's own schooling. The fourth covered parenting, gender issues, and the relationship between the mother and father. The final semistructured module included questions about work and neighborhood contexts.

The field-workers, in their participant-observation, were encouraged to keep track of these topics, but there were no set conversation topics in this work. Note that most of the data in this book are drawn from the detailed field notes taken by the field-workers. I keep direct quotes from the semistructured interviews to a minimum in order to further protect the identities of participating families.

MAIN BIRTH COHORT STUDY METHODS

Catherine Tamis-LeMonda, Ronit Kahana-Kalman, and I led the birth cohort study. Together with a small team of supervisors from the initial pilot study, I led the embedded qualitative study. In the main birth cohort study, 380 mothers were recruited in New York City: 115 Dominican, 97 Mexican, 56 Chinese, and 112 African American (see table A.2 for baseline characteristics of the sample). Researchers recruited mothers within two days after giving birth at postpartum wards in three public New York City hospitals during 2004 to 2005. These hospitals were selected because they drew patients from low-income neighborhoods with high concentrations of the four target ethnic groups. To participate in the study, mothers had to be age eighteen or older, live in New York City, self-identify as Chinese, Mexican, Dominican, or African American, and have a healthy full-term infant. These four ethnic groups were targeted for the study because together they represent over 60 percent of the population of New York City and include the largest immigrant groups in the city. Chinese participants were dropped from the study after the six-month wave owing to the high rates at which they sent their infants to live in China to be raised by relatives.

Embedded Qualitative Study

A stratified random sample of the full sample was drawn for the embedded qualitative study (stratified by ethnic group and child gender). The ethnographic study aimed to investigate the diverse pathways through which children reach different levels of early school readiness. Families were contacted by phone and were recruited to participate in additional visits with informal interviews by the same field-worker. Each family received compensation of $50 for each visit completed. The final ethnographic sample consisted of twenty-eight African American, Chinese, Dominican, and Mexican families. Of these families, seven Mexican, seven Dominican, and two Chinese families were the source of data for this book. (For the names of the mothers and focal children used in this book, see note a in table A.1 distinguishing them from the mothers and focal children in the pilot qualitative study). As described in chapter 2, the Chinese were dropped from the larger sample after we found out that the vast majority of infants were being sent back to China. We did attempt to complete the qualitative data collection for the two Chinese families who did not send their infants back to China. Because these families were not very representative of the Chinese who did send back their infants, I concentrate in this book on the experiences of the pilot qualitative study Chinese families, who included a family whose son had been sent back and then returned to the United States (Ling's family, profiled in chapter 1).

In this qualitative study, bilingual field-workers visited families in their homes every eight to ten weeks. Visits began when the infants were eight months old and continued until they were twenty-four to thirty-two months old, resulting in an average of six total visits per family. Visits consisted of a mix of semistructured interviews and participant-observation. Respondents were interviewed in the language of their choice, resulting in 39 percent of mothers being interviewed in English, 14 percent in Mandarin, and 46 percent in Spanish.

The qualitative methods for this study were the same as those used in the pilot qualitative study. When visiting families, field-workers used participant-observation and semistructured interviews in the mother's preferred language. The semistructured interview modules were slightly revised versions of the ones described earlier that were used in the pilot qualitative study.

Training and supervision methods were similar to those used in the pilot qualitative study. The supervisors in this study were myself and a team made up of field-workers in the first study, as well as additional doctoral-level supervisors: Kimberly Torres, Ann C. Rivera, Francisco X. Gaytan, and Karen McFadden.

Survey and Child Assessment Procedures

At fourteen and thirty-six months, we conducted direct assessments of the children's cognitive skills. (The measure is described later in the appendix.) In addition, at baseline, one month, six months, fourteen months, and thirty-six months, a structured survey was administered to mothers. It was conducted as an interview so that mothers with low levels of literacy could participate fully. The survey interview took between forty-five minutes and an hour. Mothers were compensated $50 for their time at fourteen months and $100 for their time at thirty-six months. The survey covered a variety of topic areas. (Measures used in this book are described later in the appendix.)

Attrition

Attrition at the thirty-six-month assessment was 28 percent, with no significant differences in rates of attrition across the ethnic groups. In an analysis predicting attrition at thirty-six months, we included a variety of baseline predictors, such as ethnicity, child characteristics (birth order, child gender), a variety of mother characteristics (age, foreign-born status, educational level, prior employment, having had children with another partner, psychological distress, perceived social support), father characteristics (foreign-born status, prior employment, having had children with another partner), and household characteristics (household earnings, public benefit receipt, marital and cohabitation status, number of people in the household, and number of biological children). With these twenty-three predictors in a model predicting attrition, only one was statistically significant at the .05 level (below chance). Mothers with higher levels of education were more likely to have been retained in the sample at thirty-six months.

SURVEY AND OTHER QUANTITATIVE MEASURES

Family Background Characteristics

Covariates were measured at baseline and included the following: maternal education (whether the mother had completed high school), whether the mother was married, whether the mother was cohabiting with a partner, the number of biological children the mother had, years in the United States, primary language spoken in the home, employment in the year prior to the child's birth, and the child's gender. A single-item measure of discomfort with out-of-home care was also used.

Neighborhood Characteristics

In chapter 4, I reported census tract–level neighborhood data based on the 2000 census in New York City. These included the median income of the census tract and coethnic concentration (based on percentages of Chinese, Mexican, Dominican, and African American or black among adults in the tract).

Resources Requiring Identification

This measure, which I use as a proxy for undocumented status, included questions about whether the mother or anyone else in her household had (1) a savings account, (2) a checking account, (3) a credit card, or (4) a driver's license. This measure was developed for this study. In the analyses, the measure was reverse-coded to represent an index of the household-level lack of such resources to more easily link to the status of being undocumented.

Social Support

The availability of social support was calculated from three questions asking the mother whether she had people in her life to whom she could go if she needed help taking care of her child, finding a job, or making ends meet. For each mother, up to three such figures were solicited. A count variable was calculated, summing each figure across the three types of help.

Autonomy in Job Duties

This variable was coded from the Department of Labor's O*NET database of job duty characteristics for 949 U.S. occupations.[1] Based on work by

Ann Crouter and her colleagues,[2] we created a scale from ten items representing self-direction and autonomy on the job.[3] These included items such as the opportunity to organize, plan, and prioritize or to think creatively (Cronbach's alpha = .96).

Wages

Wages were calculated at thirty-six months from information collected from the mother on her own earnings and the earnings of the father of her child, as well as from information on hours, both her own and the father's.

Economic Hardship

Economic hardship was measured at both the fourteen- and twenty-four-month waves using a four-item index used in the New Hope antipoverty demonstration.[4] This index assessed whether there had been a time in the past six months (yes/no) when they and their family: (1) were without telephone service; (2) did not pay the full amount of the rent or mortgage; (3) were evicted from their home or apartment for not paying the rent or mortgage; or (4) lost service from the gas, electric, or oil company because they did not make payments. These items were then summed to create an index of economic hardship (fourteen-month wave: mean = 0.49, standard deviation = 0.75, range = 0 to 3; twenty-four-month wave: mean = 0.33, standard deviation = 0.61, range = 0 to 3).

Psychological Distress

Psychological distress was measured at both the fourteen- and twenty-four-month waves using the K6, a six-item diagnostic scale that measures general psychological distress, including depressive and anxious affect (reliability as measured by Cronbach's alpha = 0.80).[5] Mothers were asked to report on the frequency of feelings of distress in the past thirty days on a five-point scale ranging from 1 ("none of the time") to 5 ("all of the time"). Sample items included: "During the past thirty days, how often did you feel hopeless?" and "About how often in the past thirty days have you felt nervous?" The sample mean and standard deviation of psychological distress was 1.89 (0.72) at the fourteen-month wave and 1.81 (0.70) at the twenty-four-month wave.

Expenditures on Toys and Books

Expenditures on children were assessed at fourteen months, using a protocol that was informed by the expenditures section of the pilot qualitative study.[6] The variable of expenditures on toys and books, representing spending on learning materials that might have an impact on cognitive skills, was defined as the amount (in dollars) of spending on these two items over the last month.

Daily Cognitive Stimulation

Mothers' reports of activities with their child were used to create an index of six cognitively stimulating activities at both the fourteen- and twenty-four-month waves, including singing songs, reading or looking at books, telling stories, listening or dancing to music, playing games that did not involve toys, and playing with building toys. Following the methods of Eileen Rodriguez and her colleagues, we gave mothers who reported engaging with their child every day in each activity a 1, and those who reported anything less were given a 0.[7] The six items were then summed to create an index of cognitive stimulation (fourteen-month wave: mean = 2.65, standard deviation = 1.39, range = 0 to 6; twenty-four-month wave: mean = 2.08, standard deviation = 1.40, range = 0 to 6).

Center-Based Care

A variable of any center-based child care at thirty-six months was created. A center was defined as a child care facility with at least ten children present in a classroomlike setting.

Child Cognitive Skills

We used the Mullen Scales of Early Learning to capture children's cognitive development at the fourteen-month and thirty-six-month waves.[8] This measure is an interviewer-administered standardized developmental test for children age three to sixty months and consists of four subscales of cognitive development: visual reception, fine motor skills, receptive language skills, and expressive language skills. Scores on each subscale are age-equivalent-normed and can be combined to provide an index of overall developmental level, the early learning composite. In reporting our results for the overall early learning composite, these scores have a mean of 100 and a standard deviation of 15. The Mullen Scales correlate highly with other measures of cognitive development in early childhood, including the Bayley Scales of Infant Development (correlation of 0.70).[9]

ANALYTIC APPROACHES

One concern about all of the analyses in this study is that the intensive data collection methods might have brought about Hawthorne effects.

That is, the very fact of being interviewed might have changed the behavior of the participants. Although this may be true, if anything this effect would have made it more difficult to find effects of undocumented status on parents and children: the potential positive effects of being observed might have been stronger for the undocumented, who were probably less accustomed to research interviewing than the documented in the sample.

Analytic Approach for Qualitative Data

Analyses in a mixed-methods study such as this one comprise iterative stages of reading previous theory and research, discussing parents' experiences in the many meetings that occurred during data collection, and multiple stages of reading and analysis. We used an adaptation of a grounded theory approach for the analyses.[10] As described earlier, a set of research questions derived from the overall goals of the Center for Research on Culture, Development, and Education determined the sets of questions asked in the semistructured interviews of the qualitative studies. Thus, prior theory and research determined the general set and sequence of topics. As the data collection progressed, however, each draft module of interview questions was revised extensively in the full-group field-worker meetings. The field-workers' and supervisors' reports of emerging and unexpected themes, as well as their knowledge of the language and conversational patterns of the parents, informed the final versions of each of the semistructured protocols.

After the theme of undocumented status emerged from our initial study of economic hardship in the data, I undertook a focused reading of all of the qualitative data. First, I indexed the main themes relevant to the analysis in an open-coding format (with themes related to the child's development in cognitive and other domains, parenting practices related to child learning, household, partner, extended family, immigration, arrival in the United States, employment, housing, neighborhood description, experiences of the country of origin growing up, transnational contact and travel, comparisons to the United States, child care, and public policy). Then, in an iterative process of writing memos and summary notes, I analyzed each of the primary themes that emerged as potentially linked to undocumented status. I brought this analysis to bear within cases (for example, analyzing social support in the context of perceptions of the neighborhood) as well as across cases (for example, analyzing all mentions of experiences of the WIC program across all of the qualitative cases). When relevant, I included counts of certain experiences (such as the central count of undocumented status of mothers and fathers or partners and the number of families in each ethnic group who had boarders living in the apartment). In general, I report these only when the counts show large differences across groups. I did not use qualitative analysis software.

Links Between Qualitative and Quantitative Data Analyses

In a longitudinal study such as our birth cohort study, it is possible for qualitative analyses to inform subsequent quantitative data collection, and vice versa.[11] As the theme of documentation status emerged in the pilot qualitative study, as well as in some of the initial visits in the main qualitative study, I added assessments in our survey of everyday experiences that might be related to documentation status. First, I included at baseline a measure of fear of consequences of using benefits. Second, I included questions about the mode of transportation used after first arriving in the United States. Third, I included the set of questions on resources requiring identification. Of these, the measure of resources requiring identification appeared to most clearly distinguish our groups in the order of proportion of undocumented that was suggested in the qualitative analysis. The other two variables were less effective owing to a combination of factors: higher rates of missing data, lack of variation, and perhaps social desirability or discomfort in answering the questions. Therefore, we decided to use the variable of resources requiring identification as the best proxy for documentation status in the quantitative analyses.

Analytic Approach for Quantitative Model

We conducted the analysis represented in figure 6.1 as follows. We used structural equation modeling techniques to estimate a path model representing the hypothesized set of relationships between institutional exclusion, economic hardship, and parenting, on the one hand, and child cognitive development, on the other. Structural equation modeling is more flexible in its statistical assumptions than regression, provides indicators of overall model fit, and can estimate paths simultaneously. Therefore, it is a useful tool for exploring multiple relationships at the same time and is often used to reduce bias in mediation analyses.[12]

We conceptualized path models such that the group with the highest proportion of undocumented (the Mexican group) was the reference group, so that comparisons could be made to a group with lower rates of undocumented status (the Dominicans) and one with no undocumented members (the African American mothers, all of whom were U.S.-born and therefore citizens). Cognitive skills were the focus, since this was the outcome on which our study and other studies differed with respect to groups with higher versus lower proportions of undocumented parents. (In other words, on social outcomes such as antisocial behavior and cooperative behavior, no differences between our groups have emerged thus far.)

We conducted path analyses using the sample covariance matrix and maximum likelihood estimation. We used the full information maximum likelihood, employing the MPlus statistical package to model and estimate all parameters.[13] MPlus uses full information maximum likelihood estimates, a strategy that yields efficient and consistent estimates in the presence of data that are either missing completely at random or missing at random, and it produces least-biased estimates in the case of nonignorable missing data.[14]

As recommended by Li-Tze Hu and Peter M. Bentler and by Rex Kline, we evaluated models using several indices of overall fit.[15] These included the comparative fit index (CFI; adequate fit > 0.90) and the root-mean-square-error of approximation (RMSEA; adequate fit < .05). By these standards, the model fit the data well: the CFI was 0.99, and the RMSEA was 0.02. We do not use the chi-square statistic because of its dependence on sample size. Comparisons of models with and without additional covariates (including employment, number of children in the household, and child gender) indicated few differences in obtained path coefficients; for reasons of statistical power, we report analyses with the reduced set of covariates.

Table A.1   Names of Mothers and Focal Children in Qualitative Sample

Families	Mother and Child
Dominican	Dolores and Gilberto[a]
	Virginia and Rogelio[a]
	Beatriz and Raul
	Mercedes and Marta
	Paloma and Stefano
	Marisa and Aurelia
	Sofia and Hermosa
	Juana and Laura
	Elena and Alberto
Mexican	Nalda and Ramona
	Flor and Linda
	Aurora and Xavier
	Margarita and Catalina[a]
	Camila and Natalia
	Blanca and Miguel[a]
	Victoria and Ruben[a]
	Alfreda and Lucio
	Emiliana and Victor
	Adelina and Federico
	Alejandra and Elisa[a]
Chinese	Ling and Guang[a]
	Chun and Ming-Sheng
	Fen and Ping

Source: Author's compilation based on data from the Early Childhood Cohort Study (Center for Research on Culture, Development, and Education 2009).
Note: All names are pseudonyms.
[a.] The case is from the pilot qualitative study.

Table A.2 Participant Characteristics at Baseline, Full Birth Cohort Sample

	Full Sample (N = 380)	Chinese (N = 56)	Mexicans (N = 97)	Dominicans (N = 115)	African Americans (N = 112)
Mother under age eighteen when first child was born	13%	0%	13%	10%	18%
Mother married or cohabiting with partner	71	98	87	68	46
Mother has high school degree	27	32	32	24	23
Mother has high school degree or GED	31	32	35	28	32
Mean number of years of education computed (standard deviation)	10.55 (3.06)	9.18 (2.74)	8.00 (3.42)	12.13 (2.03)	11.91 (1.67)
Total number of children in household	2.02 (1.28)	1.21 (0.50)	2.34 (1.25)	1.81 (0.85)	2.37 (1.67)
Household income in year prior to child's birth	$20,206 ($14,423)	$22,502 ($15,401)	$17,498 ($11,536)	$23,192 ($15,086)	$19,983 ($16,436)

Source: Author's compilation based on data from the Early Childhood Cohort Study (Center for Research on Culture, Development, and Education 2009).

Notes

CHAPTER 1

1. I use the term "undocumented" to denote not having legal documents. The terms "unauthorized" and "illegal" have also been used for this group (Bean and Stevens 2003). The term "undocumented" comes closest to the vernacular used by many members of this group themselves (for example, when they use the phrase "sin papeles," which means not having a U.S. green card or passport). Most who use it in this way understand that it means a lack of legal documents, not fake documents.
2. Passel and Cohn (2009).
3. Smith (2006).
4. Passel and Cohn (2009).
5. Liang and Ye (2001).
6. Kwong (1997); Liang and Ye (2001).
7. Zhou (2008).
8. Liang and Ye (2001); Passel and Cohn (2009); Smith (2006).
9. Motomura (2008).
10. Passel and Cohn (2009).
11. Passel and Cohn (2009).
12. Capps and Fortuny (2006); Passel and Cohn (2009); Tienda and Mitchell (2006).
13. Kao and Tienda (1995); Louie (2006).
14. Duncan et al. (2007); Raver (2002); Shonkoff, Boyce, and McEwen (2009).
15. Nisbett (2009).
16. Ramey, Yeates, and Short (1984).
17. Padilla et al. (2006); Tienda and Mitchell (2006).
18. Crosnoe (2006, 2007); Han (2006).
19. Crosnoe (2007).
20. Fuller et al. (2009).
21. Crosnoe (2006); Jackson, McLanahan, and Kiernan (2009); Landale, Oropesa, and Gorman (1999).
22. Gould et al. (2003); Hessol and Fuentes-Afflick (2000).
23. Feliciano (2005); Liang and Ye (2001); Model (2008).
24. Han (2006).
25. Qin, Way, and Rana (2008).

26. Kao (1999).
27. Ortega et al. (2009).
28. Ortega et al. (2009).
29. Kalil and Chen (2008); van Hook and Balistreri (2006).
30. Bernhardt et al. (2009); Mehta et al. (2002).
31. Ortega et al. (2007).
32. Crosnoe (2006); Hernandez, Denton, and Macartney (2008); Kalil and Crosnoe (2009); Matthews and Ewen (2006).
33. DeWind and Kasinitz (1997); Nee and Sanders (2001); Suárez-Orozco and Suárez-Orozco (2001).
34. Kasinitz et al. (2008); Portes and Rumbaut (2001); Suárez-Orozco, Suárez-Orozco, and Todorova (2008).
35. Alba and Nee (2003); Gans (1992); Portes and Rumbaut (2001); Portes and Zhou (1993).
36. Alba and Nee (2003); Portes and Rumbaut (2001).
37. Chávez (1998); Zlolniski (2006).
38. Smith (2006).
39. Kwong (1997); Liang and Ye (2001).
40. England and Sim (2009).
41. Cheah et al. (2009).
42. Lupien et al. (2000).
43. Raikes et al. (2006).
44. Loeb et al. (2007).
45. NICHD Early Child Care Research Network (2005).
46. Cornelius (1982).

CHAPTER 2

1. Burrows and Wallace (1999).
2. Lobo, Flores, and Salvo (2002).
3. Hoefer, Rytina, and Baker (2010); Passel and Cohn (2009).
4. Passel and Cohn (2009).
5. Bob Christie and Paul J. Weber, "'Birth Tourism' a Tiny Proportion of Immigrant Babies," Associated Press, September 3, 2010, available at: http://hosted2.ap.org/apdefault/f7ded15e4d4846268a17b79c1c4b7cb8/Article_2010-09-03-US-Birthright-Citizenship/id-a67be443b13143b8b18f0d32b3da3d2f (accessed September 20, 2010).
6. Kasinitz, Mollenkopf, and Waters (2002); Waters (2005).
7. Passel and Cohn (2009).
8. Passel (2006).
9. Ngai (2006); Pedraza (2006).
10. C. Wong (2006).
11. Motomura (2008).

12. White, Bean, and Espenshade (1990).
13. Capps, Ku, and Fix (2002); Singer (2004).
14. Zimmerman and Tumlin (1999).
15. Bachrach and Lipson (2002).
16. Capps et al. (2002).
17. Passel and Cohn (2009).
18. For more comprehensive histories going back further, see Massey et al. (1987); Ngai (2004).
19. Ngai (2004); Rumbaut (2006).
20. Ngai (2004).
21. Orrenius and Zavodny (2009).
22. Lee (1966); Massey and Espinosa (1997).
23. Phillips and Massey (1999).
24. Smith (2006).
25. Kraly and Miyares (2001).
26. Smith (2006).
27. Consejo Nacional de Población (2000).
28. Smith (2006).
29. Smith (2006).
30. Moya Pons (1995).
31. Garcia Coll and Marks (2009).
32. Levitt (2001).
33. Pessar (1995).
34. Levitt (2001).
35. Levitt (2001).
36. Levitt (2001).
37. Kraly and Miyares (2001).
38. Pessar (1995).
39. Levitt (2001).
40. Salyer (1995).
41. Ngai (2004).
42. Zhou (2001).
43. Liang and Ye (2001).
44. Julia Preston, "Ringleader Gets 35-Year Term in Smuggling of Immigrants," *New York Times*, March 17, 2006.
45. Julia Preston, "Trial Starts with Details of Immigrant Smuggling," *New York Times*, May 17, 2005.
46. Liang and Ye (2001).

CHAPTER 3

1. Motomura (2008).
2. Capps et al. (2007); Chaudry et al. (2010).

3. James C. McKinley, "Debate Intensifies over Deportations," *New York Times*, July 25, 2009, A13.
4. Yoshikawa, Godfrey, and Rivera (2008).
5. England and Sim (2009).
6. Perreira, Chapman, and Stein (2006).
7. Kwong (1997); Liang and Ye (2001).
8. Chin (2005).
9. Zhao et al. (2003).
10. Menjivar (2002); Suárez-Orozco, Todorova, and Louie (2002).
11. Gaytan et al. (2006).
12. Crittenden (1992); Lyons-Ruth (1996).
13. Parreñas (2005); Suárez-Orozco, Todorova, and Louie (2002).
14. Lu et al. (2000).
15. Bitler and Currie (2005); Burstein et al. (2000); National Forum on Early Childhood Program Evaluation (2007).
16. Tekin (2005).
17. Loeb et al. (2007); Magnuson, Ruhm, and Waldfogel (2007).
18. Nord (2005).
19. Chaudry (2004).
20. Zimmerman and Tumlin (1999).
21. Fremstad (2000).
22. New York State Department of Health (2008).
23. Gilens (1999).
24. Edin and Lein (1997); Yoshikawa (1999).
25. Barata, Yuan, and Yoshikawa (2010).
26. Fuller, Holloway, and Liang (1996).
27. Barata, Yuan, and Yoshikawa (2010).
28. Ramos and Yoshikawa (2009).
29. Hondagneu-Sotelo (1994, 1999); Pessar (1995, 1999).
30. Garcia and Jensen (2007).
31. Edin and Lein (1997).
32. Levy (2006).
33. Ellwood (1988).

CHAPTER 4

1. Bourdieu (1986); Coleman (1988); Granovetter (1973).
2. Small (2009).
3. Chavez (1991); Tapia (1995).
4. Evans et al. (1998).
5. DeLeire and Kalil (2002).
6. Su and Rong (2007).

7. National Bureau of Statistics of China (2009a, 2009b).
8. Menjivar (1997).
9. Yoshikawa et al. (2010).
10. Barr (2004).
11. Yoshikawa, Godfrey, and Rivera (2008).
12. Kessler et al. (2002).
13. Gershoff et al. (2007).
14. Bukowski, Newcomb, and Hartup (1996); Way (2011).
15. Crockenberg (1987).
16. Small (2009); Warren and Mapp (forthcoming)
17. Burt (2001).
18. Small (2009).
19. Aber et al. (1989).
20. Edin, Fredriksson, and Aslund (2003); Lazear (1999); Zhou (1992, 2008); Zhou and Logan (1989).
21. Borjas (2006); Chiswick and Miller (2005).
22. Chávez (1991, 1998); Hondagneu-Sotelo (1994); Zlolniski (2006).
23. Smith (2006).
24. Valencia (2005).
25. Smith (2006); Galvez (2009).
26. Galvez (2009).
27. Zhou (1992); Zhou and Kim (2006).
28. Zhou and Kim (2006).
29. Galvez (2009).
30. Galvez (2009); Smith (2006).

CHAPTER 5

1. Kalil and Ziol-Guest (2005); Yoshikawa, Weisner, and Lowe (2006).
2. Passel and Cohn (2009).
3. Yoshikawa et al. (2006).
4. Street Vendor Project (2006).
5. Bluestone (1992).
6. Chin (2005).
7. Chin (2005).
8. Lee (2008).
9. Crouter et al. (2006); National Center for O*NET Development (2006).
10. Newman (1999, 2006); Presser (2005); Seefeldt (2008); Yoshikawa et al. (2006).
11. Boushey et al. (2007).
12. Harknett and McLanahan (2004).
13. Hondagneu-Sotelo (1994, 1999); Pessar (1995).
14. Bernhardt et al. (2009).

15. Yoshikawa et al. (2006).
16. Enchautégui-de-Jesus, Yoshikawa, and McLoyd (2006); Newman (1999); Perry-Jenkins, Repetti, and Crouter (2000); Raver (2003).
17. Kohn (1969); Parcel and Menaghan (1994).
18. Crouter et al. (2006); Roy, Ramos, and Yoshikawa (2009).
19. Rivera-Batiz (1999).
20. Anne Barnard, "Admired by Many, but to Police a Killer," *New York Times*, November 28, 2008, A25.
21. Ibid.
22. Finch, Kolody, and Vega (2000).
23. Kao and Tienda (1995); Louie (2006).
24. Waldinger (1996).
25. Borjas, Grogger, and Hanson (2006).
26. Waldinger and Lichter (2003).
27. Saucedo (2006).
28. Hondagneu-Sotelo (1994).
29. Enchautégui-de-Jesus, Yoshikawa, and McLoyd (2006); Kalil and Ziol-Guest (2005).
30. Han (2005).
31. Hsueh and Yoshikawa (2007).
32. Loeb et al. (2007); NICHD Early Child Care Research Network (2005).
33. Kohn (1969).
34. Greenberger, O'Neil, and Nagel (1994); Parcel and Menaghan (1994).

CHAPTER 6

1. Robert Mackey, "Worried Girl Asks Michelle Obama if Her Mother Will Be Deported," *New York Times*, May 19, 2010, The Lede (blog), available at: http://thelede.blogs.nytimes.com/2010/05/19/worried-girl-asks-michelle-obama-if-her-mother-will-be-deported/ (accessed July 3, 2010).
2. Fuller et al. (2009); Han (2006).
3. Crosnoe (2006).
4. Karras and Yoshikawa (2009).
5. Parcel and Menaghan (1994).
6. Miller, Tessler, and van Dok (2009).
7. Bronfenbrenner (1979).
8. Loeb et al. (2007); NICHD Early Child Care Research Network (2005).
9. Ashman et al. (2002); Lupien et al. (2000).
10. Landry et al. (2001); Tamis-LeMonda, Bornstein, and Baumwell (2001).
11. Rodriguez et al. (2009).
12. Haveman and Wolfe (1995).
13. Lugo-Gil, Yoshikawa, and Tamis-LeMonda (2006).
14. Ng et al. (2010).

15. Parcel and Menaghan (1994); Yoshikawa et al. (2006).
16. Yoshikawa, Godfrey, and Rivera (2008).
17. Crosnoe (2007).

CHAPTER 7

1. Duncan et al. (2007).
2. Heckman (2006).
3. Crosnoe (2006, 2007); Han (2006).
4. Nina Bernstein, "Chinese-American Children Sent to Live with Kin Abroad Face a Tough Return," *New York Times*, July 23, 2009, A18; Su and Rong (2007).
5. Loeb et al. (2007).
6. Motomura (2008).
7. George W. Bush, transcript of televised address to the nation on immigration, *New York Times*, May 15, 2006, available at: http://www.nytimes.com/2006/05/15/washington/15text-bush.html (accessed March 15, 2010).
8. Julia Preston, "Two Senators Offer Immigration Overhaul," *New York Times*, March 19, 2010, A11.
9. Kirk Semple, "In Trenton, Issuing IDs for Illegal Immigrants," *New York Times*, May 16, 2010, A17.
10. Magnuson (2007).
11. Bernhardt et al. (2009).
12. Bernhardt et al. (2009).
13. Delgado (1993); Milkman (2002, 2006).
14. Milkman (2006).
15. Sewell Chan, "Election Remakes City Council," *New York Times*, November 5, 2009, A26.
16. Ibid.
17. Rivera (2008).
18. J. Wong (2006).
19. Dishion et al. (2008).
20. Dishion et al. (2008); Shaw et al. (2006).
21. Mendelsohn et al. (2007).
22. Alan Mendelsohn, personal communication, September 18, 2010.

APPENDIX

1. National Center for O*NET Development (2006).
2. Crouter et al. (2006).
3. Roy, Ramos, and Yoshikawa (2009).
4. Duncan, Huston, and Weisner (2007).
5. Kessler et al. (2002).
6. Lugo-Gil, Yoshikawa, and Tamis-LaMonda (2006).

7. Rodriguez et al. (2009).
8. Mullen (1995).
9. Mullen (1995).
10. Strauss and Corbin (1990).
11. Yoshikawa et al. (2008).
12. Kline (1998); Shrout and Bolger (2002).
13. Muthén and Muthén (2009).
14. Graham (2009).
15. Hu and Bentler (1995); Kline (1998).

References

Aber, J. Lawrence, Joseph P. Allen, Vicki Carlson, and Dante Cicchetti. 1989. "The Effects of Maltreatment on Development During Early Childhood: Recent Studies and Their Developmental, Clinical, and Policy Implications." In *Child Maltreatment: Theory and Research on the Causes and Consequences of Child Abuse and Neglect*, edited by Vicki Carlson and Dante Cicchetti. New York: Cambridge University Press.

Alba, Richard, and Victor Nee. 2003. *Remaking the American Mainstream: Assimilation and Contemporary Immigration*. Cambridge, Mass.: Harvard University Press.

Ashman, Sharron B., Geraldine Dawson, Heracles Panagiotides, Emily Yamada, and Charles W. Wilkins. 2002. "Stress Hormone Levels of Children of Depressed Mothers." *Development and Psychopathology* 14(2): 333–49.

Bachrach, Deborah, and Karen Lipson. 2002. *Health Coverage for Immigrants in New York: An Update on Policy Developments and Next Steps*. New York: Commonwealth Fund.

Barata, Clara M., Maggie Y. Yuan, and Hirokazu Yoshikawa. 2010. "Child Care Preferences Among Ethnically Diverse and Immigrant Families in New York City: A Mixed-Methods Study." Presented to the Seventh National Symposium of Research in Psychology (VII Simpósio Nacional de Investigação em Psicologia), Braga, Portugal (January).

Barr, Michael S. 2004. "Banking the Poor." *Yale Journal on Regulation* 21(winter): 121–237.

Bean, Frank D., and Gillian Stevens. 2003. *America's Newcomers and the Dynamics of Diversity*. New York: Russell Sage Foundation.

Bernhardt, Annette, Ruth Milkman, Nik Theodore, Douglas Heckathorn, Mirabai Auer, James DeFilippis, Ana Gonzales, Victor Narro, Jason Perelshteyn, Diana Polson, and Michael Spiller. 2009. *Broken Laws, Unprotected Workers: Violations of Employment and Labor Laws in America's Cities*. New York: National Employment Law Project.

Bitler, Marianne P., and Janet Currie. 2005. "Does WIC Work? The Effects of WIC on Pregnancy and Birth Outcomes." *Journal of Policy Analysis and Management* 24(1): 73–91.

Bluestone, Daniel. 1992. "The Pushcart Evil." In *The Landscape of Modernity: Essays on New York City, 1900–1940*, edited by David Ward and Olivier Zunz. New York: Russell Sage Foundation.

Borjas, George J. 2006. "Making It in America: Social Mobility and Immigrants." *The Future of Children* 16(2): 55–71.

Borjas, George J., Jeffrey Grogger, and Gordon H. Hanson. 2006. *Immigration and*

African American Employment Opportunities: The Responses of Wages, Employment, and Incarceration to Labor Supply Shocks. Working paper 12518. Cambridge, Mass.: National Bureau of Economic Research.

Bourdieu, Pierre. 1986. "The Forms of Capital." In *Handbook of Theory and Research for the Sociology of Education,* edited by John G. Richardson. New York: Greenwood Press.

Boushey, Heather, Shawn Fremstad, Rachel Gragg, and Margy Waller. 2007. *Understanding Low-Wage Work in the United States.* Washington, D.C.: Center for Economic Policy and Research.

Bronfenbrenner, Urie. 1979. *The Ecology of Human Development: Experiments by Nature and Design.* Cambridge, Mass.: Harvard University Press.

Bukowski, William M., Andrew F. Newcomb, and Willard W. Hartup, eds. 1996. *The Company They Keep: Friendship in Childhood and Adolescence.* New York: Cambridge University Press.

Burrows, Edwin G., and Mike Wallace. 1999. *Gotham: A History of New York City to 1898.* New York: Oxford University Press.

Burstein, Nancy, Mary Kay Fox, Jordan B. Hiller, Robert Kornfeld, Ken Lam, Cristofer Price, and David T. Rodda. 2000. *WIC General Analysis Project.* Cambridge, Mass.: Abt Associates.

Burt, Ronald S. 2001. "Structural Holes Versus Network Closure as Social Capital." In *Social Capital: Theory and Research,* edited by Nan Lin, Karen S. Cook, and Ronald S. Burt. New York: Aldine de Gruyter.

Capps, Randolph, Rosa Maria Castaneda, Ajay Chaudry, and Robert Santos. 2007. *Paying the Price: The Impact of Immigration Raids on America's Children.* Washington, D.C.: Urban Institute and National Council of La Raza.

Capps, Randolph, and Katrina Fortuny. 2006. *Immigration and Child and Family Policy.* Washington, D.C.: Urban Institute.

Capps, Randolph, Leighton Ku, and Michael Fix. 2002. *How Are Immigrants Faring After Welfare Reform? Preliminary Evidence from Los Angeles and New York City.* Washington, D.C.: Urban Institute.

Center for Research on Culture, Development, and Education. 2009. *Early Childhood Cohort Study* [database]. New York University.

Chaudry, Ajay. 2004. *Putting Children First: How Low-Wage Working Mothers Manage Child Care.* New York: Russell Sage Foundation.

Chaudry, Ajay, Randolph Capps, Juan Pedroza, Rosa Maria Castaneda, Robert Santos, and Molly M. Scott. 2010. *Facing Our Future: Children in the Aftermath of Immigration Enforcement.* Washington, D.C.: Urban Institute.

Chávez, Leo R. 1991. "Outside the Imagined Community: Undocumented Settlers and Experiences of Incorporation." *American Ethnologist* 18(2): 257–78.

———. 1998. *Shadowed Lives: Undocumented Immigrants in American Society.* 2d ed. New York: Wadsworth.

Cheah, Charissa S. L., Christy Y. Y. Leung, Madiha Tahseen, and David Schultz.

2009. "Authoritative Parenting Among Immigrant Chinese Mothers of Pre-schoolers." *Journal of Family Psychology* 23(3): 311–20.

Chin, Margaret. 2005. "Moving On: Chinese Garment Workers After 9/11." In *Wounded City: The Social Impact of 9/11*, edited by Nancy Foner. New York: Russell Sage Foundation.

Chiswick, Barry R., and Paul W. Miller. 2005. "Do Enclaves Matter in Immigrant Adjustment?" *City and Community* 4(1): 5–36.

Coleman, James. 1988. "Social Capital in the Creation of Human Capital." *American Journal of Sociology* 94(supplement): S95–120.

Consejo Nacional de Población (CONAPO). 2000. *Marginalization Index by State.* Mexico City: CONAPO.

Cornelius, Wayne A. 1982. "Interviewing Undocumented Immigrants: Methodological Reflections Based on Fieldwork in Mexico and the United States." *International Migration Review* 16(2): 378–411.

Crittenden, Patricia. 1992. "Quality of Attachment in the Preschool Years." *Development and Psychopathology* 4(2): 209–41.

Crockenberg, Susan B. 1987. "Support for Adolescent Mothers During the Postnatal Period: Theory and Research." In *Research on Support for Parents and Infants in the Postnatal Period*, edited by C. F. Zachariah Boukydis. Norwood, N.J.: Ablex.

Crosnoe, Robert. 2006. *Mexican Roots, American Schools: Helping Mexican Immigrant Children Succeed.* Palo Alto, Calif.: Stanford University Press.

———. 2007. "Early Child Care and the School Readiness of Children from Mexican Immigrant Families." *International Migration Review* 41(1): 152–81.

Crouter, Ann C., Stephanie T. Lanza, Amy Pirretti, W. Benjamin Goodman, and Eloise Neebe. 2006. "The O*NET Jobs Classification System: A Primer for Family Researchers." *Family Relations* 55(4): 461–72.

DeLeire, Thomas, and Ariel Kalil. 2002. "Good Things Come in Threes? Single-Parent Multigenerational Family Structure and Adolescent Adjustment." *Demography* 39(2): 393–413.

Delgado, Héctor L. 1993. *New Immigrants, Old Unions: Organizing Undocumented Workers in Los Angeles.* Philadelphia: Temple University Press.

DeWind, Joshua, and Philip Kasinitz. 1997. "Everything Old Is New Again? Processes and Theories of Immigrant Incorporation." *International Migration Review* 31(4): 1096–1111.

Dishion, Thomas J., Daniel Shaw, Arin Connell, Frances Gardner, Chelsea Weaver, and Melvin Wilson. 2008. "The Family Check-Up with High-Risk Indigent Families: Preventing Problem Behavior by Increasing Parents' Positive Behavior Support in Early Childhood." *Child Development* 79(5): 1395–1414.

Duncan, Greg J., Chantelle J. Dowsett, Amy Claessens, Katherine A. Magnuson, Aletha C. Huston, Pamela Klebanov, Linda S. Pagani, Leon Feinstein, Mimi Engel, Jeanne Brooks-Gunn, Holly Sexton, Kathryn Duckworth, and Crista Japel.

2007. "School Readiness and Later Achievement." *Developmental Psychology* 43(6): 1428–46.

Duncan, Greg J., Aletha C. Huston, and Thomas S. Weisner. 2007. *Higher Ground: New Hope for the Working Poor.* New York: Russell Sage Foundation.

Edin, Kathryn, and Laura Lein. 1997. *Making Ends Meet: How Single Mothers Survive Welfare and Low-Wage Work.* New York: Russell Sage Foundation.

Edin, Per-Anders, Peter Fredriksson, and Olof Aslund. 2003. "Ethnic Enclaves and the Economic Success of Immigrants: Evidence from a Natural Experiment." *Quarterly Journal of Economics* 118(1): 329–57.

Ellwood, David T. 1988. *Poor Support: Poverty and the American Family.* New York: Basic Books.

Enchautégui-de-Jesus, Noemi, Hirokazu Yoshikawa, and Vonnie C. McLoyd. 2006. "Job Quality Among Low-Income Mothers: Experiences and Associations with Children's Development." In *Making It Work: Low-Wage Employment, Family Life, and Child Development*, edited by Hirokazu Yoshikawa, Thomas S. Weisner, and Edward Lowe. New York: Russell Sage Foundation.

England, Mary Jane, and Leslie J. Sim, eds. 2009. *Depression in Parents, Parenting, and Children: Opportunities to Improve Identification, Treatment, and Prevention.* Washington, D.C.: National Academy Press.

Evans, Gary W., Stephen J. Lepore, B. R. Shejwal, and M. N. Palsane. 1998. "Chronic Residential Crowding and Children's Well-being: An Ecological Perspective." *Child Development* 69(6): 1514–23.

Feliciano, Cynthia. 2005. "Educational Selectivity in U.S. Immigration: How Do Immigrants Compare to Those Left Behind?" *Demography* 42(1): 131–52.

Finch, Brian Karl, Bohdan Kolody, and William A. Vega. 2000. "Perceived Discrimination and Depression Among Mexican-Origin Adults in California." *Journal of Health and Social Behavior* 41(3): 295–313.

Fremstad, Shawn. 2000. *The INS Public Charge Guidance: What Does It Mean for Immigrants?* Washington, D.C.: Center for Budget and Policy Priorities.

Fuller, Bruce, Margaret Bridges, Edward Bein, Heeju Jang, Sunyoung Jung, Sophia Rabe-Hesketh, Neil Halfon, and Alice Kuo. 2009. "The Health and Cognitive Growth of Latino Toddlers: At Risk or Immigrant Paradox?" *Maternal and Child Health Journal* 13(6): 755–68.

Fuller, Bruce, Susan D. Holloway, and Xiaoyan Liang. 1996. "Family Selection of Child-Care Centers: The Influence of Household Support, Ethnicity, and Parental Practices." *Child Development* 67(6): 3320–37.

Galvez, Alyshia. 2009. *Guadalupe in New York: Devotion and the Struggle for Citizenship Rights Among Mexican Immigrants.* New York: New York University Press.

Gans, Herbert J. 1992. "Second-Generation Decline: Scenarios for the Economic and Ethnic Futures of the Post-1965 American Immigrants." *Ethnic and Racial Studies* 15(2): 173–92.

Garcia, Eugene, and Bryant Jensen. 2007. "Helping Young Hispanic Learners." *Educational Leadership* (March): 34–39.

Garcia Coll, Cynthia, and Amy Kerivan Marks. 2009. *Immigrant Stories: Ethnicity and Academics in Middle Childhood.* New York: Oxford University Press.

Gaytan, Francisco X., Qing Xue, Hirokazu Yoshikawa, and Catherine S. Tamis-Le-Monda. 2006. "Transnational Babies: Patterns and Predictors of Infant Travel in Immigrant Families." In "Early Childhood Development in Immigrant Families," symposium chaired by Catherine S. Tamis-LeMonda and Hirokazu Yoshikawa and presented at the national Head Start research conference, Washington (June).

Gershoff, Elizabeth T., John L. Aber, C. Cybele Raver, and Mary Clare Lennon. 2007. "Income Is Not Enough: Incorporating Material Hardship into Models of Income Associations with Parenting and Child Development." *Child Development* 78(1): 70–95.

Gilens, Martin. 1999. *Why Americans Hate Welfare.* Berkeley: University of California Press.

Gould, Jeffrey B., Ashima Madan, Cheng Qin, and Gilberto Chavez. 2003. "Perinatal Outcomes in Two Dissimilar Immigrant Populations in the United States: A Dual Epidemiologic Paradox." *Pediatrics* 111(6): e676–82.

Graham, John W. 2009. "Missing Data Analysis: Making It Work in the Real World." *Annual Review of Psychology* 60: 549–76.

Granovetter, Mark. 1973. "The Strength of Weak Ties." *American Journal of Sociology* 78(6): 1360–80.

Greenberger, Ellen, Robin O'Neil, and Stacy K. Nagel. 1994. "Linking Workplace and Homeplace: Relations Between the Nature of Adults' Work and Their Parenting Behaviors." *Developmental Psychology* 30(6): 990–1002.

Han, Wen-Jui. 2005. "Maternal Nonstandard Work Schedules and Child Cognitive Development." *Child Development* 76(1): 137–54.

———. 2006. "Academic Achievements of Children in Immigrant Families." *Educational Research and Reviews* 1(8): 286–318.

Harknett, Kristin, and Sara S. McLanahan. 2004. "Racial and Ethnic Differences in Marriage After the Birth of a Child." *American Sociological Review* 69(6): 790–811.

Haveman, Robert, and Barbara Wolfe. 1995. "The Determinants of Children's Attainments: A Review of Methods and Findings." *Journal of Economic Literature* 33(4): 1829–78.

Heckman, James J. 2006. "Skill Formation and the Economics of Investing in Disadvantaged Children." *Science* 312(5782): 1900–1902.

Hernandez, Donald J., Nancy A. Denton, and Suzanne E. Macartney. 2008. "Children in Immigrant Families: Looking to America's Future." *Social Policy Reports of the Society for Research in Child Development* 22(3): 1–22.

Hessol, Nancy A., and Elena Fuentes-Afflick. 2000. "The Perinatal Advantage of Mexican-Origin Latina Women." *Annals of Epidemiology* 10(8): 516–23.

Hoefer, Michael, Nancy Rytina, and Bryan C. Baker. 2010. *Estimates of the Unauthorized Immigrant Population Residing in the United States.* Washington: U.S. Department of Homeland Security. Available at: http://www.dhs.gov/xlibrary/assets/statistics/publications/ois_ill_pe_2009.pdf (accessed July 14, 2010).

Hondagneu-Sotelo, Pierrette. 1994. *Gendered Transitions: Mexican Experiences of Immigration.* Berkeley: University of California Press.

———. 1999. "Gender and Contemporary U.S. Migration." *American Behavioral Scientist* 42(4): 565–76.

Hsueh, JoAnn, and Hirokazu Yoshikawa. 2007. "Working Nonstandard Schedules and Variable Shifts in Low-Income Families: Associations with Parental Psychological Well-being, Family Functioning, and Child Well-being." *Developmental Psychology* 43(5): 620–32.

Hu, Li-Tze, and Peter M. Bentler. 1995. "Evaluating Model Fit." In *Structural Equation Modeling: Concepts, Issues, and Applications,* edited by Rick Hoyle. London: Sage Publications.

Jackson, Margot, Sara McLanahan, and Kathleen Kiernan. 2009. *Mother's Investments in Child Health in the U.S. and U.K.: A Comparative Lens on the Immigrant Paradox.* Working paper WP09-24FF. Princeton, N.J.: Princeton University, Center for Research on Child Well-Being.

Kalil, Ariel, and Jen-Hao Chen. 2008. "Mothers' Citizenship Status and Household Food Insecurity Among Low-Income Children of Immigrants." *New Directions in Child and Adolescent Development* 121: 43–62.

Kalil, Ariel, and Robert Crosnoe. 2009. "Two Generations of Educational Progress in Latin American Immigrant Families in the United States: A Conceptual Framework for a New Policy Context." In *Immigration, Diversity, and Education,* edited by Elena Grigorenko and Ruby Takanishi. New York: Routledge.

Kalil, Ariel, and Kathleen Ziol-Guest. 2005. "Single Mothers' Employment Dynamics and Adolescent Well-being." *Child Development* 76(1): 196–211.

Kao, Grace. 1999. "Psychological Well-being and Educational Achievement Among Immigrant Youth." In *Children of Immigrants: Health, Adjustment, and Public Assistance,* edited by Donald J. Hernandez. Washington, D.C.: National Academy Press.

Kao, Grace, and Marta Tienda. 1995. "Optimism and Achievement: The Educational Performance of Immigrant Youth." *Social Science Quarterly* 76(1): 1–19.

Karras, Cynthia, and Hirokazu Yoshikawa. 2009. "Housing Type, Parenting, and Children's Antisocial Behavior." Master's thesis, New York University.

Kasinitz, Philip, John H. Mollenkopf, and Mary C. Waters. 2002. "Becoming American/Becoming New Yorkers: Immigrant Incorporation in a Majority Minority City." *International Migration Review* 36(4): 1020–36.

Kasinitz, Philip, John H. Mollenkopf, Mary C. Waters, and Jennifer Holdaway. 2008. *Inheriting the City: The Children of Immigrants Come of Age.* Cambridge, Mass., and New York: Harvard University Press and Russell Sage Foundation.

Kessler, R.C., G. Andrews, L. J. Colpe, E. Hiripi, D. K. Mroczek, S. T. Normand, E. E. Walters, and A. M. Zaslovsky. 2002. "Short Screening Scales to Monitor Population Prevalences and Trends in Non-Specific Psychological Distress." *Psychological Medicine* 32(6): 959–76.

Kline, Rex B. 1998. *Principles and Practice of Structural Equation Modeling*. New York: Guilford Press.

Kohn, Melvin. 1969. *Class and Conformity: A Study in Values*. Chicago: University of Chicago Press.

Kraly, Ellen P., and Inés Miyares. 2001. "Immigration to New York: Policy, Population, and Patterns." In *New Immigrants in New York*, edited by Nancy Foner. New York: Columbia University Press.

Kwong, Peter. 1997. *Forbidden Workers: Illegal Chinese Immigrants and American Labor*. New York: New Press.

Landale, Nancy S., R. S. Oropesa, and Bridget K. Gorman. 1999. "Immigration and Infant Health: Birth Outcomes of Immigrant and Native-Born Women." In *Children of Immigrants: Health, Adjustment, and Public Assistance*, edited by Donald J. Hernandez. Washington, D.C.: National Academy Press.

Landry, Susan, Karen E. Smith, Paul R. Swank, Mike A. Assel, and Sonya Vellet. 2001. "Does Early Responsive Parenting Have Special Importance for Children's Development or Is Consistency in Early Childhood Important?" *Developmental Psychology* 37(3): 387–403.

Lazear, Edward P. 1999. "Culture and Language." *Journal of Political Economy* 107(6): S95–126.

Lee, Everett, S. 1966. "A Theory of Migration." *Demography* 3(1): 47–57.

Lee, Jennifer. 2008. *The Fortune Cookie Chronicles: Adventures in the World of Chinese Food*. New York: Hachette Book Group.

Levitt, Peggy. 2001. *The Transnational Villagers*. Berkeley: University of California Press.

Levy, Santiago. 2006. *Progress Against Poverty: Sustaining Mexico's Progresa-Oportunidades Program*. Washington, D.C.: Brookings Institution Press.

Liang, Zai, and Wenzhen Ye. 2001. "From Fujian to New York: Understanding the New Chinese Immigration." In *Global Human Smuggling*, edited by David Kyle and Rey Koslowski. Baltimore: Johns Hopkins University Press.

Lobo, Arun Peter, Ronald J. O. Flores, and Joseph J. Salvo. 2002. "The Impact of Hispanic Growth on the Racial-Ethnic Composition of New York City Neighborhoods." *Urban Affairs Review* 37(5): 703–27.

Loeb, Susanna, Margaret Bridges, Daphna Bassok, Bruce Fuller, and Russ W. Rumberger. 2007. "How Much Is Too Much? The Influence of Preschool Centers on Children's Social and Cognitive Development." *Economics of Education Review* 26(1): 52–66.

Louie, Vivian. 2006. "Second-Generation Pessimism and Optimism: How Second-Generation Chinese and Dominicans Understand Education and Mobility Through Ethnic and Transnational Orientations." *International Migration Review* 40(3): 537–72.

Lu, Michael C., Yvonne G. Lin, Noelani G. Prietto, and Thomas J. Garite. 2000. "Elimination of Public Funding for Prenatal Care for Undocumented Immigrants in California: A Cost-Benefit Analysis." *Journal of Obstetrics and Gynecology* 182(1): 233–39.

Lugo-Gil, Julieta, Hirokazu Yoshikawa, and Catherine S. Tamis-LeMonda. 2006. *Expenditures on Children Among Low-Income, Immigrant, and Ethnically Diverse Families.* Working paper 2006-36. Ann Arbor: University of Michigan, National Center on Poverty. Available at: http://npc.umich.edu/publications/u/working_paper06-36.pdf (accessed October 23, 2009).

Lupien, Sonia J., Suzanne King, Michael J. Meaney, and Bruce S. McEwen. 2000. "Child's Stress Hormone Levels Correlate with Mother's Socioeconomic Status and Depressive State." *Biological Psychiatry* 48(10): 976–80.

Lyons-Ruth, Karlen. 1996. "Attachment Relationships Among Children with Aggressive Behavior Problems: The Role of Early Disorganized Attachment." *Journal of Consulting and Clinical Psychology* 64(1): 64–73.

Magnuson, Katherine A. 2007. "Maternal Education and Children's Academic Achievement During Middle Childhood." *Developmental Psychology* 43(6): 1497–1512.

Magnuson, Katherine A., Christopher Ruhm, and Jane Waldfogel. 2007. "Does Prekindergarten Improve School Preparation and Performance?" *Economics of Education Review* 26(1): 33–51.

Massey, Douglas S., Rafael Alarcón, Jorge Durand, and Humberto González. 1987. *Return to Aztlan: The Social Process of International Migration from Western Mexico.* Berkeley: University of California Press.

Massey, Douglas S., and Kristin E. Espinosa. 1997. "What's Driving U.S.-Mexico Migration? A Theoretical, Empirical, and Policy Analysis." *American Journal of Sociology* 102(4): 939–99.

Matthews, Hannah, and Danielle Ewen. 2006. *Reaching All Children? Understanding Early Care and Education Participation Among Immigrant Families.* Washington, D.C.: Center for Law and Social Policy.

Mehta, Chirag, Nik Theodore, Iliana Mora, and Jennifer Wade. 2002. *Chicago's Undocumented Immigrants: An Analysis of Wages, Work Conditions, and Economic Contributions.* Chicago: University of Illinois, Center for Urban Economic Development.

Mendelsohn, Alan L., Purnima T. Valdez, Virginia Flynn, Gilbert M. Foley, Samantha B. Berkule, Suze Tomopoulos, Arthur H. Fierman, Wendy Tineo, and Benard P. Dreyer. 2007. "Use of Videotaped Interactions During Pediatric Well-Child Care: Impact at Thirty-three Months on Parenting and on Child Development." *Journal of Developmental and Behavioral Pediatrics* 28(3): 206–12.

Menjivar, Cecilia. 1997. "Immigrant Kinship Networks: Vietnamese, Salvadorian, and Mexicans in Comparative Perspective." *Journal of Comparative Family Studies* 28(1): 1–24.

———. 2002. "Living in Two Worlds? Guatemalan-Origin Children in the United

States and Emerging Transnationalism." *Journal of Ethnic and Migration Studies* 28(3): 531–52.

Milkman, Ruth. 2002. "New Workers, New Labor, and the New Los Angeles." In *Unions in a Globalized Environment: Changing Borders, Organizational Boundaries, and Social Roles,* edited by Bruce Nissen. Armonk, N.Y.: M. E. Sharpe.

———. 2006. *L.A. Story: Immigrant Workers and the Future of the U.S. Labor Movement.* New York: Russell Sage Foundation.

Miller, Cynthia, Betsy Tessler, and Mark van Dok. 2009. *Strategies to Help Low-Wage Workers Advance: Implementation and Early Impacts of the Work Advancement and Support Center Demonstration.* New York: MDRC.

Model, Suzanne. 2008. *West Indian Immigrants: A Black Success Story?* New York: Russell Sage Foundation.

Motomura, Hiroshi. 2008. "Immigration Outside the Law." *Columbia Law Review* 108(8): 2037–97.

Moya Pons, Frank. 1995. *The Dominican Republic Today.* New Rochelle, N.Y.: Hispaniola Press.

Mullen, Eileen. 1995. *Mullen Scales of Early Learning.* Circle Pines, Minn.: American Guidance Society.

Muthén, Beugt, and Linda Muthén. 2009. *MPlus Version 6* [statistical software program]. Los Angeles: Muthén and Muthén.

National Bureau of Statistics of China. 2009a. *The One Percent National Sample Survey Summary Report* (in Chinese). Available at: http://www.stats.gov.cn/tjgb/rkpcgb/qgrkpcgb/t20060316_402310923.htm (accessed September 17, 2009).

———. 2009b. *The Third Census Summary Report.* Available at: http://www.stats.gov.cn/tjgb/rkpcgb/qgrkpcgb/t20020404_16769.htm (accessed September 17, 2009).

National Center for O*NET Development. 2006. *Updating the O*NET-SOC Taxonomy: Summary and Implementation.* Washington: U.S. Department of Labor. Available at: http://www.onetcenter.org/dl_files/UpdatingTaxonomy_Summary.pdf (accessed October 31, 2009).

National Forum on Early Childhood Program Evaluation. 2007. *A Science-Based Framework for Early Childhood Policy.* Cambridge, Mass.: Harvard University, Center on the Developing Child.

National Institute of Child Health and Human Development (NICHD) Early Child Care Research Network. 2005. "Early Child Care and Children's Development in the Primary Grades: Follow-up Results from the NICHD Study of Early Child Care." *American Educational Research Journal* 42(3): 537–70.

Nee, Victor, and Jimy Sanders. 2001. "Understanding the Diversity of Immigrant Incorporation: A Forms-of-Capital Model." *Ethnic and Racial Studies* 24(3): 386–411.

Newman, Katherine S. 1999. *No Shame in My Game: The Working Poor in the Inner City.* New York: Russell Sage Foundation.

————. 2006. *Chutes and Ladders: Navigating the Low-Wage Labor Market*. New York: Russell Sage Foundation.

New York State Department of Health. 2008. *Request for Information for Foods for the New York State WIC Program*. Albany: New York State Department of Health. Available at: http://www.nyhealth.gov/funding/rfi/wic_foods/wic_foods.pdf (accessed December 15, 2009).

Ng, Florrie F., Erin B. Godfrey, Catherin S. Tamis-LeMonda, Ronit Kahana-Kalman, and Hirokazu Yoshikawa. 2010. "Dynamics of Parents' Goals for Children in Ethnically Diverse Populations Across the First Three Years of Life." Manuscript under review. New York University.

Ngai, Mae M. 2004. *Impossible Subjects: Illegal Aliens and the Making of Modern America*. Princeton, N.J.: Princeton University Press.

————. 2006. "The Lost Immigration Debate." *Boston Review* (September–October). Available at: http://bostonrenew.net/BR31.5/ngai.php (accessed January 3, 2011).

Nisbett, Richard E. 2009. *Intelligence and How to Get It: Why Schools and Cultures Count*. New York: W. W. Norton.

Nord, Mark. 2005. "The Effect of Food Stamps on Food Insecurity: A Panel Data Approach." *Review of Agricultural Economics* 27(3): 425–32.

Orrenius, Pia, and Madeline Zavodny. 2009. *Tied to the Business Cycle: How Immigrants Fare in Good and Bad Economic Times*. Washington, D.C.: Migration Policy Institute.

Ortega, Alexander N., Hai Fang, Victor H. Perez, John A. Rizzo, Olivia Carter-Pokras, Steven P. Wallace, and Lillian Gelberg. 2007. "Health Care Access, Use of Services, and Experiences Among Undocumented Mexicans and Other Latinos." *Archives of Internal Medicine* 167(21): 2354–60.

Ortega, Alexander N., Sarah M. Horwitz, Hai Fang, Alice A. Kuo, Steven P. Wallace, and Moira Inkelas. 2009. "Documentation Status and Parental Concerns About Development in Young U.S. Children of Mexican Origin." *Academic Pediatrics* 9(4): 278–82.

Padilla, Yolanda C., Melissa Dalton Radey, Robert A. Hummer, and Eunjeong Kim. 2006. "The Living Conditions of U.S.-Born Children of Mexican Immigrants in Unmarried Families." *Journal of Hispanic Behavioral Sciences* 28(3): 331–49.

Parcel, Toby L., and Elizabeth G. Menaghan. 1994. *Parents' Jobs and Children's Lives*. New York: Aldine de Gruyter.

Parreñas, Rhacel Salazar. 2005. *Children of Global Migration: Transnational Families and Gendered Woes*. Palo Alto, Calif.: Stanford University Press.

Passel, Jeffrey. 2006. *Modes of Entry for the Unauthorized Migrant Population*. Washington, D.C.: Pew Hispanic Center.

Passel, Jeffrey, and D'Vera Cohn. 2009. *A Portrait of Unauthorized Immigrants in the United States*. Washington, D.C.: Pew Hispanic Center.

Pedraza, Silvia. 2006. "Assimilation or Transnationalism? Conceptual Models of the Immigrant Experience in America." In *Cultural Psychology of Immigrants*, edited by Ramaswami Mahalingam. Mahwah, N.J.: Erlbaum.

Perreira, Krista M., Mimi V. Chapman, and Gabriela L. Stein. 2006. "Becoming an American Parent: Overcoming Challenges and Finding Strength in a New Immigrant Latino Community." *Journal of Family Issues* 27(10): 1383–1414.

Perry-Jenkins, Maureen, Rena L. Repetti, and Ann C. Crouter. 2000. "Work and Family in the 1990s." *Journal of Marriage and the Family* 56(1): 165–80.

Pessar, Patricia R. 1995. *A Visa for a Dream: Dominicans in the United States*. New York: Allyn and Bacon.

———. 1999. "Engendering Migration Studies: The Case of New Immigrants in the United States." *American Behavioral Scientist* 42(4): 577–600.

Phillips, Julia A., and Douglas S. Massey. 1999. "The New Labor Market: Immigrants and Wages After IRCA." *Demography* 36(2): 233–46.

Portes, Alejandro, and Rubén Rumbaut. 2001. *Legacies: The Story of the Immigrant Second Generation*. New York: Russell Sage Foundation.

Portes, Alejandro, and Min Zhou. 1993. "The New Second Generation: Segmented Assimilation and Its Variants." *Annals of the American Academy of Political and Social Science* 530(November): 74–96.

Presser, Harriet B. 2005. *Working in a 24/7 Economy: Challenges for American Families*. New York: Russell Sage Foundation.

Qin, Desiree Baolian, Niobe Way, and Meenal Rana. 2008. "The Model Minority and Their Discontent: Examining Peer Discrimination and Harassment of Chinese American Immigrant Youth." *New Directions in Child and Adolescent Development* 121: 27–42.

Raikes, Helen, Barbara Pan, Gayle Luze, Catherine S. Tamis-LeMonda, Jeanne Brooks-Gunn, Jill Constantine, Lousia B. Tarullo, H. Abigail Raikes, and Eileen T. Rodriguez. 2006. "Mother-Child Bookreading in Low-Income Families: Correlates and Outcomes During the First Three Years of Life." *Child Development* 77(4): 924–53.

Ramey, Craig T., Keith O. Yeates, and Elizabeth J. Short. 1984. "The Plasticity of Intellectual Development: Insights from Preventive Intervention." *Child Development* 55(5): 1913–25.

Ramos, Maria, and Hirokazu Yoshikawa. 2009. "To Work or Not to Work: Predicting the Timing of Maternal Entry into the Labor Force After Birth Among Ethnically Diverse and Immigrant Families." Unpublished paper. New York University.

Raver, C. Cybele. 2002. "Emotions Matter: Making the Case for the Role of Young Children's Emotional Development for School Readiness." *Social Policy Reports of the Society for Research in Child Development* 16(3): 1–18.

Raver, C. Cybele. 2003. "Does Work Pay Psychologically as Well as Economically? The Role of Employment in Predicting Depressive Symptoms and Parenting Among Low-Income Families." *Child Development* 74(6): 1720–36.

Rivera, Ann C. 2008. "WIC and Food Stamps Programs: Low-Income Families'

Decisions About Whether to Participate." Chapter of Ph.D. diss., New York University.

Rivera-Batiz, Francisco L. 1999. "Undocumented Workers in the Labor Market: An Analysis of the Earnings of Legal and Illegal Mexican Workers in the United States." *Journal of Population Economics* 12(1): 91–116.

Rodriguez, Eileen T., Catherine S. Tamis-LeMonda, Mark E. Spellmann, Barbara A. Pan, Helen Raikes, and Gayle Luze. 2009. "The Formative Role of Home Literacy Experiences in the First Three Years of Life in Low-Income Families." *Journal of Applied Developmental Psychology* 30(6): 677–94.

Roy, Amanda L., Maria Ramos, and Hirokazu Yoshikawa. 2009. "O*NET Occupational Classifications in a Low-Income, Ethnically Diverse, and Immigrant Sample." Unpublished data. New York University.

Rumbaut, Rubén G. 2006. "The Making of a People." In *Hispanics and the Future of America*, edited by Marta Tienda and Faith Mitchell. Washington, D.C.: National Academy Press.

Salyer, Lucy E. 1995. *Laws Harsh as Tigers: Chinese Immigrants and the Shaping of Modern Immigration Law, 1882–1924*. Chapel Hill: University of North Carolina Press.

Saucedo, Leticia M. 2006. "The Employer Preference for the Subservient Worker and the Making of the Brown-Collar Workplace." *Ohio State Law Journal* 67(5): 961–1022.

Seefeldt, Kristin. 2008. *Working After Welfare: How Women Balance Jobs and Family in the Wake of Welfare Reform*. Kalamazoo, Mich.: W. E. Upjohn Institute for Employment Research.

Shaw, Daniel, Lauren Supplee, Thomas Dishion, and Frances Gardner. 2006. "Randomized Trial of a Family-Centered Approach to the Prevention of Early Conduct Problems: Two-Year Effects of the Family Check-Up in Early Childhood." *Journal of Consulting and Clinical Psychology* 74(1): 1–9.

Shonkoff, Jack P., W. Thomas Boyce, and Thomas S. McEwen. 2009. "Neuroscience, Molecular Biology, and the Childhood Roots of Health Disparities: Building a New Framework for Health Promotion and Disease Prevention." *Journal of the American Medical Association* 301(21): 2252–59.

Shrout, Patrick E., and Niall Bolger. 2002. "Mediation in Experimental and Nonexperimental Studies: New Procedures and Recommendations." *Psychological Methods* 7(4): 422–45.

Singer, Audrey. 2004. "Welfare Reform and Immigrants: A Policy Review." In *Immigrants, Welfare Reform, and the Poverty of Policy*, edited by Phillip Kretsedemans and Ana Aparicio. Westport, Conn.: Praeger.

Small, Mario Luis. 2009. *Unanticipated Gains: Origins of Network Inequality in Everyday Life*. New York: Oxford University Press.

Smith, Robert Courtney. 2006. *Mexican New York: Transnational Lives of New Immigrants*. Berkeley: University of California Press.

Strauss, Anselm, and Juliet M. Corbin. 1990. *Basics of Qualitative Research: Grounded Theory Procedures and Techniques.* Thousand Oaks, Calif.: Sage Publications.

Street Vendor Project. 2006. *Peddling Uphill: Conditions for Street Vendors in New York City.* New York: Urban Justice Project.

Su, Yu, and Lian Rong. 2007. "A Study on the Psychological Development of Overseas Left-Behind Children Ages Three to Five in Changle, Fujian." Master's thesis. Fuzhou, China: Fuzhou Normal University, Psychology Department.

Suárez-Orozco, Carola, and Marcelo Suárez-Orozco. 2001. *Children of Immigrants.* Cambridge, Mass.: Harvard University Press.

Suárez-Orozco, Carola, Marcelo Suárez-Orozco, and Irina Todorova. 2008. *Learning a New Land: Immigrant Students in American Society.* Cambridge, Mass.: Harvard University Press.

Suárez-Orozco, Carola, Irina Todorova, and Josephine Louie. 2002. "Making Up for Lost Time: The Experience of Separations and Reunifications Among Immigrant Families." *Family Process* 41(4): 625–43.

Tamis-LeMonda, Catherine S., Marc S. Bornstein, and Lisa Baumwell. 2001. "Maternal Responsiveness and Children's Achievement of Language Milestones." *Child Development* 72(3): 748–67.

Tapia, Javier. 1995. "Making a Living: The Microeconomics of U.S. Mexican Households." *Urban Anthropology* 24(3–4): 255–80.

Tekin, Erdal. 2005. "Child Care Subsidy Receipt, Employment, and Child Care Choices of Single Mothers." *Economics Letters* 89(1): 1–6.

Tienda, Marta, and Faith Mitchell, eds. 2006. *Hispanics and the Future of America.* Washington, D.C.: National Academy Press.

U.S. Bureau of the Census. 2000. *Census 2000: Summary File 3 (SF 3)–Sample Data* [database]. Available at: http://factfinder.census.gov/servlet/DatasetMainPage Servlet?_lang=en&_ts=308156835405&_ds_name=DEC_2000_SF1_U&_program =DEC (accessed November 19, 2010).

Valencia, Ernesto Lucario. 2005. "La Celebración de la Virgen de Guadalupe en La Ciudad de Puebla." *Revista de Antropología Experimental* 5(16): 1–6.

van Hook, Jennifer, and Kelly Stamper Balistreri. 2006. "Ineligible Parents, Eligible Children: Food Stamps Receipt, Allotments, and Food Insecurity Among Children of Immigrants." *Social Science Research* 35(1): 228–51.

Waldinger, Roger. 1996. *Still the Promised City? African Americans and New Immigrants in Postindustrial New York.* Cambridge, Mass.: Harvard University Press.

Waldinger, Roger, and Michael I. Lichter. 2003. *How the Other Half Works: Immigration and the Social Organization of Labor.* Berkeley: University of California Press.

Warren, Mark R., and Karen L. Mapp. Forthcoming. *A Match on Dry Grass: Community Organizing as a Catalyst for School Reform.* New York: Oxford University Press.

Waters, Mary C. 2005. "Assessing Immigrant Assimilation: New Empirical and Theoretical Challenges." *Annual Review of Sociology* 31: 101–25.

Way, Niobe. 2011. *Deep Secrets: Boys, Friendships, and the Crisis of Connection.* Cambridge, Mass.: Harvard University Press.

White, Michael J., Frank D. Bean, and Thomas J. Espenshade. 1990. "The U.S. 1986 Immigration Reform and Control Act and Undocumented Migration to the United States." *Population Research and Policy Review* 9(2): 93–116.

Wong, Carolyn. 2006. *Lobbying for Inclusion: Rights Politics and the Making of Immigration Policy.* Palo Alto, Calif.: Stanford University Press.

Wong, Janelle. 2006. *Democracy's Promise: Immigrants and America's Civic Institutions.* Ann Arbor: University of Michigan Press.

Yoshikawa, Hirokazu. 1999. "Welfare and Work Dynamics, Support Services, Mothers' Earnings, and Child Cognitive Development: Implications for Contemporary Welfare Reform." *Child Development* 70(3): 779–801.

Yoshikawa, Hirokazu, Anna Gassman-Pines, Pamela A. Morris, Lisa A. Gennetian, and Erin B. Godfrey. 2010. "Racial-Ethnic Differences in Effects of Welfare Policies on Early School Readiness and Later Achievement." *Applied Developmental Science* 14(3): 137–53.

Yoshikawa, Hirokazu, Erin B. Godfrey, and Ann C. Rivera. 2008. "Access to Institutional Resources as a Measure of Social Exclusion: Relations with Family Process and Cognitive Development in the Context of Immigration." *New Directions in Child and Adolescent Development* 121: 73–96.

Yoshikawa, Hirokazu, Thomas S. Weisner, Ariel Kalil, and Niobe Way. 2008. "Mixing Qualitative and Quantitative Methods in Developmental Science: Uses and Methodological Choices." *Developmental Psychology* 44(2): 344–54.

Yoshikawa, Hirokazu, Thomas S. Weisner, and Edward Lowe, eds. 2006. *Making It Work: Low-Wage Employment, Family Life, and Child Development.* New York: Russell Sage Foundation.

Zhao, Ying, Aimin Niu, Guifa Xiu, Matha Garrett, and Ted Greiner. 2003. "Early Infant Feeding Practices in Jinan City, Shandong Province, China." *Asia Pacific Journal of Clinical Nutrition* 12(1): 104–8.

Zhou, Min. 1992. *Chinatown: The Socioeconomic Potential of an Ethnic Enclave.* Philadelphia: Temple University Press.

———. 2001. "Chinese: Divergent Destinies in Immigrant New York." In *New Immigrants in New York*, 2d ed., edited by Nancy Foner. New York: Columbia University Press.

———. 2008. "The Ethnic System of Supplementary Education: Nonprofit and For-Profit Institutions in Los Angeles' Chinese Immigrant Community." In *Toward Positive Youth Development: Transforming Schools and Community Organizations*, edited by Marybeth Shinn and Hirokazu Yoshikawa. New York: Oxford University Press.

Zhou, Min, and Rebecca Y. Kim. 2006. "The Paradox of Ethnicization and Assimilation: The Development of Ethnic Organizations in the Chinese Immigrant Community in the United States." In *Voluntary Organizations in the Chinese Dias-*

pora, edited by Kuah-Pearce Khun Eng and Evelyn Hu-DeHart. Hong Kong: Hong Kong University Press.

Zhou, Min, and John R. Logan. 1989. "Returns on Human Capital in Ethnic Enclaves: New York City's Chinatown." *American Sociological Review* 54(5): 809–20.

Zimmerman, Wendy, and Karen C. Tumlin. 1999. *Patchwork Policies: State Assistance for Immigrants Under Welfare Reform*. Washington, D.C.: Urban Institute.

Zlolniski, Christian. 2006. *Janitors, Street Vendors, and Activists: The Lives of Mexican Immigrants in Silicon Valley*. Berkeley: University of California Press.

Index